Life and Letters
of John Bacchus Dykes

Life and Letters of John Bacchus Dykes

Originally edited by
J. T. FOWLER

New edition edited by
IAIN QUINN

WIPF & STOCK · Eugene, Oregon

LIFE AND LETTERS OF JOHN BACCHUS DYKES

Copyright © 2021 Iain Quinn. All rights reserved. Except for brief quotations in critical publications or reviews, no part of this book may be reproduced in any manner without prior written permission from the publisher. Write: Permissions, Wipf and Stock Publishers, 199 W. 8th Ave., Suite 3, Eugene, OR 97401.

Wipf & Stock
An Imprint of Wipf and Stock Publishers
199 W. 8th Ave., Suite 3
Eugene, OR 97401

www.wipfandstock.com

PAPERBACK ISBN: 978-1-5326-9465-3
HARDCOVER ISBN: 978-1-5326-9466-0
EBOOK ISBN: 978-1-5326-9467-7

Manufactured in the U.S.A.   03/19/21

There are in this loud, stunning tide
Of human care and crime,
With whom the melodies abide
Of the everlasting chime;
Who carry music in their heart
Through dusky lane and wrangling mart,
Plying their daily task with busier feet,
Because their secret souls a holy strain repeat.

—*St. Matthew*, John Keble

"Les pourquois de la terre seront les Alleluias du ciel."

John Murray, Albemarle Street, London, 1897.

Contents

Introduction to This Edition | ix
Acknowledgements | xii
Introduction | xiii

1. Early Days | 1
   1823–1843
2. Cambridge | 11
   1843–1847
3. Malton and Early Durham Days | 28
   1848–1857
4. "These Are They" | 41
   1857–1862
5. St. Oswald's | 53
   1862–1866
6. Church Music | 71
   1866–1869
7. In Memoriam M. H. D. | 84
   1870–1873
8. The Trial | 113
   1873–1874
9. Through Pain to Peace | 131
   1874–1876
10. Spiritual Letters, Etc. | 162

Appendix 1: The Bishop of Durham and the Vicar of S. Oswald's | 211
Appendix 2: Dr. Dykes' Published Hymn-Tunes | 225
Index | 245

Introduction to This Edition

Joseph Thomas Fowler's 1897 edition of the *Life and Letters of John Bacchus Dykes* remains a critical document when assessing the musical life of the Church of England in the nineteenth century. It is filled with details concerning Dykes' involvement with the first edition of *Hymns Ancient and Modern* (1861) and the compositional process behind many of the hymns that are today well-known across several denominations, in addition to others that occur in only a few hymnals. Many of Dykes' contributions to hymnody have drifted from current usage but will perhaps reemerge in future hymnals or even in hymn-anthems. Dykes' style of hymn writing is very much of the third quarter of the nineteenth century and students of the period will observe the progression from the choral writing of Thomas Attwood to John Goss, the influence of Mendelssohn followed by Dykes and John Stainer. The commanding use of chromaticism that can be observed in his tune *Melita* gave the hymn a tremendous legacy because of the alliance of words and text that can quickly fasten an emotional response when singing, as can be seen later with the hymn tunes of Stainer and Charles Hubert Hastings Parry. However, Dykes' role as a writer of text as well as a composer of tune places him in a distinct position in nineteenth-century studies especially given his prolific output. In this regard, his commentaries on the theological understanding of texts by other writers who are composing verse for the layperson to sing in services are also of special importance. Indeed, it may be argued that when reading the *Letters* it is easy to see a complementary overlap between Dykes' life as a priest and his ongoing work as a writer of hymns.

The *Letters* also afford the reader a glimpse into the parish life of the Church in the north east of England in the nineteenth century. St. Oswald's Church in Durham, where Dykes served and is also buried, continues to be an important ecclesiastical centre in a great cathedral city. Dykes' commentaries capture the life and challenges of a parish priest during an era of liturgical renewal in the Church of England and also point to the differences of parish and cathedral life as he experienced them.

The publication of the correspondence between Bishop Baring and Dykes that defined much of Dykes' later years and which caused so much abiding upset to him would have been as startling to many a parishioner in 1897 as it would be today, even though the book was published twenty years after Dykes' death and eighteen years after Baring's death. The presentation of the argument between the two men as laid forth by Fowler in the main body of the text is, perhaps unsurprisingly, sympathetic to Dykes. While it could be suggested that Fowler's overall portrayal of Dykes is overwhelmingly positive between the letters themselves and Fowler's commentary, the close proximity of the dates in the published correspondence suggests that there was no overt intention to portray Dykes in any light other than that in which he appeared in person to Fowler. Dykes appears as a relatively humble parish priest blessed with a considerable skill as a composer of hymns who worked, and arguably suffered, for the betterment of the Church as a whole. This ministry was supported by a tremendous self-discipline and the high principles that come to the fore in both his critiques of other hymn texts, and of friends and parishioners who strayed from their faith, together with his determined correspondence with Bishop Baring.

Fowler points out the importance of including the correspondence with Baring, and it will be for readers to determine the nature of these exchanges between the relative verbosity of Dykes and the taciturn responses of Baring. To this reader, the tenor of Dykes' letters were surprising on first reading, coming as they do after the spiritual letters and the larger volume, a significant portion of which deals with grief. The letters demonstrate an especially assertive side to Dykes that is only otherwise demonstrated in his gentle disciplining of laypersons and in his concerns regarding hymn texts.

In seeing the 1897 publication as something of a memorial to Dykes, Fowler presents a great deal of material for scholars and general readers to consider. This edition has amended the many editorial inconsistencies in the first edition related to the transcription of the diary entries and letters with the exception of the dates on letters which have been left as they originally appeared. The curious but also inconsistent use of one sentence paragraphs that are directly related to the material of the previous paragraph have been left in place because in reading the larger volume it becomes apparent that this relates very directly to Dykes' own thinking and his thinking through of matters.

Some readers will have encountered the ecclesiastical world of nineteenth-century England through the Barchester novels of Anthony Trollope, or perhaps the works of Thomas Hardy or George Eliot. It would be remiss not to comment that much content from those narratives will seem familiar to those readers when encountering the following pages of Dykes' life including the many fascinating turns in the development of Dykes' ministry. Indeed, more will be familiar in terms of parish life than will be unfamiliar and this helps us see how close those authors were to the truth. For those with an intimate knowledge of Durham, these texts are something to treasure especially to anyone who has walked the same paths as Dykes himself.

I began by noting that this is unquestionably an important historical document but I conclude that it is also at times a riveting discourse for anyone with an interest in church life, England in the nineteenth century, the hymnody of the English nineteenth century, and the nature of an individual commitment to parish ministry. Dykes emerges as a figure that may well be an inspiration to many embarking on ministry, whether clerical or musical, and it is hoped that this text will be a source of reference to both scholars and those who seek to further the work of the Church.

Iain Quinn
Tallahassee
July, 2020

Acknowledgements

I am indebted to Judith Bauer, Adam Cobb, Laura Gayle Green, Barbara Lee, and Arianne Johnson Quinn for their assistance with the preparation of this edition.

Introduction

My own share in the production of the present volume has been very small. It is really the work of a sister and niece of Dr. Dykes, who do not wish their names to be published, and it is at their request that I have looked over the manuscript and proof-sheets, and that my name appears on the title-page.

It has been said that no man's life ought to be written until twenty years after his death, and there is often much to be urged in favour of this opinion. The lapse of years reveals whether a man's work has been a living work; besides, had the present Life been published soon after Dr. Dykes' decease, it would have been painful to Bishop Baring, and might possibly have been the means of stirring up strife. Even now some may think that the correspondence between Dr. Dykes and the Bishop ought not again to be published. Yet it seems only fair to Dr. Dykes' memory that the true story should now be put into permanent form, after this considerable lapse of years, and told in his and the Bishop's own words.

It is believed that the Life and Letters of Dr. Dykes will be found to possess great interest, as bringing before us the mental development of one trained in the early Evangelical School; of one who, while moving with the Catholic Revival, maintained a certain independence of judgment, and held fast that which was best in the doctrines he had received in early life. But to many these Memoirs will appear, more especially, as a manifestation of singular musical talent, in alliance with genuine piety.

With Dr. Dykes, music was a part of his religious life, but, as a true musician, he also thoroughly enjoyed, at proper times and within due limits, every form of really good music. For many years he directed an amateur choral society in Durham, the members of which met at each other's houses in turn. Two characteristic points in his management may here be recorded. We always practised sacred music in Lent, to the exclusion of all other, and, during the rest of the year, whatever else we had, Orlando Gibbons' "Silver Swan" was always in the programme. For, as Dr. Dykes would say, it would be soon enough to leave it out when we had done it properly.

The accounts of the *genesis* of several of his tunes will attract all lovers of Hymnody, and the Sunday evenings at St. Oswald's Vicarage, after service, when many of them were tried over for the first time, will ever be a delightful memory to all who were privileged to take part in those little gatherings.

And, in this connection, his correspondence with Mr. Monk, Sir Henry Baker, and other musical friends, as well as with the Rev. E. H. Bickersteth, now Bishop of Exeter, will be read with great interest, an interest greatly extended through the enormous popularity of *Hymns Ancient and Modern,* in the editing of which work he took so active a part, not only in the musical settings, but in the help which he gave to the Words Committee. The author of the tunes to which are constantly sung such hymns as "Come unto Me, ye weary," "Nearer, my God, to Thee," "Christian, dost thou see them?", "Holy, Holy, Holy," "Jesu, Lover of my soul," "Lead, kindly Light,"—has helped the religious life of millions.

Some persons may be surprised that so devoted a servant of the Church should have written music for the use of Nonconformists; but his view was, that if St. Paul could rejoice and thank God that Christ was preached "every way," even of envy and strife, he might not only thank God that Christ was preached even in outward separation from the Church, but help any of His followers to sing His praises. Some idea of Dr. Dykes' attitude towards Nonconformists may be gathered from what he wrote in 1870 (p. 190). It may be observed that he did not give leave to Unitarians to use his tunes, but only to those who "worship Christ as God."

Few men have ever left such a mark on a parish as Dr. Dykes did on St. Oswald's, in conjunction with his first colleague, J. W. Kempe; and there is no doubt that, under God, Dr. Dykes and he together made St. Oswald's to be what it was. Dykes was the theologian, Kempe the ritualist, and each supplied that in which the other was less fully equipped, while both were men of remarkable personal influence.

What Dr. Dykes was in his parish may be gathered, in great measure, from the present volume. One of his characteristics, that has not been mentioned, was his great dislike to any sort of advertising of preachers' names, and even on ordinary occasions he would not let his own family know who was to preach, but, if asked, would playfully put them off with some enigmatical reply.

The Processional Cross, mentioned on page 104, a crucifix with figures of SS. Mary and John, has so remarkable a history as perhaps to claim a record here. It was found in a portmanteau left in a coach and was never inquired for. The late Mr. Caldcleugh, of Silver Street, had possession of it for many years, and after his death, his widow, a devout communicant at St. Oswald's, presented it to Dr. Dykes for the church. It was then sent to Messrs. Barkentin & Krall, of Regent Street, to be repaired. The nimbi, and the label over the head of the central figure were supplied, the old work gilded and silvered, and a new staff and knop made. It has been in constant use up to the present year, and has been valued, not only for its sacred use and intrinsic beauty, but as an interesting link between the earlier and the latter days of our national Church.

To all who knew Durham during Dr. Dykes' time, or, at any rate, to all who had the advantage of knowing him as a friend or as a pastor, his singularly engaging personality remains, after two-and-twenty years, as a vivid and cherished recollection.

In his *Life and Letters* we seem to have him amongst us once again; and to have been allowed to take any part, however slight, in the publication of so deeply interesting a record, has afforded me greater pleasure than I am able to express.

J. T. F.
Bishop Hatfield's Hall, Durham
October, 1897

1

Early Days
1823–1843

Hull—Birth of J. B. Dykes—Family life—St. John's Church—Education—
Music—A crisis in life—Death of his youngest sister, Caroline—Removal to
Wakefield—Death of his brother Phillip

In the old town of Kingston-upon-Hull there is a district called "The Groves." It is now a wilderness of streets and business premises; but in the early part of the present century it was a pleasant suburb, with its trees, gardens, and good houses, and the River Hull (purer and cleaner than it is now) flowing through it.

Here, in the "Old Ivy House," on March 10th, 1823, John Bacchus Dykes was born, and was baptized by his grandfather, the Rev. Thomas Dykes, at Sutton Church, to which parish "The Groves" then belonged. His second name, Bacchus, was originally a surname, belonging to his maternal ancestors.

His grandfather, the Rev. Thomas Dykes, an excellent and devoted clergyman of the old Evangelical school, had settled in Hull in 1790. Finding that the spiritual needs of the growing town required more church accommodation, he devoted a sum of money left him by his aunt, Rose Dykes, to building a church. He had much opposition to encounter from the Corporation, who at first objected to the undertaking; but by the help of the famous William Wilberforce, himself a native of Hull, the difficulty was overcome. Of this church, consecrated, under the name of St. John, by Archbishop Markham in 1791, Mr. Dykes remained incumbent for fifty-seven years. He had married the daughter of the eminent surgeon, Mr. William Hey, of Leeds. They had three children, Thomas, William Hey, and Mary.[1]

William Hey Dykes, the father of the subject of this memoir, married in 1816 Elizabeth Huntington, daughter of Bacchus Huntington, a surgeon in Hull, and granddaughter of the Rev. William Huntington, Vicar of Kirkella, near Hull. At the time of their marriage, both were twenty-three years old.

Mr. William Dykes, who had settled in Hull, was engaged first in shipbuilding, and then in banking, and on his appointment as manager of the Hull Branch of the "Yorkshire District Bank" (now "The Yorkshire Banking Company"), he moved into the Bank House, opposite St. Mary's Church, Lowgate.

The fourteen children, nine boys and five girls, were all born in Hull. John was the third son, and fifth child. He was a bright, quick boy, affectionate, full of fun, but very sensitive. His father and mother made it their first care that the home should be a happy one, and, by their genuine goodness, set an example to the household. The mother's sweet and gentle disposition endeared her to her children, while the father's sound sense and loving discipline won their respect and affection. He entered into all their innocent pleasures and encouraged in them a love both of nature and of art, thus adding much brightness to their home lives.

Their mother prepared herself in the early years of her married life to teach her children the rudiments of Latin and Greek. As their number increased, it became evident that the boys could not be sent to the best public schools. Moreover, their father much preferred that they should remain at home. Fortunately, at that time there was a most excellent school in Hull, the "Kingston College," the headmaster of which was Mr. Henry Ralph Francis (a grandson of Sir Philip Francis, the supposed author of "The Letters to Junius"). There the Dykes boys received a thoroughly good early education.

John was remarkable in the family group as a sensitive child of excitable feelings, with much mental power. He learnt by heart with the least possible trouble, and was his mother's pride, from the quickness

---

1. Who afterwards married the Rev. John Dale Wawn, Vicar of Stanton, Derbyshire.

with which he could repeat long lists of dates, names, and events. It used to be said that he was heard quietly repeating the counties and kings of England to himself in church; but in excuse for this it must be stated that the long, dull services in those days were most trying for little children, especially when they and the servants were seated in the high gallery, where they could not easily hear.

His talent for music soon developed itself, and he could play by ear almost anything that he heard. But he was so sensitive about it that it was with great difficulty he could be persuaded to play before strangers, and he would hide himself under the piano, or anywhere, to avoid notice.

A kind aunt undertook to teach him his notes, but it was not such an easy matter, as playing by ear came so readily to him. He was also taught the violin and piano. He soon overcame all difficulties, and at ten years old played the organ in his grandfather's church. It was curious to see the small, pale child—for he never was tall or robust-looking—trying to reach the pedals, and bringing so much power out of the organ. His schoolmaster, Mr. Francis, feared that the music would interfere with his graver studies; but the number of prizes he brought home showed that any such fears were groundless.

The daily family life was very regular. The father and mother were always up at six o'clock—this enabling them to have a quiet time for prayer and reading before the business of the day began. Then, after their cold baths, came the walk before breakfast, when a procession of father, mother, and those children who were old enough, was to be seen every fine morning on one of the piers or country roads.

The children were brought up on plain, wholesome food; no delicacies were allowed. Butter, in those days, was considered unwholesome for children—a wise consideration when there were fourteen of them. One piece of bread-and-butter was, however, allowed on Sunday, if the children were good.

After bank hours, when there was more time to devote to country rambles, another walk was taken; and the father's knowledge of botany and geology made the walks interesting and instructive.

The life in Hull was a happy time for the children. Their grandfather, the Rev. Thomas Dykes, was not only incumbent of St. John's Church, but in 1833 he was appointed Master of the Charter House, Hull, where he settled; and the garden of the Master's house was a favourite meeting-place for the grandchildren.[2] There and at the Botanic Gardens they met their special playmates—Dr. Bodley's children, and the family of the Rev. W. Keary. St. John's was, of course, the family church. It is a large, almost square, red brick edifice, with a small tower, close to the old docks and the Wilberforce Monument. The only architectural idea seems to have been to build it to hold as many people as possible; and it was a sight not to be forgotten to see the church crowded with an attentive congregation, for it was capable of holding from fifteen hundred to two thousand people. There were galleries the whole way round, including an organ gallery at the east end, under which was a very small Altar, almost hidden by a high three-decker pulpit.

In those days the life of the Church seemed centred in the old Evangelical party. People came from all parts of the town to attend the services at St John's. One pew was set apart for the dissenting ministers, many of whom thought it wrong to hold their meetings during church time; believing in John Wesley's saying, that if they left the Church, God would leave them. They came regularly to the Holy Communion, then administered only on the first Sunday in the month; before which, the old clerk gave out: "A collection will now be made for the poor, as it is usual on 'Sacrament Sunday.'"

Amongst the great excitements of the year were the Church Missionary Society meetings, which were held in St. John's Church. A large platform was erected in front of the pulpit, and hiding the altar. It was nearly the height of the galleries, covered with green baize, and with a flight of steps up to it. Chairs were placed all round it, and a table in the middle, with decanters of water and glasses; while a dish of oranges was laid for the refreshment of the speakers, though the memory of the oldest inhabitant cannot record that they ever ate one in the church.

The meetings lasted long, but were thought very interesting; the morning one began at eleven o'clock, and was not over until between one and two o'clock.

The Dykes children always gave something at the collection, added to which a halfpenny was given to each for any cake that could be bought for that price, to eat during the meeting—quite sufficient to allay the pangs of hunger; for a gingerbread elephant could be purchased for a halfpenny. And these, when made by Bessy Capes, an old family servant, then a confectioner in Whitefriargate, were most excellent. The meetings excited

---

2 There were twenty-four, twelve boys and twelve girls, then living or visiting in Hull.

much enthusiasm in the minds of the children, and in very early times, John and his sister Fanny, with a favourite cousin, arranged to go out as missionaries, taking with them a barrel organ and a box of lucifer matches, a great wonder, in those days of tinder and flint. These were to attract and astonish the natives, so that they might be more easily converted.

John had a clear soprano voice, and, as he could read music easily he was most useful in the family concerts, which were generally arranged to take place before the little boys went to bed. Their solos were practiced beforehand, and a programme settled. The father had a beautiful tenor voice, and played the flute and French horn. Most of the brothers and sisters could take their parts, when, after bank hours and the evening meal, either oratorios, glees, or part songs were practised.

In September 1834, when John was eleven years old, a grand musical festival was to be held in Holy Trinity Church, Hull, conducted by Sir Henry Smart. To quote the programme, it was "For the completion of the magnificent East window of Holy Trinity Church, and for the benefit of Hull General Infirmary." There was much practising to be done by the chorus, and John had such a reputation for reading music that the lady sopranos smuggled him in amongst them to help them, hoping he would not be seen by the conductor. However, Sir Henry Smart soon discovered the boy's voice, and would not allow them to keep him, no doubt much to his disappointment. The first solo singers were engaged, with an excellent band and chorus; but, before the Festival, Mr. William Dykes went up to London, and there, at her father's house, he first heard Clara Novello sing. She was then only fifteen years old, and looked very young, but he was so charmed with her voice and style of singing that he wrote at once to the Festival committee, and, on his recommendation, they engaged her. She came down to Hull, accompanied by her mother.

The members of the committee, who met the London coach, of course concluded that the mother was the singer, and great was their dismay when she explained that the engagement had been made with her daughter. However, they were so delighted with the beauty of her voice, and her pure style of singing, that they at once justified Mr. Dykes in his choice.[3]

On March 18th, 1835, there is the following notice in his eldest sister's diary:

> John made his first *début* on the orchestra.

---

3. This was Clara Novello's first appearance in public.

and, on May 27th in the same year:

> Mr. Knight (Vicar of St. James' Church) called to ask Papa and Mama if they had any objection to allow John to become organist at his church, as it was the decided wish of his congregation, who preferred his playing to others who had played there before. He spoke in the highest terms of John, and said he believed he would soon become the best organist in a hundred miles round. Mama, of course, declined.

He was then twelve years old.

The younger sisters have a lively recollection of being made useful as organ-blowers in early times. When he became a more accomplished organ-player, an hour, or more, was spent on Saturday afternoons in tuning the reeds, when he was going to play on Sunday. This was easy work, as a professional organ-blower was provided, and the sister had only to strike the notes.

Another excitement in the year was the Sunday School Anniversary, when all the Sunday Schools met together in St. John's Church. A fresh set of original hymns was printed every year, and to these the Dykes children contributed. The authorship, however, was kept a profound secret; though, as the hymns for the Selection Committee were brought by their uncle, Mr. Frederic Huntington, their source was guessed. To these early productions we attribute the taste for hymn and tune writing which developed itself in after years, especially in Dr. Dykes, whose juvenile hymns are unfortunately lost, and in his sister Mrs. Alderson, who afterwards wrote the Almsgiving hymn "Lord of Glory, Who hast bought us," and the Passion hymn "And now, belovèd Lord, Thy soul resigning," both in *Hymns Ancient and Modern*.

On Sunday afternoons, after his public work as Superintendent of Christ Church Schools, the father had a Greek Testament class for his boys, while the mother held a Bible class for her servants. The little ones, too, were not forgotten, but were duly told the beautiful Bible stories, taught the Church Catechism, and Watts' hymns.

Amongst the favourite evening amusements (especially when friends came in to help, and during the Christmas gatherings) were the games of "questions and answers" in poetry. In these games, though the compositions of all the brothers were good, John's were especially clever. On Christmas Eve, 1840, the last time the fourteen children met, all were assembled, but John was ill, and could not come downstairs, so his papers were sent up to him to write. His illness was not at first thought to be serious, but the next day he was worse, and soon became delirious. His uncle, Mr. Frederic Huntington, and Dr. (now Sir James) Alderson, were sent for, and they pronounced the illness to be scarlet fever. The children were all dispersed at once among relations and friends. John was in great danger, and for some days hung between life and death. Just at the crisis, when he was thought to be dying, he remembered an old friend, Samuel Knight (son of the Rev. James Knight, of Sheffield), whom he fancied he had neglected, asked for paper and pens, and wrote the following note:

> My Dear Samuel,
>
> In five minutes' time, so may it please the Almighty, I shall be in Heaven; my affection for you has never flagged the least, and that we may meet again is the earnest prayer of your devoted— Give my love to your beloved brothers.

By God's mercy he recovered; though the fever left a delicacy in his throat, and weakness in his voice, which he felt much in after years. But the lessons taught by his illness were never forgotten, as he then learned to take more sober, earnest views of the responsibilities of his renewed life. Proper sanitary precautions were, in those days, not understood, and the dispersed members of the family, after being away a month, all returned home, except three who had not been well.

The day after their return, January 29th, 1841, Caroline, the youngest daughter, a clever, intelligent, thoughtful girl of twelve years old, was seized with the fever; she soon became delirious, and two days running she was bled! Such was the treatment for fever at that time. On the third day, February 1st, she died. In her conscious moments she begged to have the twenty-seventh (her favourite) Psalm read to her, and kept repeating verses from it, with prayers, until her happy spirit was taken by the angels into Paradise. Her death, the first death in the family, was keenly felt by all the members—and those who had returned home were again dispersed, and sent away for a longer time.

This was a year of change. In October the children were startled by the announcement that they must leave Hull and all their friends and old associations. Their father had been appointed manager of the "Wakefield and Barnsley Union Bank" in Wakefield, a more lucrative post, which was an important consideration as expenses increased, and the future of nine sons was to be provided for. On November 5th the removal began. Of course, the children assured one another that they should never be happy again; and when some of them tried to be cheerful as the train neared Normanton, the others thought them very unfeeling. John was especially broken-hearted; but time healed the wounds, and their spirits soon began to revive.

The new Bank House, in Westgate, had to be arranged, and the pretty country near Wakefield was a delight to them after the flat neighbourhood of Hull. Then there came a visit from three of the Hull clergy, Mr. King, of Christ Church, Mr. Scott, of St. Mary's, and Mr. Knight, of St. James', who brought presentations to Mr. William Dykes—a timepiece from the Sunday-school teachers, and silver plate from the town of Hull, in recognition of his services.

Before leaving Hull, John had been presented with a gold watch and chain; and on the gilt-edged paper accompanying it was the following inscription:

> "A list of the subscribers towards a testimonial, to be presented to Master John Dikes on the occasion of his leaving Hull, by the congregation of St. John's Church in that place, in acknowledgement of his services for several years as assistant Organist."

At Wakefield the boys went to the "Proprietary School," then under Dr. Fennell and Mr. Garvey, two very able teachers. In his first year, 1842, John gained a prize for English verse. Next year he won three prizes.

But now a great trial came. On April 5th, 1842, the father, mother, and children were returning from their afternoon walk, by the Silcoates fields, where they had gone to buy plants for stocking their garden. They were met by a messenger with the news that Philip, the fifth boy, thirteen years old, who had been playing with his brother Charles by a pond near Sandal Castle Hill, had fallen into the water, and was drowned. Charles, having in vain tried to save him, rushed off for help; but before the body was recovered, life was gone. That afternoon had been fixed for a concert, and the boys had their songs practised, ready for it. The song that Philip had prepared was "Angels, ever bright and fair, Take, oh! take me to your care."

The time had now come when the boys must be sent out into the world. Their parents had so much feared its temptations, that when Mr. Carruthers (the Conservative Member for Hull), in early days, had offered to procure a cadetship in the East India Company for Thomas, the eldest son, it was refused. Their great desire was that the boy should become a clergyman; probably, if they could have foreseen that he would afterwards become a Jesuit priest, their opinion might have altered. He went up to Cambridge in 1840, entered at Clare Hall, and was ordained in York, in 1847, to the curacy of Gleadless, near Sheffield.

William Hey, the second son, studied as an architect in London. While there he became influenced by the Church revival, which had taken such hold on the many earnest, devoted priests who were striving to put new life into the Church of England, and to teach her children to realise her true position; William attended Mr. Dodsworth's church in London, and was much struck by his preaching, and that of Dr. Pusey, Mr. Marriott, and others whom he heard.

On his first visit home after the removal to Wakefield it was rumoured in the family that William had become a Puseyite. This, of course, much distressed his parents, and resulted in a long correspondence between father and son. But the arguments of the son at last convinced his father that the dreaded Puseyites were only enlightened Evangelicals, and that it is only by adding apostolic order to evangelical truth that the true life of the Church can be maintained. From that time the family gradually embraced those deeper views of the Christian life which spring from a truer grasp of Sacramental truth. William as an architect, and John as a musician, strove to devote their talents to the glory of God, and the good of His Church. The other sons, as they grew older, followed in their steps.

In Wakefield the family at first attended Holy Trinity Church, where the father was honorary choirmaster, and some of the sons sang in the choir. But they also thankfully availed themselves, after a time, of the more frequent services at the parish church; and the early morning walk was taken to matins at the beautiful old Chapel on the bridge.

At Holy Trinity Church John frequently played the organ. The incumbent, the Rev. C. G. Davies, was devoted to him; and when Mr. Davies was afterwards appointed to a church in Plymouth, he kindly offered to allow John to read with him for the three months before he went to Cambridge. There, on July 13th, 1843, John settled, as Mr. Davies' guest, and remained until he went up to Cambridge, in October. He was then twenty years old.

In a letter to his mother, he says:

> Those *foolish* people in Wakefield are actually going to make me a present. I felt quite vexed when I heard about it; for it just seems as though I had played with the expectation of getting some compensation, instead of for my own pleasure. However, I have come to a better frame of mind, and think a nice present a very agreeable sort of thing.

> Mr. Fennell wrote to ask Mr. Davies what he thought I should like, and we have decided it should be half music and half other books; at least, I should exceedingly like *The Fall of Babylon, Palestine, St. Paul,* and Weber's *Oberon*. With the rest of the money they must do what they like.

During his visit to Plymouth, and when he first went to Cambridge, a short diary was kept, in which occurs (July 1843) the first notice of any of his musical compositions:

> A letter from M. T. thanking me for a copy of my waltzes which I had sent her, with an Arietta.

But his brother Frederic sends a much earlier recollection:

> I remember his writing a song to Tom Moore's words, "As down in the sunless retreats of the ocean,"

which he dedicated to Miss Harriet Spence, in Hull. I was entrusted by him to leave it at her father's house, which I did, and caused John some agonising moments when I told him that the white roll which contained the MS. was addressed to Miss *Hariot* Spence.

2

Cambridge
1843–1847

"Dikes Scholarship"—Arrival in Cambridge—Visit of the Queen and Prince Albert to Cambridge—University Musical Society—Professor Thomson (Lord Kelvin)—Evening party at Trinity Lodge—Reading party—Jenny Lind—J. B. Dykes' degree—He misses a Fellowship—Fire at Cambridge—John Parry—*Elijah*—Death of his grandfather, the Rev. T. Dykes

IN entering on his University life, John Dykes' great fear seems to have been lest he should be led into idleness or extravagance, and lest his music should interfere with his more solid studies. To guard against these dangers, he laid down definite rules for his daily work, arranging his reading so as not to be interrupted. His spiritual life, too, was not forgotten, and he gladly availed himself of such helps as the University afforded. He frequently attended the evening services at the churches of St. Michael, Holy Trinity, or St. Giles, to hear the preaching of Professor Scholfield, Carus, or Harvey Goodwin. But his special delight was the University sermon, and on his scholarlike theological mind profound impressions were made by Dr. Mill, Dr. Wordsworth, and Professor Blunt.

He was entered at St. Catherine's Hall, Cambridge, with a view to his obtaining one of the Yorkshire Scholarships there. He had already received the "Dikes Scholarship," founded by the town of Hull, and presented to his grandfather on his eightieth birthday—December 21st, 1840—in recognition of his services to the town during his fifty-seven years' ministry at St. John's Church. The scholarship was also for the benefit of his descendants. The change of spelling in the name Dykes must be explained. A rich old gentleman, who spelt his name *Dikes*, was a friend of old Mr. Dykes' grandfather. He promised to leave him a large fortune if he would change the *y* into *i*, in his name. This he did. The old gentleman died, but never left him the fortune; only the legacy of a deformed name. The Rev. Thomas Dykes requested that this might not be perpetuated by his descendants, and begged that his own name might be spelt with a *y* on his coffin.

John Dykes' arrival in Cambridge took place on an auspicious day. The town was *en fête*, in honour of Prince Albert, who, accompanied by the Queen, had come to receive the Doctor's Degree, conferred upon him by the University. In a letter to his sister Fanny, John Dykes writes:

> I arrived in London between ten and eleven at night; put up at the "Golden Cross," went to Novello's next morning, and set off by the Cambridge Coach at 9.30.
>
> All the road was covered with triumphal arches, etc., so that it looked quite gay and lively. We reached Cambridge at 3.30. The first thing I noticed was a knot of undergraduates, and, as the Coach drove on, their number increased, till, when we put up at "The Hoop," almost every other person was a 'Varsity man.
>
> Coming up quite fresh, as I did, you cannot tell how pleased I was with the appearance of all the men. All were in full Academicals, so that the streets looked gay with all the different uniforms. We made the best of our way to Tom's[1] rooms, but his door was sported. We heard that the Queen was in King's College Chapel, so we got up to the top of the College and waited there till the service was over. Nor did we wait long; for in a very few minutes, the three state carriages drove up to the doors of the chapel, and soon the doors were thrown open and out walked, surrounded by hosts of Doctors of Law, Divinity, and Music, Noblemen, Fellow Commoners, etc.—all in their different costumes—Her Majesty and the Prince; then they walked to their carriage, and made the best of their way to Trinity, to dine.
>
> . . . We set off and soon arrived at the noble and illustrious foundation of St. Catherine's Hall, which was illuminated by a gigantic Catherine Wheel, and other tasty devices. The next morning I made the best of my way to "King's," for the purpose

1. His eldest brother.

of surveying quietly the Glorious Chapel, and very glad I was I had done so, for I had not been there ten minutes when it was reported that the Queen and Prince Albert were coming to look at the Chapel, and consequently the gates were shut against the populace. As soon as the report got wind, I and those few who had the good luck to be in King's grounds at the time rushed into the Chapel, and to the door of it very shortly drew up the state carriages, and out came Her Gracious Majesty and her Royal Consort, and walked into the Chapel. I of course had a splendid view, and saw her quite plainly. I followed her to her carriage, and with a few more undergraduates walked by the side of it all the way to King's gate. It was open and went very slowly. She was teasing her husband about his new Doctor's robe and kept smiling and bowing graciously upon us. When we arrived at the gates, I ran on to St. John's, and, by means of a ticket which Corrie had given me, got into the grounds, where in five minutes the Queen and suite followed. All the Johnians were arranged in a long file at each side of the path to meet her, and didn't we nearly bawl our lungs out, much to her amusement. After all this, I went about the streets, meeting first one old schoolfellow and then another. On Saturday evening I went with Bodley and Trueman to Trinity College Chapel, and very much delighted I was. The view of the Chapel was most beautiful; it was surplice night, and the long row of candles and white surplices had a most imposing effect.

It is an immense organ, and a very beautiful one; and I had indeed a treat in hearing our Professor[2] play. Before the anthem, he played a long extempore introduction, working in the most splendid manner on the subject of the anthem; and at the end he played one of Bach's most difficult fugues. He let me try the organ after the service.

The following are short notices from his Diary:

*November 9*th. Went to a private meeting of the Peterhouse Musical Society. They fixed that I was to take the piano. Went to Walmisley's Madrigal Society. A rich treat, several of Morley's "Ballets," and choruses from the *Antigone*.

Mr. Carus' meeting on Sunday night.

These meetings he appears to have attended regularly.

---

2. Professor Walmisley.

Sunday, Nov. 25th. Chapel, reading Greek Testament. Began Doddridge's "Rise and Progress." It is certainly a most excellent book. St. Mary's, admirable sermon. Huntington, Wray and I went to Carus', where was Mr. Latrobe, who gave us a missionary lecture.

Nov. 26th. At lecture this morning I drew up a declaration, stating, that until the end of the term I would agree to pay a shilling to the boat club, every morning when I was not at the College gates at, or before, seven a.m.

Nov. 29th. Lecture at 10. On my return was reading Euclid most piously, when a gyp came to tell me that old Proctor wanted to see me. I posted off, and found I had got the scholarship, whereat I was much pleased. Huntington came home with me, and brought a friend of his, Cust, who seems a very nice fellow.

In 1844 he writes to a sister:

I had a deputation almost as soon as I got up, to ask me to take the Presidentship of the University Musical Society, now vacant by the departure of Blow. I asked for time to think about it, and then sent and declined it, in consequence of the reading, etc. (was not this good of me!). I am very glad, however, that I did, for we have prevailed on that splendid fellow Thomson,[3] of Peterhouse, to take it. It will be no end of a feather in our caps, to have such a man as our representative in the University.

Again, he writes:

Our Musical Society is getting on famously. Walmisley is going to join us. He says it is the most splendid affair since he came to the University.

In April, in a letter to his sister Lucy, he writes:

I am bringing home a friend who plays the cornet in our band, and rejoices in the very *un*common name of Thomson. He is a great friend of mine, and a very nice fellow, indeed, and, what is more, a most gentlemanly man.

The friend came, and delighted his hosts with his simple, good-natured kindliness. They have a lively recollection of how he made a flying machine with umbrella whalebones, persuaded an egg to stand alone, and performed wonderful experiments, besides joining in the family concerts.

---

3. Professor, afterwards Sir William Thomson, and now Lord Kelvin.

The following is a quotation from the *Dictionary of Music and Musicians*, on the "University Musical Society":

> The first Concert given by the newly named Society was held on May 1st, 1844. It included Haydn's "Surprise Symphony"; and Mr. Dykes, of St. Catherine's College, sang John Parry's "Nice young Man," and, for an encore, the same composer's "Berlin Wool." The Mr. Dykes who thus distinguished himself was afterwards well known as the Rev. J. B. Dykes, the composer of some of the best modem hymn tunes.[4]

His talent for singing, and clever arrangement of humorous songs, was very great, and, with his natural fund of humour, and his genial, pleasant manners, made his society much sought after. We are indebted to Lord Kelvin for the following interesting particulars of the early history of the "Cambridge University Musical Society," which began as the "Peterhouse Musical Society."

To Mrs. Cheape[5]

The University, Glasgow
February 23rd 1896

The first president of the Peterhouse Musical Society was G. E. Smith, who remained President until his death in 1844, when it had become the C.U.M.S. He came up to Peterhouse as an undergraduate, at the same time with myself, October 1841.

Blow, an undergraduate of a year later, succeeded him, and retired in 1845, when I became President. Blow was a splendid violin-player, and he continued as first violin in the C.U.M.S. till 1846. He became a clergyman, and lived to about 1874.

When I left Cambridge in 1846 to enter on my professorship here, your brother John succeeded me as President.

I still came up from Glasgow in the May term, and continued my part (as 2nd Horn) in the orchestra, till (as far as I recollect) your brother retired in 1847 on leaving Cambridge. He was succeeded by E. W. Whinfield, of Trinity, an excellent violoncello player, of whom your brother thought very highly.

A Jubilee Commemoration of the first fifty years of the C.U.M.S. was held at Cambridge in 1893, and I find a menu card of a dinner given on the occasion in King's College Hall on June

---

4. *Dictionary of Music and Musicians*, vol. iv.
5. Dr. Dykes' sister.

12th, with some pencilled notes on the back of it for a reply to the toast "Prosperity to the C.U.M.S."

"Founded 22 years after the birth of *Der Freischütz*

"17 years after the birth of *Oberon* and death of Weber

"16 years after the death of Beethoven. Mendelssohn still alive

"These were our gods:

"1843: G. E. Smith, Cornet, Founder, and first President

"1844–45: Blow, Violin and President

"1845–46: Thomson, 2nd Horn and President. Macdonnell, of Magdalen, 1st Horn and Secretary

"1846–47: Incomparable John Dykes, Musician and President

"1847: Whinfield, 'Cello and President"

I well remember my first visit to your father's hospitable house in Wakefield, with your brother, in the Easter Vacation, 1844. I can never forget the kindness I received from all your family, including the extreme good nature of your father in giving me some instructions in the French Horn, and allowing me to play on it in his study when he was out at the Bank, and the, if possible, more extreme good nature of the rest of the family, in tolerating the noises that came from that room during many hours of each day of my visit. I also remember well being taken to a friend's house in Wakefield,[6] and being delighted with selections from *Don Giovanni*, instrumental and vocal, in which your father played the Horn part.

I am glad to hear that there is to be a published memoir, and a collection of your brother's hymn tunes, of which the general public knows just enough to have some appreciation of their extreme beauty.

A letter, written by John Dykes to one of his sisters, describes, with graphic detail, an evening party at Trinity Lodge.

Cambridge
May, 1845

But I must now give you a slight account of my visit to Dr. and Mrs. Whewell, as I promised you. On the Thursday evening, after dressing myself with the most consummate nicety and precision, and looking as angelic as any unhappy undergraduate might be well expected to do, I sallied forth from the walls of St. Catherine's, at a quarter to nine, and soon found myself before the great entrance of Trinity College. I had just reached

---

6. Hatfield Hall, near Wakefield.

this when a carriage drove up, out of which issued two ladies and two gentlemen. I thought I could not do better than follow this party, which I did, and soon found myself in a large square Hall. My first impulse was to follow them; but as I didn't know who they were, I did not like to join the party, and thought I would wait until I could see some servant, who would introduce me upstairs. Well, I waited and waited, looking this way and that way until, on a sudden, I espied a door open at the farther extremity of the Hall, and out of it, to my horror, I saw Mrs. Whewell in a grand scarlet polka sort of cloak, issue, followed by a huge string of ladies, all leaving the dining room. I turned my back most vigorously to them all, and though I heard them nearing, and nearing me, and felt the gowns sweeping by my trousers, yet I pretended to be so vigorously searching in my great-coat pockets on the table, as not to be in the least aware of anybody's being near me. As soon as they had passed I, by degrees, began to turn my head round, but very meekly and gently at first, for fear of any of them seeing me—and at last, having quite turned it, I perceived them going up the aforementioned flight of stairs. Well, thought I, come, I'll be plucky and follow, and so, as soon as they had fairly got out of sight, having put on my white kids, and given my hair a rub and pulled down my coat, and pulled up my choker, and looked at my boots and taken out my pocket handkerchief, and put it in again, and pulled down my wristbands, and given myself a sort of general stroke all down, I walked to the stairs and began to run most boldly up them. But I had only managed to get about halfway up when my courage failed me. I saw before me, brilliantly lighted rooms, and then thought, how can I go in by myself? Who is to introduce me? and with these pleasing meditations, I quietly walked down again. I wished myself most earnestly safe in my rooms, and was seriously meditating a desperate bolt back, when I espied a flunkey, to my joy. He came to me and asked me my name, and told me to follow him, which I did. He led me up the stairs, through a large lighted room, full of ladies, into the drawing room, a most magnificent and noble room. Here, to my surprise, I found nobody but the party whom I had at first followed, and whom I recognized as the father and mother-in-law of the Vice Chancellor, and two strangers whom I did not know.

This being the case, I began to amuse myself with admiring the room, which was certainly a most magnificent one. It is what is called the Queen's drawing room, and is only used on special occasions. It is hung with crimson velvet hangings—has a lofty pendant roof, and has its walls covered with gigantic oil paintings of kings, queens, etc., and was then most brilliantly lighted. Well, I had not been half a minute thus engaged, when the old Mrs. Vice Chancellor (whom I had met before, but who I did not think would recognise me, and therefore did not take any notice of) came up to me and said, " Mr. Dykes, will you allow me to introduce you to my daughter and her husband, who wish to be introduced to you." So I said I should be most happy, and having been introduced we went on talking most sweetly, till Mrs. Whewell and all her ladies entered the drawing room. Mrs. W. immediately went up to my old friend Mrs. S., and shook hands with her and the rest of her party; and then looked most intently at me. I consequently returned the gaze, and there we stood staring, till Mrs. S. again helped me, and introduced me to Mrs. Whewell—who began talking most amicably. I began to feel myself now tolerably comfortable, and discovered amongst the train of ladies, several of my acquaintance; but I could not help thinking that all of them stared rather hard at me. I just looked at my clothes again, and thought they all appeared (as the poem says) "extremely neat," and was beginning to sing inwardly, "Away with melancholy," when my mistake flashed across my mind.

I found that every member of the University (of whom, by this time, there were many present) was dressed in full academicals, whereas I was only in common evening dress. I cannot express to you how dreadfully annoyed I felt. I didn't know where to put myself, because I thought it would appear such a great insult to Whewell. But while there is life there is hope. W. had not as yet left the dining room, so I went to my good old Mrs. S. again, and when I found her at liberty for a moment, I begged her to excuse me, but asked her if I had not made a great mistake in coming upstairs in un-academicals. She said I certainly had, and she would advise me, if I could, to slip out, make my way to the Hall, and put on my gown. I accordingly followed her advice, and, watching my opportunity, while Professor and Mrs. and the Miss Frizzlewigs were being announced, I stepped out, put on my gown, came back, and then, for the first time, felt happy. The drawing room kept filling and filling with Professors, masters, fellow commoners, noblemen, etc., till at last Dr. Whewell and his clique of dining friends came up, at which point, I suppose, the evening began. I have not time to enter into particulars. It was, however, a regular formal state party—the reason of its being given was, there had been an election that day, for the office of University Librarian, and many old masters had come up for the purpose of voting; and Cambridge was, of course, very full.

Blow was there, and I think that, as far as I could make out, he and I were the only two *plain undergraduates* there (of course I don't include fellow commoners, etc., in the term *plain*).

There is a piece of etiquette kept up at Trinity Lodge, which I believe is kept up nowhere but at court—viz: that no *male* sits down all the evening. So of course I had to stand on my legs all night. We had some music during the evening: Walmisley and Blow played a magnificent P.F. [pianoforte] duet of Onslow's, which took up nearly half an hour, and which acted as a nice accompaniment to conversation! Then some lady who was staying at the lodge sang a song, and very nicely she sang it. This being finished, I saw, from the other end of the room, Mrs. W. apply her glass to her eye, and take a sweep of the room, and stop in the direction where I was standing. I immediately began talking very vigorously to some young ladies near whom I was,—but it was all no go. I was petrified by Mrs. W. coming up to me and saying, "Mr. Dykes, will you go to the P.F. and sing something." I, of course, had to say, "Certainly, Madam," and then began to rack my brain for something to sing. Of course I dared not sing anything comic, so I luckily thought of that song of Kreutzer's, "Ah from out those gloomy valleys" with which, by the bye, Walmisley was delighted. But I am tired of writing, so must finish my narrative when I get home. Here is a programme of our last concert. The trio was most splendid, and the concert went off admirably. Walmisley played the P.F. Solo; he is really a magnificent player. You see I came out in the Russell line, this time, instead of the Parry. We're in the midst of the races. I have already lost about six or seven pounds in weight, and we have four more races.

His second long vacation was spent at Bangor, with a reading party, when he sent several amusing letters home. One of them, thirteen sheets in length, beginning, "Brevity is the soul of wit," gives an account of the party being lost on Snowdon, and remaining there all night.

He returned to Wakefield with his friend Mr. Wray, who in after years was his valued curate, and with whom he formed a lifelong friendship.

In 1846 he went to Keswick with his tutor, Mr. Percival Frost, and a reading party. There they were lost on Scawfell for several hours and being without food it is reported that one of the party was reduced to eating grasshoppers.

To His Sister Lucy
Keswick

... We all finish with Mr. Frost (tutor) next Monday, so that I shall soon have to think of departing. What glorious weather we have had! This is certainly far the best time of the year for this sort of scenery. I can't tell you how beautiful everything looks.

"I have made another ascent up Skiddaw and went up with the Vicarage party and a few others. It was one of the nights of the harvest moon, and we came down by moonlight. Wasn't it romantic and glorious?

I went to dinner at Barrow House the following day and met all the party at dinner—there were no less than five Dykes's! We had such fun over it. I took down a Miss Frances Dykes to dinner, and we made out that, if we were not cousins, we ought to be. They play and sing most beautifully, and seem a regular musical family, and a very clever one; three of the brothers are Fellows at Cambridge.

Two days ago, Mr. Frost and some more of us accomplished the ascent of Saddleback. We walked about 8 miles on the Penrith road, and ascended from there. It is a splendid mountain, worth 50 Skiddaws. Half way up there is a very deep black tarn, so dark that you can see the stars in it at noonday, and in it two immortal fish, that have been known to exist there ever since the time of the flood! A little way from the tarn is a long, splendid ridge—Razor Edge—several hundred yards in length, so narrow that you can only get along in some places by striding over it, and as it is a great height and very steep it is rather dizzy work.

The following letter, written to his sister Fanny during a Cambridge vacation, is interesting as showing the marvellous power which Jenny Lind exercised over all who heard her:

Dulwich Hill House,
Camberwell, London

Many thanks for your last epistle. In reply, I have to commence with a dismal piece of information, viz., I have had my pocket picked and am penniless.

The circumstances of the case I will now briefly unfold. Last Thursday, Wray, Thomson, and I left Cambridge for London, and in the evening *of course* all went to hear Jenny Lind. Well, on coming out of the Opera house, judge my dismay to find my purse vanished. It is the first time I have ever gone to one of those places with my purse in my pocket, and I promise you it shall be the last. It was almost unavoidable this time . . .

But of course, you want to know how I liked Jenny Lind. Why, I can only say that you must hear her before you can at all form a conception of her powers. What most of all struck me was the thorough *genuineness* of all her singing. She sings so thoroughly "*con amore*," and without, apparently, the slightest exertion to herself. I have never heard a voice half so lovely, or a style half so chaste and pure.

She has immense power, and apparently an immense compass of voice, and executes the most extraordinary and difficult passages with the greatest possible ease, and with such a happy and placid countenance that you can hardly think it is she who is singing. And then, her acting is such, that she completely carries you away with her. In fact, she raises the people to such a pitch of enthusiasm that they seem as though they were all, to a man, about to turn lunatics. However, enough of her for the present.

The next day we went to the Exhibition, and very much I was pleased. We saw divers other things and dined at Wray's rooms. Next morning, I wrote a note to the Treasurer of the Philharmonic Society and informed him that I was the conductor of the Cambridge University Musical Society and would be greatly obliged for a ticket for the Philharmonic rehearsal that morning. He met me at the door of the Hanover Square rooms and said he should be very happy to introduce me. And so he did; and didn't I just enjoy it! We had the Sinfonia Eroica, and upon my word, it nearly drove me mad. What a grand, wild, extraordinary, and sublime production it is. We had also Haydn's 5th Symphony— an overture of Sterndale Bennett's—a scena from *Der Freischütz*; in fact, the whole programme of the concert, which you may see in the *Times*. I heard Herr Pisheck then; I had never heard him before. He is the first mankind singer I have ever heard. After that I went with Thomson to the Royal Institution, Albemarle Street, and he got Faraday to introduce us to his lecture, which took place a little after three. There was a most fashionable attendance, and a most interesting lecture on divers branches of natural philosophy—chemistry to wit, acoustics, electricity, etc.

That done, we went again to Wray's to dinner, and afterwards went out to divers mathematical instrument makers, to look over all the new instruments which are being invented, and to get some for the Glasgow College. After church, on Sunday morning, I went to Aunt Lucy's, dined there, and had an invitation to spend a few days there. On Monday I went, and here I am (Tuesday) just about to dine, after which I am going with

Aunt Lucy and Uncle D. to hear JENNY LIND!! again, in *La Sonnambula*. It is very pleasant stopping here. I have nice quiet mornings, when I read Divinity, etc., like anything, and then we drive out, etc. Kindest love to all.

Johannes

Wednesday morning. I *must* write another Postscript. The opinion I formed of Jenny Lind's singing on hearing her the other night in *La Figlia del Regimento* was far, far below the mark. To say that her *Sonnambula* is "*perfection*" "*divine*," and anything of that sort sounds but tame, but I really cannot say anything else. She nearly drove us all crazy. The accounts you see in the papers of her are really not the least exaggerated, but (I think) far below the reality. The Queen was there last night, and Prince Albert, the Duke and Duchess of Cambridge, the Grand Duke Constantine of Russia, and the *grander* Duke of Wellington, Prince Louis Napoleon, etc., etc. Oh that angelic Jenny Lind!

Great was the disappointment in the family when, on January 23rd, 1847, there came a letter from Cambridge containing only these words:

I'm a spoon.

They were so sure this meant the "wooden spoon," that the next day it was a little consolation to find that he had come out the last of the "Senior Optimes," and was the "silver spoon." He writes a few days before this:

The list comes out on Friday morning; I can seriously give you no chance of even a decent place for myself. You must not be surprised if you do not see my name at all.

This was written after a few days' illness, brought on by sitting up too late at night, reading. Again, he writes:

The conferring of degrees is certainly a very amusing ceremony. We had all to appear in full black, white chokers, bands, and hoods, etc. And it was a mightily imposing function. The Senate House was crammed, and I can assure you there were three very splendid cheers for "the Silver Spoon."

Since that day I have met with a very fearful *sell*. You must know that there is, at present, a Yorkshire Fellowship vacant, one of the Fellows having married about two months ago. Well, I have always heard that our Dons were anxious to give it to me. I, of course, have never liked to cherish the idea knowingly, and have always attempted to do that difficult thing—fancy I had no chance for it. But, having lately been told by nearly everybody that I was sure of the Fellowship, and being continually congratulated by the College servants that I was about to become a Fellow, I could not help getting gradually wedded to the notion.

Still more was I beginning to feel sure of it when, as soon as the degrees had been conferred, and I had returned to my rooms, the Vice Chancellor sent for me. I immediately rushed in a great state of excitement to the Lodge, where were the Master and Missis seated. He asked me to sit down, and first congratulated me on my degree, and said he was perfectly satisfied with it, and then told me there was a Yorkshire Fellowship vacant, and that he strongly advised me to try for it, in fact, almost in so many words told me I could have it. But now for the sell. I asked him when the examination was—he said about the end of March. I immediately asked him if it must necessarily be then, for I knew that the fellowships were limited to men under twenty-four years of age and that I should be twenty-four on the tenth of March. He said yes! that the examination must take place after the eighteenth, because on the 18th is the second Tripos day, till which day none of those who had taken their degrees this year are full Bachelors by the Will. I told him that I could not possibly try for it, as I should be over age on the eighteenth. He seemed much surprised, and really very sorry; but the Law is decided. The Candidates must be full Bachelors and under twenty-four.

I never have had such a damp thrown over me in so short a time. Fancy being so near a Fellowship, and there being not one single reason against my having it but being born eight days before my time. I have no end of sympathy from the good people in the Town and University . . .

My only chance is, if I could date my birth from my baptism . . . The day after we all took our degrees, we each, in our College, gave ten shillings towards a relief fund for the poor Irish, by way of a Thankoffering for being safely made B.As.

Another letter states that, in spite of all efforts, and much good will, the fact of his being just over age prevented his obtaining the Fellowship. About this time, he wrote as follows to his sister Eliza, from Cambridge:

On Saturday night, at about 12, as I was just retiring to my couch, being clothed with my "*robe de nuit*," and just composing myself with a soft and sober little conversation with my P.F., I was startled by loud cries of *"Fire! Fire!"* from different parts of the town. I immediately slipped on whatever came first and rushed into the court, where the whole Heavens seemed one brilliant crimson colour.

Corrie gave orders for the gates to be thrown open, and for all to go who wished, so, of course, off I sallied, towards the market place, whence the flames seemed to issue—and on arrival there found one of the grandest fires I have ever seen. The whole town seemed brilliantly illuminated, and the fire seemed spreading with fearful rapidity. It originated in a warehouse behind a large shop in the Market Place, close by Trinity Church, and in a situation surrounded *most closely* on all sides with houses, some of them very good ones indeed. When I arrived there, the utmost consternation seemed to prevail, as it appeared next to inevitable that Trinity Church and the whole of the Market Place must be consumed. Families and furniture were being removed with the greatest haste on all hands, and the sight was truly awful, though inconceivably exciting. But no time was, of course, to be lost. Members of the University came streaming from all sides to the spot, and soon everyone was at work, some carrying away furniture, others working at the engines, others running to every house anywhere near, and bringing all the buckets that could be got; others up to their knees in water at the different water sources in the neighbourhood, filling their buckets, which were passed one from another along long lines of men to the different fire engines, from whence, having been emptied into them, they were passed along other lines, empty, back to the reservoirs to be refilled.

Upon my word I can give you no idea of how splendidly the university men worked; and, while the townspeople stood gazing listlessly on in mute astonishment, there was not such a thing to be seen as an idle university man. And to such purpose did they work that this fire, to the surprise of everybody who knew anything about the matter, was completely brought under by 3 o'clock on Sunday morning, at which time I wended my way home, being fairly tired out. Everybody who knows anything about that sort of thing says that, had not the measures taken been most prompt and decisive, and the exertions on all hands next door to superhuman, nothing in the world would have saved a great part of Cambridge.

On Monday night, I heard Parry; and had no end of a long talk to him between the parts and after the concert. He was exceedingly kind in showing me one or two of his dodges.

Our first concert for this term comes off on Friday.

In May 1847, he went to London to hear the *Elijah*, and wrote the following account of his impressions:

S. Cath. Hall
May, 1847

Well, I went to London and I heard the *Elijah*, and I can safely say that I was never more delighted in my life. Several of the choruses did not go quite so steadily as I could have wished and hoped, and I did not think that there were nearly sufficient violins to support such a weight of chorus and brass. However, I was so excessively delighted and absorbed by the magnificence, grandeur, and excessive beauty of the oratorio itself that I was well-nigh entirely blinded to the defects which there certainly were in the performance of it. I think the scene of Elijah and the priests of Baal, where they are vainly invoking their god—the scene, moreover, on Mount Carmel, where Elijah sends his servant to look towards the sea, and there is first "nothing," then, a "little cloud," and then the sound of "abundance of rain," and the scene also on Mount Horeb, where the "Lord passed by," and there is an earthquake, a fire, and then a still small voice—are perfectly unequalled in musical description by anything I have *ever* heard, or could possibly have conceived. And especially the last-mentioned chorus, "Behold the Lord passed by." I do seriously think it impossible for there to be a grander conception. It is throughout sublimity personified.

...

We've got a debating society in Cath. Hall now, and I really am going to try if I can open my mouth at it, for I have never made a speech in my life, and have not the least notion of putting more than 5 or 6 words together.

On August 23rd, 1847, at the age of eighty-five, the Rev. Thomas Dykes died. A large family gathering assembled at his funeral, in Hull, where he was buried in the vaults of his own church, St. John's. The demonstration in the town showed how much he was beloved. The shops were closed, the blinds drawn down, and thousands of people lined the streets, as the procession passed from the Charter House to St. John's Church. By his sweet, lovable character, and by his holy, consistent life, he had won the respect of all. To him, at all times, came numbers of people, clergy and laity, "to open their griefs," and ask advice. He was the valued friend of William Wilberforce, Charles Simeon, Joseph Milner, Richard Waldo Sibthorpe, and other good men of that day. His grandchildren still retain and greatly prize two silver cups given to him by William Wilberforce, of whom the town of Hull is so justly proud.

In the autumn of this year, 1847, John Dykes and his youngest sister visited his old friend, the Rev. C. G. Davies, who, having left Plymouth, was then vicar of Tewkesbury Abbey. On November 11th his sister distinctly remembers being quite alarmed, on going into the vicarage drawing-room, and finding her brother at the piano, his eyes overflowing with tears, as he played one of the *Lieder ohne wörte* (the Duetto). He had just heard of the death of Mendelssohn. It seemed to him a most irreparable loss.

Before going to Tewkesbury, he had been to Cambridge to pass the voluntary theological examination, and the following quotations from letters to his sister refer to his future plans:

> Redcar
> *Sep. 16, 1847*
>
> When you write to Mr. Davies, will you say . . . it will give me great pleasure to come for a few days, before you return, and bring you home. Justin Martyr progresses wonderfully, and Wray and I are getting on very respectably for the Voluntary (we read all the morning and a good part of the evening).
>
> Wray has got a Curacy at Darlington and is going to be ordained on Sunday week. I have written about a Curacy at Malton, but have not yet received a reply.
>
> The letter you sent me was from Thomson, written from the monastery on Mt. S. Bernard.

> Redcar
> *Sep. 27, 1847*
>
> I have finally settled to take the curacy of Malton. The reason of my being previously undecided was, my having heard from Mr. Carter that I should have *two* full services to perform every Sunday, and my fearing that I should not be able to prepare two sermons weekly.
>
> He, however, has set my mind at ease by informing me that the two services are in different churches (one in New, and the other in Old Malton), and that one sermon will do capitally for both. In fact, I believe it is the general custom there to preach the same sermon in the two different churches. The salary is £100 a year, and everybody speaks in the highest terms of Mr. Carter.

Returning home for Christmas, he joined for the last time in the amateur theatricals and charades, which were frequently arranged for the Christmas gatherings, and in which he had always taken an active part. In scenes from Shakespeare, Sir Walter Scott, or Charles Dickens, he showed a natural gift for acting, which also seemed inherent in his brothers. His amusing songs, too, gave great pleasure to all who heard them; but all these were given up after he was ordained. One of his old college friends (the Rev. J. A. L. Airey) tells us:

> I remember we tried hard, when he was staying with us in Durham, to get him to sing one of his humorous songs, with which he delighted our concert audiences in Cambridge, but he said he had made up his mind, on taking Holy Orders, to forswear them all for ever.

3

Malton and Early Durham Days
1848–1857

Ordination—Curacy at Malton—Lecture on "Sound"—Priest's Orders—Minor canonry—Precentorship of Durham—Letters to future wife—Marriage—Birth of eldest son—*Credo* in F—Literary work

On January 16th, 1848, John Dykes was ordained Deacon in York Minster, by Dr. Musgrave, Archbishop of York. On the 21st he settled at Malton—his first and only curacy. There he devoted himself earnestly to his work in the parish. There also he met his future wife, Susan, daughter of George Kingston, Esq., who afterwards proved a true helpmeet for him; and partly from his correspondence with her, some of the events of the next few years can be gathered.

His vicar at Malton, the Rev. William Carter, was a most earnest and devoted clergyman, for whom Mr. Dykes retained great respect and affection. Besides his parochial work, Mr. Carter took pupils at St. Michael's Vicarage.

The following is a quotation from a home letter:

> Mr. Carter has just been out of town for something like a fortnight, and I have, in consequence, had to do all the parish work alone, besides coaching his pupils. So I have been spending my days at the Vicarage . . . The Parochial work has been very heavy

lately; three have just died within four days; and I have three more who may go off at any moment.

Again, he writes, to his sister Eliza:

Malton
1848

How are you to expect a young man who has to study for his priest's orders; who has to prepare two or three sermons, alternately, for each Sunday; who has a thousand other things to do—and is, by his nature, always in a hurry—how are you to expect him to be a steady correspondent? . . . I am just put down to give a lecture at the Mechanics' Institute here, some time in February, on "Sound." Will you please ask the Pater if he will be kind enough to look amongst his numerous books—if he has any which I can find of assistance in the composition thereof. I can deliver it at your Church Institute afterwards, if you like.

Later, to the same sister he writes:

The Lecture went off highly satisfactorily: the chief fault was that it was too long. It occupied two and three-quarter hours. But (as Oliver Goldsmith once said with regard to a letter of his) "I had not time to make a short one, so I made a long one"; I will, however, condense and curtail it, before I read it to your learned body.

The lecture delivered, both in Malton and Wakefield, proved a great success. He worked steadily at Malton during the year but was able to come home for the next Christmas gathering, as, in those days of less frequent services, his vicar could more easily spare him. He preached at the Wakefield Parish Church on Christmas Eve, and this was the last Christmas he spent with his family, as he soon began to prepare for a home of his own.

On December 21st, 1848, he was ordained Priest by the Archbishop of York, in Bishopthorpe Parish Church, receiving his Priest's orders before he had been a year Deacon.

He remained at Malton until July 1849, when he was appointed to a minor canonry in Durham Cathedral. There were two vacancies at that time; the other being filled by the Rev. Edward Greatorex, who is still a Minor Canon of the Cathedral, and Rector of Croxdale. This resulted in a lifelong friendship between the newly appointed colleagues.

The following home letter contains an account of his first arrival in Durham:

South Street, Durham

There were only two of the Prebendaries in residence, on my arrival. So, on the Friday morning, after prayers, I called on them, and left a card for each, viz., for Archdeacon Raymond and Dr. Townsend. In the afternoon I received an invitation to dine with the former that evening, at 6.30. But my luggage had not arrived, and I had not an evening coat. However, I borrowed one from my friend Airey, which was about a mile too big for me—and in which I looked exactly like the pictures of John Browdie—and I went. There were present only one of the Proctors of the University—a Mr. Henderson (a tremendously clever man), Dr. and Mrs. Townsend, Archdeacon Raymond, Archdeacon Scott, and a young lady whose name I never caught. I was perfectly amazed at the wonderful amount of information which these old gentlemen seemed to possess on every subject—almost—in the world. They kept up one incessant flow of most interesting intellectual conversation. I have rarely enjoyed such an evening in my life.

On Sunday my duties in the Cathedral commenced. I am to go on now for a fortnight. I got through very well, and am now beginning to get quite at home with the Cathedral service. On Sunday evening, I went to the Galilee Chapel, at the West End of the Cathedral, and Dr. Townsend preached a most impressive sermon on the subject of the Cholera. He asked me into his house afterwards, and a most delightful evening I had. He is a most kind old gentleman and knows almost everything! He showed me his Library, which is a most tremendous one, and he has given me leave to make any use of it I like. On Monday I went to dine with Airey. On Tuesday all my luggage came. Tomorrow I expect the Dean will return home, as also Henry of Exeter, who is one of our Canons, and is now coming into Residence.

I like Durham exceedingly. The view from my window is hardly to be equalled in England. It is most magnificent, as is also my daily walk to and from the Cathedral. My window exactly faces the glorious West End of the Cathedral; and I am separated from it only by the river, on the richly wooded banks of which it stands. My walk is about seven minutes, rather brisk work down a footpath through a rich wood to the River, across the Bridge—and up again through the beautiful wood on the other side, to where the old Cathedral towers aloft. Then through the

Cloister, to the Minor Canons' vestry, whence, having robed—I proceed into the glorious building itself. I cannot tell you how much I enjoy the daily Service there. I feel as if I could never tire of it. We had Mendelssohn's *Te Deum* on Sunday—and right beautiful it was. I am beginning now to have callers and shall be inundated with them. There are not less than eight Clergymen close by me. I shall have very first-rate *mankind* society, and shall be able now fully to appreciate it, having my mind set at rest with regard to the feminine portion of the creation!

I wish you could just see the view from my window this moment! It is glorious! Lit up so splendidly with the sun. I am going to pay a visit to my Parish Priest, to ask him for a slice of the Parish to visit the sick in. I can't afford any more paper, for I am not yet Precentor, and I must not be extravagant!

On November 19th, 1849, Mr. Dykes was appointed Precentor of Durham Cathedral, a fact which he announces in the following letter to one of his sisters:

South Street, Durham
Nov. 19, Monday, 1849

. . . I am at present busily engaged in deciphering an old MS. Troubadour song for Dr. Gilly, and I have a great deal of trouble with it. It's most heathenish looking stuff. Dr. Gilly, you know, is the Waldensian man, and a most delightful and excellent man he is. He has only lately come into residence, but I like what I have seen of him immensely. He has lately discovered a new translation of the New Testament; the *oldest vernacular* version that has ever yet been found, and one whose existence has hitherto been unknown, in the language of the Troubadours; the old Romaunt, Romance, or Provençal language. It is a most interesting and valuable discovery and invests the Troubadours themselves with a great deal of interest. They are a class of men, he makes out, who are very much misconceived and underrated, and he is going to give a lecture on them, and especially on their sacred poetry—on Wednesday night: as an illustration for which I am now grinding at this song.

Almost all our Canons are now in Residence, and I have got to know something of them all by this time. I was dining with one of them, a little time ago, Dr. Ogle, and met there one of the most accomplished feminine musicians I have ever seen, viz., his daughter Lady McDonald, a fascinating young widow . . . She, Greatorex and I sang divers trios, etc. One of them you must certainly get; it is for Treble, Tenor, and Bass, by Lindpainter, "Sweet the thought, thou star of night." I think it is one of the most lovely things I have ever heard. The night, however, of which I am speaking, there was a great crowd of people, and we couldn't have our music in peace; so Canon Ogle asked us to come to dinner a few nights afterwards, to have a quiet musical evening, and we tried *Elijah, Lauda Zion,* and I don't know what besides. The party consisted of the vice master of the University (a Cambridge Senior Wrangler) and his wife; a son and daughter-in-law of Lord Rosendale's, the Honorable and Rev. Francis Grey (vicar of Morpeth and son of Earl Grey), and his wife, Lady Elizabeth, sister of the Earl of Carlisle—besides Lady McDonald and her brother—the Member for the County of Northumberland. However, notwithstanding they were all such grand folks, we had some very jolly music.

I am thinking seriously of starting a small establishment and trying a little bachelor housekeeping. The fact is there is at present a very pretty cottage[1] to be let, about a mile out of Durham, with a nice bit of garden and a very fine prospect, and houses of every description are so difficult to meet with here. I shall want some instructions in the art and science of house-furnishing, and gardening, and servant hiring if I do, but I have not made up my mind yet.

Well, my dear, I am very happy to inform you that I have this morning been appointed Precentor of Durham. I am exceedingly pleased, as I had begun to fear that they were not going to make a fresh appointment yet. I am of course to have sole management of the Choir—and also (a thing which I am very glad of, as being an important part of a clergyman's office, and as being also likely to give me a moral influence over the boys)—I am to have the superintendence of the religious instruction of the boys. I shall have £100 year extra, for my office, so that I shall now have about £330 a year, or, counting my surrogacy, £340. Moreover, if any of the singing boys like to learn Latin, they are to come to me for it, and I am to have eight guineas a year extra for each boy. Don't you think I am very fortunate? I am sure I ought to be wonderfully thankful for all this. If you are writing to Hull, will you be so kind as to tell Aunt Mary of my good luck, and ask her to let my friend Jane Burn[2] know, as Jane made me promise, when I left Hull, that I would let her know if I got the Precentorship.

---

1. Hollingside Cottage.
2. An old pensioner in the Charter House, Hull.

The following extracts, quoted from letters to his future wife, give a picture of his daily life at Durham. In one we have an account of his playing the cathedral organ for the first time. In after years he frequently played it, when help was required. And in his own church, St. Oswald's, it was no uncommon thing for him to accompany the musical parts of the service.

South Street, Durham
Oct. 29, 1849

I have now begun again my regular system of rising at 6.30. The very moment the tap comes at the door, I jump out of bed; and by the time I have begun to think exactly where I am, I find myself nearly half drowned by my shower bath; which has a most wonderful and salutary effect, in restoring consciousness, and dissipating drowsiness. I am always *downstairs* before 7.30, have thus an hour's quiet reading before 8.30, when I breakfast. My breakfast generally takes me till about 9.30, as I lounge over it, have a little light reading, or learn a verse or two of Keble; and after breakfast, I have a good practice of my scales, which, together with a little extemporaneous rattling over the keys, takes me till it is time to go to the Cathedral. After service, if I have anything to do in the town, I go and do it; if not, I come home, put on my reading-coat, sit on a little high stool, before a grave-looking reading desk, both of which I have lately purchased, in order to ensure myself preservation from sleep—and then I have some good stiff reading, till about 2.30. I am at present engaged with Hooker's [*Of the Laws of*] *Ecclesiastical Polity*; and I have divers other good, stiff, solid books to wade through. When I have finished that, I always have a pencil in my hand, and mark at the side every passage which I think worth re-reading, to facilitate reference to it. In the middle of this, I indulge myself with a bit of bread and butter and a glass of sherry, and, when finished, I start out for a good brisk walk, from which I get back just in time to read over the lesson, to see that there are no hard names in it, and get to the Cathedral by 4 p.m. Vespers concluded I proceed home, just turning first perhaps for a few minutes into the news room, to see what is going on in the world; and then I have my dinner. After dinner, provided I do not go out anywhere, I have a good practice at my music, instrumental and vocal, and this, with anything else that may turn up, takes me till tea, after which I have a little general reading:—history, biography, until the time comes for Keble and Greek Testament; with which I conclude, somewhere between 11 and 12.

Durham

I have lately been personifying on two occasions, the Chancellor of the Diocese of Durham, and attending upon the Bishop[3] in his place, at two consecrations. When the Chancellor cannot appear, the principal surrogate of the Diocese appears for him, (i.e. Mr. Raine, for whom I am deputy). He was unwell, so I had to turn Chancellor! and read the sentences of Consecration. The 1st Consecration was that of a little Church a few miles from Stockton, called Thorpe, near the seat of the Marquis of Londonderry. He came in a carriage drawn by six greys and preceded by outriders; then came the other carriages containing the Ladies from Wynyard. I had an invitation to luncheon at the Marquis', and was introduced to the Bishop there, who made himself wonderfully agreeable. What a magnificent place it is. The Marquis took us over the house, and I was quite aghast at its splendour! I slept the next night at Stockton and attended the consecration of a Churchyard there. I enjoyed the little trip very much, and considering I had all my expenses paid, and two guineas into the bargain, I don't care how soon I have to go again.

I have been lately taking duty at the workhouse, for my friend Airey, who has been very ill. They have daily service there as well as Sunday ditto, so that there has been plenty to do. He has just made me a present of Jeremy Taylor's *Life of Christ*, in 3 vols., printed by Pickering. But I must really get to work again at Dr. Gilly's song.

Durham
Sunday, 1849

What do you think I have been doing this afternoon? I have actually played the organ at the Cathedral. Poor Henshaw (the organist) was looking so ill this morning and told me he ought not to go out of doors at all today—and begged to be let off playing the last voluntary. I suggested that the Anthem should be changed to one that could be sung without organ—he seemed pleased at the suggestion—or else I said, if you will permit me, I shall be most happy to take the organ myself. To my astonishment he consented, so I got the key at once and set off. It happened, while I was there, that the doctor called and asked me to prevent Mr. Henshaw turning out again to-day—so I went home, swallowed my dinner, and went in a most tremendous state of excitement to try over the music. I think the service

---

3. Bishop Maltby.

went uncommonly well. We had to pay our formal visit to see the Dean after, and he congratulated me most heartily on my appearance in a new character—and both he and the choir seemed much pleased with the performance.

But I was tremendously nervous at playing for the first time on Sunday afternoon, and have got a splitting headache in consequence, which I hope may soon be better.

Shortly after this Dr. Henshaw (the organist) had an accident, and was laid up for six months, during which time Mr. Dykes took the organ for him, besides his own work as Precentor.

On New Year's Day, 1850, he writes to his future wife:

> I am just reading my Grandfather's life, which has lately been published with some of his sermons, and am deeply interested in it; not because there is anything at all extraordinary in it or any striking events; but because, remembering him as well as I do, and having so frequently admired his truly heavenly and Christian disposition, as well as personally experienced his unwearied kindness, I find it very instructive and interesting to trace the gradual development of his character.

Again, he says:

> By the bye remember that procrastination is one of my greatest, if not my greatest besetment; so take care and never allow yourself to offend in that point: you must select some other besetment for yourself from which I am comparatively free. It is a most tiresome failing, and I wish most heartily I was rid of it, as it causes a world of annoyance.

On May 1st he first occupied Hollingside Cottage, in the parish of St. Oswald's, Durham, a description of which has been given in a former letter. The following letter from his new home was written to Miss Kingston on the first evening he settled there.

> I cannot go to bed on this the very first night at the Cottage, without entreating you to join in the earnest prayer that the Divine Blessing may rest upon me in this house, to which, by His Good Providence, I have at last arrived. That I may acknowledge Him and seek His heavenly guidance in all my ways and doings; and that He may in mercy direct my paths, that this house may be, (as it were)—a little Temple devoted to His service, and hallowed by His Blessed Presence; and, that if it shall seem good to Him to grant me my earnest request and bring you safely to

me here, we may both have Grace given us to give up ourselves, Body, Soul, and Spirit, to His Blessed Service, and to seek His Favour, as better than life itself: and being united to each other in the gentle bond of a tender and indissoluble affection—may be united still more closely to Him; and be His in life, His in death, and His through all eternity.

On St. James' Day, July 25th, 1850, John Dykes was married to Susan Kingston at St. Michael's Church, Malton, and after their wedding tour in the English Lakes, he brought his bride to their charming home, Hollingside Cottage, near Durham. This was an ideal home for a newly married couple; a one-storeyed house, with a deep verandah round it, overgrown with creepers, and surrounded by a rather large garden, on pretty, undulating ground. The walk from the cottage to the Cathedral was a very pleasant one—through a wood, then along the riverbanks, and so up to the glorious building.

This house gave its name to the hymn-tune "*Hollingside*," written a few years later for the first edition of *Hymns Ancient and Modern* to the words, "Jesu, lover of my soul."

On August 14th, 1851, their eldest son, Ernest Huntington, was born and on September 18th was baptized at St. Oswald's Church.

In December of the same year occurs what seems to be the first notice of any of his Church Music, when Mr. Dykes had brought his wife and baby to the family home in Wakefield, and we find that his "*Creed*" was practised. This *Creed* (unpublished) is in the key of G. It is still in use in Durham Cathedral.

In April 1851 he was much distressed by the sad tidings that his eldest brother, the Rev. Thomas Dykes, had resigned his curacy at Holy Trinity Church, Hull; and then, that he and his fellow curate, Mr. Barff, had been received into the Roman Catholic Church. The chief causes which had led to this change were, the Great Gorham Controversy, the secession of Archdeacon Wilberforce, and the loss of his wife, to whom, after a very long engagement, he had only been married three months. John Dykes spared no pains in trying to persuade his brother to reconsider his decision, and a long correspondence passed between them; but it is doubtful whether the elder brother was allowed to read the letters, as the answers were so entirely unsatisfactory, and wide of the mark. One letter of fifty pages, written by John, is mentioned during a family excursion in Wales as being read aloud, and not finished after an hour and a half's reading. Thomas Dykes became a Jesuit priest, and died at Bournemouth, in 1888, much beloved by his people.

Mr. Dykes had been asked by the Editor of the *Ecclesiastic and Theologian* (the Rev. Thomas Chamberlain of Christ Church, Oxford) to contribute articles for his review. This he was glad to do, as, having no definite parochial work except that which he voluntarily undertook, he had time for the study of theology, in which he was intensely interested. In his dread of becoming worldly and careless, he also looked upon this literary occupation as a call from God to make himself useful.[4]

One of his duties as Precentor was to preach in the Cathedral every Ash Wednesday; the Precentor receiving five pounds for the sermon. On Ash Wednesday, 1852, he writes:

> I have had such difficulty with my sermon this time. For, having forgotten how long a sermon ought to be, I found I had written about three times too much; and have had such hard work to compress it into proper size and shape.
>
> Dr. Townsend sent for me after the service and informed me that I had given them "a most admirable and excellent discourse," but there were many things quite new to him. He begged I would lend him it to examine into some of the points, so I gave it to the old Doctor.

The following extract is from a letter written to his wife, then staying at her mother's house with her little boy, in Malton, after her father's death:

---

4. The following is a list of Mr. Dykes' articles, so far as they can be ascertained:
1851–52. "Antichrist and the Babylon of the Apocalypse"—four articles.
1853. "Williams and Hengstenberg on the Apocalypse"—four articles.
1854. "The Lord's Prayer and the Beatitudes;" "Lee on the Inspiration of Holy Scripture."
1855. "Interpretation of the Psalms."
1856. "Symmetrical structure of Holy Scripture;" "Rowland Williams' Rational Godliness;" "Internal Structure of the Sermon on the Mount;" "Rowland Williams' Pamphlet;" and "Lord Arthur Hervey's Sermons."
1857. "Auberlin on Daniel, and the Apocalypse" three articles; "Warnings of the Apocalypse to the Churches."
1858. "The Voice of the Last Prophet;" "Miracles of Antichrist;" "Antichrist."
1859. Sermons by Kingsley and Stanley.
Many letters of grateful thanks were sent to the Editor from those whose books Mr. Dykes had reviewed. Amongst others from Isaac Williams, Rowland Williams of Lampeter College, Professor Forbes, Charles Kingsley, etc.

Sep. 27, 1853

I am now full of business; being master of the boys, Precentor, Librarian, Organist, and resident acting Surrogate. I have the Organist's work on my hands, besides my own, which is by no means slight just at present; but I am beginning to write for the *Ecclesiastic* again . . .

Martin, (one of the choristers) is here at present; poor lad, he played truant last night, and told something like a story, (if not a decided one) by way of accounting for it. And I have been giving him a thrashing in consequence. His Father cautioned me to do it, in fact I told him, only the other day, that I would, if he did so again, and this is the very first night after my exhortation; so I am obliged to keep my word, though it grieves me most sincerely to do it. He is such a quaint, bonny lad, I am so fond of him.

Hollingside Cottage soon became too small for an increasing family, and Mr. and Mrs. Dykes removed into a larger house in "Old Elvet," Durham. In spite of the multifarious activities of his life, Mr. Dykes, as the following letter to his wife shows, found time for other work. That he should have been selected to do it is no slight proof of his practical gifts:

Durham
Sep., 1853

. . . There was a notice awaiting me, on my return to Durham, informing me that I had been proposed a member of a Committee in Elvet to consider the Sanitary Condition and suggest such measures as might be expedient, to prevent the spread of Cholera in the town. We had a large meeting—Sneyd in the chair. Every house in Durham is to be examined, and nuisances reported. Anthony Wilkinson, Stoker and I are deputed to examine every house in Old Elvet to-morrow. The accounts from Newcastle are very bad. I had a walk with Archdeacon Bland and Maltby between afternoon church and Galilee, and I have been taking tea at Dr. Townsend's since . . . The Cholera is the great subject of conversation at present . . . The account you heard of the Newcastle surgeon is quite correct. But a far more melancholy case has just occurred at Hexham. A Dr. Fairbridge (I think that is the name)—who has been very energetic lately in seeing after the sanitary regulation of the Town, was suddenly seized himself, and was dead in a few hours. His eldest daughter was next seized, and in less than a day was dead. His other daughter followed and also died, and at last the poor mother caught the disease and was just dead, when the letter in which I saw this account was written.

Meanwhile he continued his literary work. In his letter, written to his brother-in-law, the Rev. John Cheape, who was then laid aside from active work, he alludes to his review of a book which at the time was famous:

Durham
1856

I have just been sending to the press a review of Rowland Williams' "Rational Godliness." He is an ex-fellow of King's, Cambridge; and vice-principal and Hebrew Professor of Lampeter Theological College. Some of his sermons are striking and beautiful.

Unfortunately, he has most loose notions on the subject of the Inspiration of Holy Scripture. It strikes me these notions are spreading fearfully. The devil seems to have a great many "irons in the fire" at present. There is a great movement going on in the English Church, and he evidently wishes to meet it, and to thwart it somehow.

He seems at present to be instituting a series of experiments in different quarters, in order to test the assailable points, and to collect data, to enable him to elaborate some more definite and concentrated mode of attack. It behoves us all to be prepared, holding fast to the "Shield of Faith," and the "Sword of the Spirit"—the two great weapons of defence and offence—"praying always with all prayer." I fancy this last great spiritual engine is too much underrated by all of us. Preachers and Controversialists, and Reviewers, go on fighting the Battle of the Lord, and if the cause of Truth seems to triumph, they are apt to think it is their own arm which has prevailed to subdue Amalek; forgetting, perhaps, many a retired, unnoticed, unheeded Moses, whose Prayers in the Mount are the real cause of the success of the Combatants. The Church needs both the Meditative and the Practical, the pray-ers as well as the fighters; and may it not be for this very end, that some are kept back from the possibility of *active* work, that they may then more give themselves to contemplation and devotion, and strengthen by their prayers the hands of their Brethren?

With regard to yourself, my good fellow, you must never allow yourself to think that you are "laid on the shelf" and rendered useless. Nobody is "laid on the shelf" so long as he has life, and faculties. You are placed exactly where you are, for some all wise, all merciful purpose; you are just where you should be. Your malady (whatever it is) has been sent you for some good end, by One Who loves you with an everlasting Love. It is merely yours to strive and pray, that this good end may be abundantly realised in you. I presume you know I am shortly about to change my abode again: we dread the removal, but it will be decidedly satisfactory to have no rent to pay. The Chapter is putting the house into decent repair, and I think it will be a very comfortable one. Kindest love to L. and kisses to the God-daughter. I often think of you all.

4

"These Are They"
1857–1862

Early deaths of brothers—Their influence on his spiritual life and musical compositions—Death of his brother George—Birth and death of his fourth child—"Nearer, my God, to Thee."—Deaths of his brothers William and Charles—Anthem, "These are they"—Mus. Doc. Degree—*Hymns Ancient and Modern*—Notice of Durham life, by Rev. E. Greatorex

No life of Dr. Dykes would be complete without some allusion to the early deaths of so many of his brothers, to whom his spiritual help was of the greatest service. His life was so bound up with theirs, that the grief he felt at their sufferings and their loss quickened his own perceptions and feelings, and may account, in some measure, for the sympathetic character of so many of his hymn-tunes and other musical compositions.

As instances, we may mention his tunes to the words,

"Now the labourers task is o'er"
"How bright those glorious spirits shine"
"Ten thousand times ten thousand"
"Lead, kindly Light"

and the anthem, of which we shall shortly speak—"*These are they which came out of great tribulation.*"

In August 1857, Mr. Dykes visited the Farne Islands in company with his friends, Mr. Greatorex, Sir Frederic Ouseley, Mr. Wood, and Mr. Maude. This visit is alluded to in a letter to his brother George, who was then very ill. To this brother, who was a surgeon, he was of the greatest service in helping to prepare him for his death. He writes:

> I feel very anxious to know how you are—I fear not improving. Well! be it so, or be it not, remember you are in the Hands of One, Who is alike Infinite in Wisdom, and Infinite in Love, and whatever He does, must be best. It is in Love that He has permitted this sickness to visit you—it is in Love that He suffers it not to leave you. It is the Hand of your Heavenly Father that is upon you for good. He does not take His Hand off, only because it is better for you that He should not do so . . .
>
> Do not think by my letter that I am wishing to kill you outright! No, my dear fellow, God grant (if it be His Blessed Will) that you may be long spared to us. All I would venture to impress upon you is this—that in your present state, the issue is at least doubtful, and that it will be infinitely happier, and better for you to face the *worst* (so the *world* would call it—not *you* I hope) and so be prepared for either issue. If you are prepared to die, you *must* be prepared to live; but it does not follow, that because you are prepared to live, you are therefore—to die! So accustom yourself to face "The king of terrors"—(as he is faithlessly called)—with good heart. For since Christ has died, he is "king of terrors" no longer: but merely the Angel of Mercy, sent to conduct you (so soon as you are quite ready for it) to your true Home, your happiness, your everlasting rest.
>
> I don't think I have very much news to communicate. I have been absent from Durham a fortnight, returning last Monday evening. The first week I was with Greatorex, Maude, etc., at the Farne Islands; and enjoyed my stay there very much. I had a great deal of talk with Maude, who has got a most tremendous Roman twist, and I trust that what I have said may not be altogether lost upon him. At all events I was deeply gratified by his voluntarily, and unasked, giving up to me a book of Romish devotions—which he had been long in the habit of using, on the first leaf of which was written, "Given to the Rev. J. B. Dykes, as a pledge of greater fidelity, and more reverent obedience" (*i.e.* to the teaching of H.[oly] Scripture and the Church of England). God bless you, my dear fellow.
>
> Believe me ever
> Your very affectionate brother
> John

"These Are They"

The following are quotations from a letter to his friend the Rev. Canon Thompson, Vicar of Datchet, Windsor, written at this time:

> I have had several walks with Freeman, since I wrote. He is a first-rate fellow. He has given me his new work, "The Holy Eucharist regarded as a Mystery." It is an admirable book; you *must* read it. It throws a great deal of light on many important questions . . . We like our Bishop[1] well. He is rather a low Churchman, in his heart of hearts, but he is thoroughly anxious to do good, and further any *real* work that may be going on in the Diocese.
>
> I have just heard again from George, poor fellow; he tells me that, humanly speaking, he has only a month or two to live, and begs me to come over and see him at Filey, as he says he finds it so difficult to prepare for death.

His brother George died at Wakefield on October 13th, and left every assurance that he had found peace with God, and that his death (to quote Mr. Dykes' letter) was the entrance to "his true Home, his happiness, and his everlasting rest."

On November 1st another little boy was born at Durham, and baptized November 30th (St. Andrew's Day). He was named George Lionel Andrew. A few weeks later, when Mr. Dykes was at Wakefield, visiting his brother Arthur, who was there laid up with an attack of hemorrhage, he received a telegram from Durham, to tell him that the baby,—whom he had left quite well,—was dead. He hastened home, and found that the child had been suddenly seized with croup, and suppressed measles, and died before his father could be sent for; he was barely three months old, and was laid to rest in the burial-ground of the Cathedral.

Early in the year 1859, Mr. Dykes went to Wakefield, and on February 29th conducted a performance of the *Messiah* there; the proceeds of which were devoted to the restoration of the Parish Church.

On June 1st he visited the Rev. John Sharp, at Horbury, and preached there. The special object of this visit was to make his first confession. The hymn-tune which he named "*Horbury*" was written at this time, to the words, "Nearer, my God, to Thee," and it was, to him, a perpetual reminder of the peace and comfort he found there. Previously to this we have only notices of one or two tunes, written for the "West Riding Lunatic Asylum." One of these, to the words, "Dark shades of night," was a great favourite with the inmates. He had also written thirteen tunes for

---

1. Bishop Longley.

the Hon. and Rev. John Grey's[2] *Hymnal*, the first edition of which was published in 1857. Eight more were added in the second edition, making in all twenty-one of his tunes in this *Hymnal*.

In an obituary notice published in the *Literary Churchman*, the late Canon Ashwell, referring to this time, says of Mr. Dykes:

> Dr. Dykes was a most thorough student of Holy Scripture, and his knowledge was both wide and accurate. But of all the books of Holy Writ, the one which engrossed him the most was the Apocalypse, and it came out strongly in his sermons.
>
> In his case it was the natural outcome of the devoutness of his mind, and of his intense realization of the world unseen. Dr. Dykes was unworldly in the sense of living above the world, and that view of the unseen side of this world's present history, which is opened out by the Apocalypse, was naturally congenial to him. He drew to it instinctively, and, as was natural, such thought and studies drew his life and character further within the veil. Still he was not a mystic, but a practical Christian;—a high Churchman, as he could not help being, and with a touch of the ascetic temper too.
>
> A very remarkable sermon on "Natural and Supernatural life" was preached in his turn, as Precentor, in Durham Cathedral, on Ash Wednesday, 1859, when he was thirty-six years of age, and his character fully formed.

When asked to publish this sermon, at the earnest request of some of the undergraduates, Dr. Dykes at first hesitated, but then said he supposed he "must regard it as a sort of call." The following criticism, from a Church paper, is given:

> A very interesting and thoughtful discourse on John xvi. 16, in which the preacher interprets "ye shall not *see* Me" (οὐ θεωρεῖτέ με) as referring to the departure of our Lord from His disciples beyond the range of their bodily sight; and "ye shall *behold* Me" (ὄψεσθέ με) as implying that spiritual illumination which was to be the immediate effect of the Pentecostal visitation. And from the words that follow,—"A little while, and the *world* seeth Me no more; but *ye* see Me: because I live ye shall live also," he deduces that the spiritual *sight* of Himself to be enjoyed by His people, is the consequence of a spiritual *life* communicated to them from Himself. And this introduces the distinction between the natural and supernatural life, which is the subject-matter of the

---

2. Rector of Houghton-le-Spring.

sermon. It follows from the position thus taken, that there must be natural and supernatural modes of sustaining life, and hence the place of the Eucharist in the Christian system. The sermon is very carefully compiled, was published by request, and has passed to a second edition in a very short time,—a rare achievement for a single sermon.

During the year 1860, two more of the nine brothers passed away.

William Hey, the second son, who was settled in York, as an architect, had never recovered from a severe chill, caught when skating on the Ouse, in the winter of 1855. While trying to rescue a friend, who had fallen into the water, he also fell in. It was nearly twenty minutes before either of them could be taken out; and the chill resulted in a lingering cold, which ended in consumption affecting the throat, so that, at the last, he was unable to swallow any food. He continued his work until ten days before his death, when he returned home, to be nursed by his mother and sisters. Strange to say, he never spent a day in bed in his life, and now, on September 19th, 1860, he had come into the drawing-room, laid himself down on the sofa, and died, as his brother John (who had come two or three days before) was administering the last consolations of religion to him. He was buried in the churchyard of Thornes, near Wakefield, by the side of his brothers George and Philip.

Another son, Charles Edward, who was then curate at the parish church in Barnsley, hearing of William's increased illness, had also come over to Wakefield, and was with him to the end. Two months afterwards their happy spirits were together in Paradise. Charles was strong and healthy and had never known illness. He was a man of considerable ability, and, though quiet and reserved, possessed a great fund of humour. Devoted to his work, he was much beloved by his people, especially the poor, whom he visited with unceasing care and attention. He was then very anxious about a working man, who had been a great drunkard, and was dangerously ill with typhus fever. He spared no pains in visiting him night and day, and ministering to his wants, until he himself caught the fever. The working man recovered, but on November 11th, after a few days' illness, the priest who ministered to him died. The parishioners, in token of their love and gratitude, at their own express wish, paid the expenses of the funeral, and also put up a gravestone in the churchyard of St. Mary's, Barnsley, from a beautiful design which Mr. Bodley had kindly given for his brother William's grave.

The following letter from John Dykes to his wife gives an account of the illness and death of his brother Charles:

Wakefield
Nov. 13, 1860

We have this day consigned to his last earthly resting-place, our dear brother Charles: or rather, I should say we have consigned to the tomb his frail *body,* there to sleep in calm, unconscious repose, till the Archangel's Trump wakens it up to new life, beautified, glorified, and fashioned like unto Christ's glorious Body, and it rises to be united once more to his now happy spirit, to enjoy an Eternity of bliss, in the Kingdom of our God and Saviour.

We left Wakefield at nine o'clock. Alder (Charles' vicar) met us at the Barnsley station, and we proceeded to the Church. The burial service was read by one of the neighbouring clergy, Alder not feeling equal to the task of going through it. As we entered the Church, the music, and associations of the place, quite overpowered me, and I had a good cry.

After the sad but most comforting service was over, we drove to the vicarage, where my old schoolfellow, and College friend, Alder, showed us every conceivable kindness. He says wherever he goes, throughout his Parish, he hears one universal cry of regret at dear Charles' departure: and admiration of his steady, single-hearted, consistent course.

The more I hear of the dear fellow, the more I am convinced what a true-hearted, earnest, genuine Christian he was. He was only twenty-nine when he died. He appears to have been, of late, really always at work, morning, noon, and night, always in his Master's service.

Naturally reserved, and taciturn, as he was, I am glad that he has left a tolerably copious diary behind him, from which we shall be able to learn something of his inner life.

Dear fellow, he seems to have had this fever on him for many days—without any one being aware of it. He worked resolutely on, till he could work no longer.

Feeling instinctively that he was going to break down, he appears to have visited as many people as he could during the week. He administered Holy Communion to a girl in consumption, on the Friday, and told her he feared she must not look to see him, for some time; for he felt very ill. We hear of other sick people to whom he said the same. The Church where he preached on Sunday (and where he had to take the whole duty morning and afternoon) was two or three miles from Barnsley. Feeling very feeble, he ordered a fly to convey him there, (a *most unusual* thing for him). He seems from his Diary to have made it a matter of prayer, that he might be supported through the services. He went through the duty so steadily, that none of the congregation even dreamed that anything was the matter with him. He went home, and instantly sent for the doctor. In a few hours he was in raging delirium. The doctor said from the very first that it was a hopeless case.

And so he is gone! He rests at last from his labours. He rests his calm, peaceful, eternal Rest, in the arms of his loving Redeemer.

God's blessing rest upon you all.

In a letter on the same subject to his youngest sister—November 26th, 1860, he writes:

I think the great lesson we learn by dear Charles' mysterious removal, is the importance of scrupulously discharging—and being contented with—the duties (however unostentatious) of that particular and limited sphere, where God places each of us. There was nothing showy about Charles' work. It was, however, the work his Master set him to do—and he *did* it for *Him;* and his Loving Lord has accepted it and taken him to his reward. God grant that we may, all of us, be found at the last to have done our work with a like fidelity, and single-heartedness.

During the autumn of 1860, Mr. Dykes first heard of the projected publication of the new hymn-book, to be called *Hymns Ancient and Modern,* and at the request of some friends he wrote the following letter to Mr. Monk, the musical editor:

Durham
Oct. 12, 1860

... You will I trust pardon the liberty I am taking, in addressing you, being personally a stranger to you.

I venture however at the request of Mr. Twells and also of Mr. Wilkins to send you a few MS. Tunes for your inspection, thinking it is possible that some of them might do for your forth-coming book. I may perhaps, in case I can find time, send one or two more tomorrow. Of course you will fully understand that you're not, *in any sense whatever,* bound to accept any one of the accompanying Tunes. I trust that in your responsible position of Musical Editor of the work, you will (in respect of them, as of all others) adopt none but such as you deem really worthy of admission.

I am sorry that I knew nothing of the musical arrangement of the work till just now. I should have felt so happy if I could have, either in the way of suggestion, or otherwise, rendered any little aid whatever to the musical committee. I understand that you are now in an advanced state of progress. However, I just send up these slight contributions, in case they may be of any service.

The "*Dies Irae*" has given me much anxious thought. I am convinced that no single *unvarying* melody will bear to be sung to it throughout, without becoming thoroughly wearisome, and somewhat marring the grandeur of the words. The slight variations which I have introduced do not add to the difficulty of the composition. I have been *most* anxious to keep it as easy as I possibly could, consistently with the necessities of the words but I think they will be found to relieve the Hymn considerably.

The other Tunes I have at different times written, finding myself unable to discover suitable music for the Hymns. Some of them are sung in the Galilee of Durham Cathedral, and are very popular.

As the following letter to Sir Henry Baker shows, his tunes were accepted: but no one at that time realised what great help he would give in future editions and revisions of the hymnbook.

In the first edition seven of his tunes were published. Twelve more were specially written for the Appendix, and twenty additional ones for the second edition. Thus, thirty-nine tunes were written for *Hymns Ancient and Modern*, and, with those obtained from other sources, made a total of fifty-five published in this popular hymnal.

Durham
March 20, 1861

My best thanks are indeed due to you for your very handsome present, and also for the kindly notice you have been pleased to make of me in your preface.

I have esteemed it a great privilege to have been permitted to offer any aid, however humble, to a work in which I feel so warm an interest. The book really seems to have turned out admirably; my first copy reached me yesterday, and I have hardly yet found time to look through it. The book seems beautifully got up, the types so clear and good.

The seven tunes by Mr. Dykes published in the first edition of the hymnbook were—

"O come and mourn with me awhile" (*S. Cross*)

"Holy, Holy, Holy, Lord God Almighty" (*Nicæa*)

"Our blest Redeemer" (*S. Cuthbert*)

"Jesu, lover of my soul" (*Hollingside*)

"Nearer, my God, to Thee" (*Horbury*)

"Day of wrath, O day of mourning" (*Dies Irae*)

"Eternal Father, strong to save" (*Melita*)

In the year 1861 the University of Durham conferred on Mr. Dykes the honorary degree of Mus. Doc. in recognition of his musical talent. He was presented to the Warden and Proctors by Sir Frederic Ouseley, in whose Collection had appeared the anthem, "*These are they which came out of great tribulation,*" which established his fame as a composer of Church Music.

This anthem had been partly composed when Dr. Dykes was staying for a holiday with his wife and little children at a farmhouse in Flamborough where the only instrument available in the house was an old harpsichord. When, in 1858, Sir Frederic Ouseley applied to him to provide an anthem for a book he was about to publish, Dr. Dykes completed "*These are they.*" No one who has heard it sung in our great cathedrals and parish churches can fail to be touched by the pathetic beauty of this anthem.

He had been requested—as there was at that time a great dearth of suitable hymns and tunes for children—to set Mrs. Alexander's beautiful hymns to music. But, finding that Dr. Gauntlett had already done this, his attention was turned to the small collection published by Masters,—*Hymns for Infant Children.*

In a letter to his sister Lucy, dated, Durham, June 27th, 1861, he says:

> Sir Frederic Ouseley left me on Friday night; I have enjoyed his visit thoroughly. We were always so fully occupied, while he was with us, that I never found time to make him write for the Juvenile Tune book; only he quite takes to the idea and has promised to send his contributions.

In September, Sir Frederic Ouseley invited Dr. Dykes to stay with him at Tenbury, and preach at St. Michael's Church; but the following letter to his sister Fanny explains his reason for giving up the visit:

> Durham
> *Sep., 28*
>
> Another thing has kept me here. Our dear friend and neighbour Cordelia Durham, who has been in a decline for nearly ¾ of a year, and whom I have ministerially attended for some years past—has this last week suddenly become rapidly worse and is evidently in a dying state. She had several times expressed an earnest wish, that if God willed it, I should be with her at the last—and I felt if I went to Tenbury, there would be no human possibility of finding her alive on my return . . . I therefore wrote to Sir Frederic begging him to entrust the sermon which I had undertaken to preach to other hands.
>
> Poor Cordelia cannot live, humanly speaking, more than a day or two. I have been with her twice a day, and I must say I never knew what a Christian deathbed might be, till I saw hers.
>
> She has always been what the world would call a very high Churchwoman, and has availed herself of all the means of grace provided in the Church, and she has lived strictly and religiously up to her high profession. She was always a most humble-minded soul and thought most lowly of herself.
>
> She is now without a doubt, without a fear, in such a state of "Perfect Peace" as I could hardly have thought attainable on Earth. She feels and knows her sins are forgiven—she feels Christ's presence with her—she seems to have no Will but only His—and merely to be waiting on in calm hope till the time when He is pleased to release her from the burden of her decaying and worn-out body, and to take her to dwell with Him for ever—here is the case, alas! how rare, of one who has never lost Baptismal grace, but whose life has been a continual advance in Holiness.

Of Dr. Dykes' life at this time as Precentor and Minor Canon of the Cathedral, the Rev. Edward Greatorex has kindly supplied the following recollections:

> J. B. Dykes was elected Minor Canon of Durham on the 20th of July, 1849, and came into residence almost immediately after his appointment. In the following November he was made Precentor, the office which he so ably filled till his presentation to the Vicarage of St. Oswald's.

It was during his Precentorship that he became known as a composer of Sacred Music and laid the foundation of that musical reputation which he well deserved.

In the early days of his Minor Canonry and Precentorship he made many friends by his cheerful and kindly manner, and was soon valued, not only for his social and musical qualities, but for the depth and earnestness of religious character which pervaded his life. His first sermon in the Cathedral (the Precentor being the Preacher on every Ash Wednesday) was spoken of on all sides, as being the production of no ordinary mind, and, both by the Canons and the University tutors, was mentioned with great approval.

The Dean and Major Canons were men of considerable note, and some of great force of character; they showed great appreciation and personal liking for their new Minor Canon. Besides Dean Waddington, the residents in the College were Doctors Townsend, Gilly, and Ogle: Archdeacons Thorp and Raymond, Mr. Douglas and Professors Jenkyns and Edwards—Bishop Philpotts of Exeter coming only for his close residence. It was with the first two Canons that Dykes was most intimate, who, though belonging to a different theological school, were most kind and hospitable friends.

The Precentorship was, as might be expected, not altogether a bed of roses. Many prejudices had to be met, and improvements had to be very carefully introduced; but by degrees the services were improved by the introduction of new music, by weekly choir practice, and by bringing the singing boys into choir in an orderly manner.

Between 1850 and 1860, he became acquainted with Sir Frederic Ouseley, by meeting him at the room of a mutual friend, who was a student of the University. This acquaintance soon ripened into an enduring friendship and produced as its first fruits the well-known anthem "*These are they,*" which was published in the first volume of Ouseley's *Collection of Special Anthems*. He had, previously to this, written the anthem "*O God, forasmuch as without Thee,*" which is frequently sung in Durham Cathedral, but has not been published. He also, in the earlier part of his Durham life, wrote several songs, amongst which was a setting of Longfellow's "*Excelsior.*" These compositions have not been published.

During the whole of the period, between his coming to Durham and his presentation to St. Oswald's, he was always actively employed, and had the greatest dislike to anything like waste of time or idleness. To supply in some degree the want of practical work he would visit the old people of the Bishop's Almshouses and was ever ready to assist a Brother Priest when he could properly be away from the Cathedral services. He kept pace with all the stirring ecclesiastical events of the period, and was, with his intuitive power of looking to the result of things, a very valuable member of a clerical Brotherhood which was formed in 1857 for discussion on Church matters and mutual help.

He was, of course, in great request at Choral gatherings, which were then in their infancy, for they had nowhere attained their present gigantic proportions till after his succession to St. Oswald's.

His Durham life was, to a superficial observer, a quiet and uneventful one, but beneath the surface lay a great work; his very social life was working good; by his steady adherence to the Church's rules, and by his never failing cheerfulness, and placidity of temper, he drew many to see the beauty of the system he upheld, and gained the influence for which he was so remarkable.

Edward Greatorex
Durham Minor Canon 1849–97

5

St. Oswald's
1862–1866

Dr. Dykes appointed Vicar of St. Oswald's, Durham—Resigns Precentorship—Tunes for Chope's *Congregational Hymn—and Tune—Book*—Prize tunes—Birth of his youngest child—Death of his father at Ilkley—Death of his brother Arthur—Funeral at Eastbourne—Easter at Brighton—Tunes for *The Holy Year*—"Lead, kindly Light"—Retreat at Horbury—Norwich Church Congress—Tunes for Grey's *Hymnal*

On the banks of the River Wear, immediately opposite the glorious Cathedral, stands the interesting old church dedicated to St. Oswald. One side of the vicarage is in Church Street; the other, and most attractive side, looks into the pretty garden, overhanging the riverbank, and commands a beautiful view of the Cathedral towers. Here were the drawing-room and the vicar's study; out of the low windows of both, a step led into the garden.

To this living, on September 18th, 1862, Dr. Dykes was instituted. It was presented to him by the Dean and Chapter of Durham; and here he lived and worked, a faithful parish priest, until his last illness compelled him to leave the home and parishioners he loved so well.

Sir Frederic Ouseley, in a letter dated September 11th, 1862, writes:

> I am terribly sorry that you are about to resign the Precentorship—I know no man better qualified for such an office: This is no mere compliment, but a genuine expression of strong feeling on my part, which would come out. I liked to think of you as my best coadjutor in matters choral.

He was succeeded in the Precentorship by his friend, the Rev. Edward Greatorex, but he still retained the minor canonry. From this time, he began to keep a Diary, which was a great help to him in his work; and from it we gather many of the events which follow.

> *Nov. 20*th. Went to the Grove to congratulate Greatorex on his succeeding to the Precentorship—then to Cathedral. Had to take a "lower room," and change my side. Felt it rather a wrench to find myself and the Precentorship sundered.
>
> It is God's Will, it shall be mine!
>
> *Dec. 19*th. Prepared for school distribution. Felt very nervous; got up a small speech. Am sadly let down by my want of fluency and self-possession. Have nothing to say and cannot even say that nothing. This singular deficiency probably permitted to keep me humble, and more constantly and consciously dependent upon God.
>
> *Oct. 31*st. Sent off the last batch of Tunes to Chope.

These tunes were written for Mr. Chope's *Congregational Hymn—and Tune—Book,* in the second edition of which there are twenty-eight of Dr. Dykes' tunes. Mr. Chope had previously offered prizes for the best tunes to the hymns,—"Rock of Ages, cleft for me," and "Jerusalem the golden." For these Dr. Dykes had competed and had been successful in gaining the prizes. The tunes are published in Mr. Chope's book.

In quoting these Diaries, we omit the daily routine of parish work, which would become tedious to the general reader, and confine ourselves to special points of interest. Suffice it to say that, as a pastor, Dr. Dykes was unremitting in his attention to the sick and dying, in going after the wandering sheep, in keeping up the daily services, and frequent celebrations of Holy Communion, so far as his strength would permit; and also in giving "ghostly counsel and advice" to the many who came to him and "opened their griefs," seeking the benefit of Absolution.

> *Nov. 29*th, *1862.* Cathedral. My Anthem—"*O God, forasmuch.*"

This anthem, to the Collect for the Nineteenth Sunday after Trinity, had been written earlier for Durham Cathedral, and is still used there, but has not been published.

> *Nov. 30th*. Preached from St. Matt. 21.5. "Thy King cometh," &c., alluding to Christ's Sacerdotal work—His coming in the "Water and Blood."—Shall not be surprised if I have given offence—cannot help it. God knows I do not mean it. I must preach what my Great Vicar puts into my mind to preach. Offertory for distressed operatives in Cotton Manufactory districts. About £45. Thank God!
>
> *Dec. 26th*. Played my own Anthem, "*These are they.*" Went very well.
>
> *June 26th, 1863*. Came home, found Alan Greenwell had called to make a most handsome proposal. That, on his return from Germany, he will become my curate, and work in the Parish gratuitously. It would certainly be a grand thing for the Parish, and a wonderful support and comfort to me. Oh Lord, if this proposal comes from Thee, Blessed be Thy Name for it. Overrule this matter, I beseech Thee, as shall be best for us all, and most conduce to Thy Glory.
>
> *June 26th*. Have thought much lately of the Love of God and determined to pray more definitely for it. I feel this a great deficiency. My love is so cold.
>
> *June 29th*. Had more happiness and fervency in prayer than I have enjoyed for a long time. Hope to pray more for God's Love.
>
> *July*. Achieved two sermons, but have found it hard work, I write so slowly, and think so slowly. I have no fluency of thought or diction. Never mind—my Master knows my deficiencies. If He has work for me—He will enable me to do it.

In September, there was to be a great meeting of choirs in Durham Cathedral, which Dr. Dykes was to conduct. We give the account of the Festival from his Diary:

> *Sep. 10th*. Prayed especially for Blessing on my Holy Communion of the day, and also on our great Choral Festival. Administered Holy Communion to Mr. Elliot. Rehearsing Service. Thank God it is such a beautiful morning. Choirs came in slowly. Two thousand voices. Felt anxious as to how we should be able to keep all together. But (D.G.) the Chief Musician helped me through His Gracious aid.
>
> The Rehearsal passed off most satisfactorily. The whole of the Cathedral was a dense, surging mass of living beings.

> Thought it quite impossible the service could go on, and the Bishops and clergy come to their stalls. However, our Lord helped us. I gave the signal, and away we went. Thank God, everything was most satisfactory. There was really no hitch. The whole mass kept together throughout. It was a great success, for which I felt humbly grateful.[1]
>
> *Friday, Sep. 18th.* On this day, a year ago, I was instituted to the cure of souls. Alas! what deep cause for penitential sorrow for my negligence, and what humble cause for thankfulness for the undeserved mercies which have followed me.

In October he attended the Manchester Church Congress, and on his way back went to see his father and mother, who had left Wakefield and were then living at Ilkley.

> *Oct. 22nd.* Met Snowdon; he was walking to Keighley. Accompanied him nearly three miles on the road. Most beautiful day; passed a large stone Latin Cross,[2] standing by itself, on the Moors. Went to it and enjoyed a short season of happy private prayer, kneeling down before it.
>
> Went on my way refreshed—said Matins. The views of the valley of the Wharfe as you come in sight of Ilkley on this road are most splendid.
>
> *Oct. 27th, Durham.* A little after ten, met Mrs. Kingston on the stairs who congratulated me on the birth of a son. (Thank God.) May the little one be His for ever.
>
> *Sunday, Nov. 22nd.* In the afternoon went to Church for dear baby's Christening. Mr. Elliot and Dr. Holden Godfathers, and Mary Chaytor Godmother to my dear little boy, whom we called John Arthur St. Oswald: and whom may God Almighty bless and preserve; employing him in His service here and giving him a crown of glory hereafter. Lord Jesus, preserve this newly made member of Thine Own Mystical Body from soiling his baptismal robes.

And now the time came when his father's long and useful life was drawing to a close. His health having failed, he had resigned the Bank at Wakefield in favour of his son, Mr. Frederic Dykes, and established his home at Ilkley. His rest, at the age of seventy-one, was well-earned, for besides his daily work in the Bank, he had helped, as treasurer or secretary, nearly forty different Societies.

> 1. This was the first choral festival in Durham Cathedral.
> 2. To any who know the Keighley road at Ilkley, this Cross will be a familiar object.

Dr. Dykes makes the following entry in his Diary:

Monday, January 11th, 1864. On coming down to breakfast found a letter from L. announcing the death of my dear Father. He died very suddenly and quietly at Ilkley, on Sunday morning just after breakfast. Eternal Rest and Peace be with him! Well! his last few years had been in some sense, but labour and sorrow. His weakness and trials are for ever over. He is at rest! God grant that I may follow him, as he followed his Master. God support and comfort and bless dear Mother. How can I be sufficiently thankful to God for giving me such a Father, and such a Mother.

The letter which was written, the same day, to his mother, on the death of his father, is given in the last chapter.

Wednesday, Jan. 13th. Up at 6.15, off at 7.35 to the station. Fine sharp frosty morning. Read Bishop of Brechin's sermon, till I arrived at Thirsk; then Jean Ingelow's Poems. Full of beauty. Her power of language seems very great; and her ideas full of grace, and originality. She is a true Poet. Left luggage at Arthington, and walked, said Matins, and had a thoroughly enjoyable walk. Arrived at Ilkley between two and three o'clock. Found dear Mother looking so nice, such a placid, trustful, and even cheerful expression of countenance. The power of God's Grace, and reality of Christ's promise of comfort, apparent in her very look. Lucy also there, and my little Goddaughter Emmie. Went to see my dear Father. There is the Grace of God asserting its victorious Presence in his countenance. Love and Peace triumph over all. God be thanked for giving me such a Father. God grant that in health and strength I may devote my powers to Himself, as he ever did, so that my work may not have to be begun, when his began to draw to an end.

Read several letters, a very nice one from Tom, a most touching and beautiful one from Arthur, who has been very unwell lately.

Coach came, bringing Eliza, Fanny, Fred and Ned.

Jan. 14th. William Huntington[3] came, and soon the funeral cortège was ready to start. First the Vicar. Then a company of bearers; (there being no hearse in Ilkley) carrying the coffin on their shoulders.

The church looked very nice with its Christmas decorations. The choir (who had requested that they might give their services) chanted the 90th Psalm, and after the lesson sang the

---

3. Rector of St. John's Church, Manchester, cousin of Mrs. Dykes.

quaint but beautiful Easter Eve Hymn, "So rest my Rest."[4] Was impressed by Mr. Snowdon's reading of the service. He said the first verses a little distance *from* the grave, while the coffin was being lowered, then at the prayer of committal stooped down and said the solemn words—"Forasmuch, etc."

Well! it was soon all over, the last look given into the resting place—and we were off again. Another, and he the best, the head, the stock of our large family. Well! the other Home is rapidly filling; God in mercy grant that none of us may be shut out from *that*. Grant that none of us may fall away. Which of us will be the next? He alone knows. Lord! help us all to live in daily preparation for death.

About two months after his father's death, Dr. Dykes' youngest brother (Arthur) was taken to his rest. We feel no apology is needed in giving a short account of the life of this brother, to whom Dr. Dykes had been as a father. They were kindred spirits, especially in their love and gift of music. Arthur was a fine pianist, and richly gifted as an extemporiser. Had he lived, he might have made his reputation as a composer, for he had already written several good hymn tunes, and also songs. After leaving Durham, where he had been living in St. Oswald's Vicarage, he was entered at St. Catherine's Hall, Cambridge, in 1856. There he soon obtained one of the Yorkshire Scholarships. He gave great promise of future success, and hoped, in due time, to take Holy Orders. But after a residence of little more than a year at Cambridge, his health broke down, exposure and exertion in rowing brought on hemorrhage, and, though he recovered, and returned two or three times to Cambridge, yet, on each occasion, the weakness showed itself, and at last, in 1859, he abandoned all idea of continuing his University career. Through the kindness of relations, he travelled abroad; first to the South of France, and then to Madeira. While there he heard of his brother Charles's sudden death and wrote the following touching letters—the first to his mother, the second to his sister, Mrs. Alderson.

Funchal, Sollways
December 4th, 1860

I received Fred's and your letters yesterday. You did well not to keep me in suspense. It has quite broken me down. God help us, we are indeed brought low. It is awful to rouse up and find that it is real, and not a horrid dream. Our best, our noblest, our

4. Mercer's Hymns were then used in the Ilkley parish church.

cleverest, gone. It must be and is well, well for him who fulfilled a long time in a few years and worked all the hours of his day. And well for those of us who can take it to be well. But inexpressibly bitter. No doubt you must be the chief sufferer.

If it is hard for a brother, what must it be to you?

Our first thought is, let us go with him, that we may also die with him, but this must not be yet, though doubtless, soon for some of us, and not far off for any. God knows how I loved him, and not the less that one felt so reserved with him, for I am sure there is no family in the world that love one another more than ours, and yet our friends know more of us than we do of one another.

But we are bound by a closer bond than friendship, one that needs not confidences nor proofs, but is satisfied with loving, and being silent. So I know he felt towards us, and I feel the shake of his hand still, and see his sincere eye, when he bade me goodbye.

There is no family that love one another more, and yet God has chosen to chastise us with His rod; to lose health or wealth is hard, but to lose a loving heart from among us is terrible; and yet I see as you do, that He has been very kind; for in two, I would say three cases (were it not that I am still by His mercy alive), who should, humanly speaking, have been dead these two years— were it not that He is still digging about me, in hopes that I may bear some fruit before finally cutting down—in two cases He has given us long warning of what He was about to do.

He has distributed over two years the grief that He might, if He had chosen, have sent us now in one day. It may be we did not take to heart George and William's deaths sufficiently. But no doubt there are infinite reasons for this. Each of us must draw his own conclusion from it, for to each of us the trouble is sent.

Let me speak my own feelings on the subject, for it is a comfort to write them down; it is unbearable to be amongst strangers, unable to unburden oneself, and forced to keep in, and hide one's overloaded heart, with no one to speak a word of sympathy to me. You do not know what I would give to be with you now.

The bright sun and beautiful country are terrible, they seem cruel. We may see him again as a glorified being, but never as Charles, never as Charles that was the good walker up the hills, at the Lakes. This is the bitterness, never to see him walking without his hat, and the first—or not to see him on Christmas Eve. We may talk as we will of Angels, but we are men, and yet on the earth, and we cannot tear our feelings from the earth. The dearest places must now become hateful, because they are haunted by the remembrance of him. Who can bear the Lakes again? Nay, it will be bitterness even to come back to Wakefield again, for it is hardly home now. There is a new Home which is beginning to usurp the place of Wakefield. "The Silent Land."

We have almost as many there as here now, but who knows anything of it, except by guess and hearsay? And only their spirits are there.

Only part of them to meet us when we die. It is easy for you who have lived so long in the world, to know for a perfect fact that there is no happiness in it, but it is hard for one at my age to give up finally that hope that has kept me alive so long.

The hope that there are brighter days, that there is such a thing as friendship and love; that earth is a reality. Did we love him too much? Is it wrong to love one's relations? These are questions which have come to me during the last three or four years. Are the monks and hermits right after all? It would seem so, for God must have the whole of our hearts. We are punished for loving a brother, as if it were a sin.

I know the answer to this is plain, but sense fights hard against Faith. If we loved God more than our brothers, the grief would be less. Time will heal our grief, but it is indeed all but unbearable at first. Please write often to me, for I must have some aim to try to get better, for I have kept up by thinking of Wakefield, and friends! Now I dare hardly think of it, or them. Our youth has become age, the clouds return after the rain.

Forgive me for talking in a way that may pain you, but I must speak to somebody. I wish one could be certain that it was in love, not in anger, that God's Hand is lifted up again, and again. My evil conscience tells me that it is in anger. And I can at times only despair, or at least talk with my lips, comforting words that find no response, but only a sinking fear at heart. But I feel so blind, so weak, so miserable, and yet at the same time so proud, so self-confident, so defiant, that now, when such a blow has fallen, I can only feel utterly broken down, knowing neither what I am, or what will become of me.

This is what I feel now our darling has been taken away, for there was none of us like him, the bravest, the truest, the sweetest of all fourteen. And now the three schoolfellows, Philip, Charles, and George, are together again, and there is Cousin Charlotte there, so he has not gone among strangers. And God help us that are left. Write soon and ever believe me

Your most affectionate son,
Arthur

Jan. 6, 1861

Well, Christmas will be over with you now. I hope it was not a very sad one, because I still have an intense clinging to that time. For though all our late troubles have been towards the end of the year, from the time when Papa's health failed to the last sore trial, yet I feel to love it almost better than ever. I was talking about it to a clergyman who came to see me, and he did not approve of Christmas gatherings, because they sooner or later must become bitter and melancholy. But I stuck up for them. We shall have them because Christ was born, and with Him hope, and in honour of those who have been found ready and worthy to be taken. The more necessary, too, that we who are left should oftener meet—and love one another more, and show it while we are still together. No one can look on this trouble in this same light. We must each draw our own lessons from it.

If I do wonder or grieve at all, it is not for myself, but for those who seem so little to have required such heavy blows; but I am quite sure Mama draws her own lessons and comforts from it, and I bless God that He makes her to bear up. With regard to myself, all I can say is, "Thou Lord, in Thy very faithfulness hast caused me to be troubled." For this I do feel from the bottom of my heart. I said to myself before leaving Wakefield, nothing but a miracle can make any change in me, I feel so utterly hardened; brother after brother, friend after friend, are dying. Sentence of death is on me myself. And yet I cannot feel anything but this hideous callousness. For three or four years I have felt more and more desperate. I have known perfectly well where the fault lay. I knew and had argued (a thousand times) the case, but it always ended where it began. I had never been willing or able to say from my heart, that I would give up friends, relations or even life itself, if it was necessary. I could not say this after every trouble. I have always found a relief in mixing with my friends, and joining society again, and this has ever been my stumbling block, for I could not do without admiration and sympathy. However, having to bear this alone has, I trust, made me turn where I feel now peace may be had; and I have felt perfect confidence and happiness since. I am glad I am not in Wakefield, for I should have shrunk back from the effort as of old. There was only one thing left—"To cast all my care on Him Who cares for us," and to resign one's self like a child to His guidance.

I have had to say I know nothing; I can do nothing. I have no hope in this world—I will give up everything, even life itself; and so, in weakness, I have been strengthened, and can only hope that He will lead me on.

> I always admired Charles so much for his real wisdom, which I felt so deficient in; for whereas he had more talents by far, and had exercised them more than any of us, and was calculated, if he had chosen, to do great things in the world, yet he thought better to remain perfectly unknown. Such humility, such meekness, such an absence of vanity, I have never known. He had ambition, but gave up everything for Christ. I noticed every year a great change in him, from the time he was so silent, satirical, and reserved. He felt this to be false shame and pride, and conquered it, and became more open, real, hearty, sincere, and truthful every day. He acted thoroughly up to his belief. I wish one of us could say the same, because I feel so insincere, so vain and full of false pride and all manner of abominations. I admired him, but had never courage to say, as he had done, "I will put all aside—the false mask—and act as I know it to be right." But then his whole life was one of singular purity and gentleness. He had the single eye, and I have never heard of his ever having done anything either at College or elsewhere, for which he had cause to be ashamed. I do not feel it to be a matter of wonder that God should call him away when he was doing so much good, for I am sure he is doing more good where he is now, for us on earth, than he could do while he was in the corruptible body, which weighs down the soul.
>
> He has sowed the seed and ploughed; let others get the Harvest in. It matters not, he is nearer to us than ever; and now what we must do is to be thankful.
>
> Well, I must say farewell; it is nearly bedtime, though one does not feel much inclined for bed after lying on the sofa all day. I have twelve letters to answer and my spirit sinks at the prospect, and only two days to do it in.

On his return home Arthur Dykes, finding that he could not remain in the North of England, went to Bournemouth and Eastbourne; but his health gradually failed. His cousin, Mr. Joseph Dowson, most kindly placed at his disposal his country house, Holywell Lodge, at Meads, near Eastbourne, and invited his mother and sisters to be with him, and minister to his last needs.

We continue the extracts from Dr. Dykes' Diary:

> *Monday, March 7*[th]*, 1864.* A letter from Eastbourne. Dear Arthur has received my letter and sends me his warm thanks for it. He seems to be in a delightful frame of mind, and looks forward to the release, like a child looking forward to his holidays. God be thanked for His mercy to him.

The letter referred to in the Diary was the last Dr. Dykes wrote to his brother. The letter and its answer, which Arthur Dykes dictated (being too weak to write), are given in the last chapter.

Monday, March 21st. Heard at breakfast of the death of dear Arthur; he is to be buried at Eastbourne on Wednesday. Felt much perplexed what to do, not liking to leave Holy Week services. Prayed for special guidance; received kind promises of help, so determined to go to Eastbourne. Arrived there on Tuesday at 9.30. Found Mother, F. and L. Much grieved to find dear Arthur's coffin fastened up. I had earnestly hoped to look upon his face once more.

Wednesday, Mar. 23rd. Beautiful morning. Walk on the Downs. Went to meet Fred, Edward, and Sanderson. The day bright, but a cutting wind. Well! the dear boy was soon consigned to his last earthly resting-place—"Earth to earth, dust to dust." But, blessed be God, in sure and certain hope of the joyful rising again. Another of our large family laid asleep: who will be the next? Lord, Thou knowest!

Mar. 25th. Good Friday—Feast of the Annunciation. Most delicious walk to Beachy Head. Glorious Spring morning, the sea so blue all round, except where it rolled to the beach, and surrounded the base of the white cliffs, like waves of molten silver.

Tried to spend most of my time in private prayer and fix my thoughts on the Death and Passion of my Redeemer. Morning service. Evensong at three. Called at the Vicarage. I think the most cheerful drawing-room I have ever seen. Nice kind family; thanked Mr. Pitman for his kindness to dear Arthur; then went to the cemetery and bade farewell to his last resting-place.

Saturday, Mar. 26. Went to take a last look, and offer up a last prayer, at the bedside where dear Arthur had fallen asleep. Felt so thankful I had been able to see the bed and the room, so as to realise where he passed through his final struggle. Oh! that I may be stimulated and encouraged by his memory. Parted from Mother, F., L., and E., at Lewes. Lord Jesu! watch over them during their journey, grant us all a happy meeting again on earth, and a final glorious reunion in "Thy Heavenly Kingdom."

During his last illness, the simple faith of Arthur Dykes had deeply impressed the Rev. Thomas Pitman, the vicar of the parish in which he died at Eastbourne. Writing to Mrs. Cheape, Dr. Dykes' sister, on August 30th, 1864, Mr. Pitman says:

I fear you vastly overate my poor services to your dear brother. For my own part I can assure you I am the debtor rather than the creditor. For to see such simple Faith growing stronger and stronger as the outward man decayed, was to me a most valuable lesson, and one which for my own and my people's sake, I think I shall not readily forget. Would that it were oftener my privilege to minister to like spirits as his in the like extremity of our humanity. How often as I pass the house, in which you lived at Meads, do the several scenes within it, while you were there, rise up before me. Especially those in which I trust we had the presence of the Almighty Comforter, aiding our poor devotions. What a sea of troubles you have gone through! But the way to the Kingdom is through much tribulation! and so you may still be supported by the knowledge, that God is lovingly leading you, by His Fatherly Hand, to the Haven where you would be...

Easter was now close at hand, and Dr. Dykes, who was greatly in need of change and rest, accepted an invitation to spend a few days with his cousins at Brighton. The following extracts are taken from letters written to his wife during this short holiday.

12, Brunswick Square, Brighton
Easter Eve, 1864

Monday was one of the most magnificent days I have ever seen. The good old Mr. Pitman preached in the morning at Eastbourne old church...

The singing though simple was rather nice, and they had a very pretty quadruple chant, which I fixed in my own mind was by Herbert Oakeley, even as I discovered it so to be. After Church, we took a very pleasant walk, round by New Eastbourne, and so, by the cliffs, to the village of Meads, in which Holywell Lodge is situated. After which we examined the church, and paid a visit to the old Vicar, who lives in the very nicest Parsonage House I have almost ever seen. Then we went to the Cemetery to bid adieu to dear Arthur's Grave, then a pleasant walk by the fields home.

The next morning, we all travelled together as far as Lewes. Then we parted, my dear Mother, the girls and Emily going to London, I to Brighton.

12, Brunswick Square, Brighton
Easter Day, 1864

Many happy returns of this Holy Day. All best Easter blessings be upon you and yours; you are continually in my mind and prayers.

In the evening [Easter Eve] we went to St. Paul's Church at 8.30,—we arrived there half an hour before the service but the Church was almost full.

I was perfectly amazed when I entered. The Church was a perfect *blaze* of light and flowers, the decorations were splendid. On the chancel arch (which was one unbroken pattern of rich floral device) stood a large Cross some 8 or 10 feet high, made of nothing but daffodils; with the blaze of lights full upon it, it looked like gold. There were camellias and cinerarias and geraniums, in fact every variety of flower. I had never seen anything like it before and felt quite bewildered with the sight. As soon as 9 o'clock struck, the organ pealed forth a triumphant sort of prelude, leading into the old Easter Hymn, "Jesus Christ is Risen to-day."

As soon this began, a large surpliced procession issued forth from the sanctuary doors, (some forty, I should think, of Priests and Choristers) singing this Hymn, accompanied by the full organ, and all the people taking it up. The effect was glorious. Oh! what a change from the morning service! How I wished some of my Durham friends could have been present and heard and witnessed all! The Hymns and Chants were most thrilling. The anthem, "Blessed be the God and Father" (Wesley), was not quite so good. The sermon was from the text, "I will sing unto the Lord, for He hath triumphed gloriously," and was a capital one. The service finished with "Worthy is the Lamb."

I felt a strange mixture,—delight and sorrow through all— delight at seeing such a *glorious* service in the Church of England, and such signs of life!—and sorrow at comparing all this with our shortcomings in the North. This morning, the first Celebration of Holy Communion was at 5, the 2nd at half-past six, the 3rd at eight, and the 4th after midday Matins. My four cousins and myself attended the 8 o'clock Communion at St. Michael's. The service was most beautifully and solemnly conducted. The Altar was lighted up for Celebration; the Altar cloth was Cloth of Gold. I stayed also during the midday Celebration; not of course to communicate, but to worship and pray. I have never enjoyed any services so much in my life. They have moved me more than I can tell; I found myself constantly in tears. Yourself and my own dear Parish have been much in my thoughts and prayers. God grant that even in the North, we may yet "Arise and shine"!

March 31st: Brighton. Packed up—had a delicious turn near the sea.

> I felt loth to leave, and have been much pressed by my dear cousins, and also my wife, to stay a little longer, for my health's sake. Think I ought to go, and trust I am doing right in leaving.
>
> Bade all goodbye. God bless and preserve them for their great kindness to me.—Off to London. Got to Dr. Quain's at two.

Probably from the effects of over-work during Lent, Dr. Dykes' voice had been so weak that he became uneasy about the continued hoarseness. Dr. Quain was always most generous and kind in giving his advice, and to him he used to go when his health failed.

> *April 1*st. Dr. Quain examined me, and says that my chest and lungs are, as yet, all right; but I am delicate and must take care. I am to take Cod liver oil and wine, live generously, have plenty of sleep, and exert my voice only a little. He seems to agree almost entirely with what Cleaton says.
>
> *Durham, May* 25th. Letters from Charles Camidge. School feast tune. Made a new "Sun of my Soul."
>
> *June 23*rd. Visitation. Service at 11. Dinner in Hall. Felt foolishly and sinfully nervous, lest, as Incumbent of St. Oswald's, my health should happen to be drunk, and I compelled to answer. Oh! that I were not so utterly unable to speak; that I had at least some share of the gift of correct and ready utterance. I feel sure I should be more useful. And yet God knows my deficiencies, and He can work through me just as well without the aid of the gift as with it. This is one of my great trials. God over-rule it of His mercy, to be one of my blessings.

To His Wife, on the Anniversary of Their Wedding Day

S. Oswald's, Durham
Sunday, July 24, 1864

I cannot let to-day pass over without sending you a line to greet you on our wedding day, to wish you many, many happy returns of it, and to send you my dearest love. We shall be separated once again in body: not in spirit.

Dear me, how many years it seems since we started off together to the Castle Howard Station, full of hope and glee and pleasant anticipations. Well, all that has passed. And though the light-hearted gaiety of springtime is over—still, it has only given place to something, perhaps better, and more really wholesome—the calm, sober happiness of maturer life. We have found that all was not to be sunshine—although God has given us a large share of it. But we have found, also, how even the clouds and rain have been ever brightened up with bright gleams of mercy. I am sure we can both say that "goodness and mercy have followed us" all the days of our married life. And I feel humbly confident that the same goodness and mercy will still encompass our onward path, that, if heavier trials should be before us, fresh grace and strength will be given us to bear them, and that *all* things shall mysteriously work together for our good.

Among all the many, many undeserved temporal mercies which surround *me*, there is none for which I so earnestly and constantly thank God as for my dear wife . . .

May God supplement my poor love with the rich outpourings of His Love, filling you with a growing peace and happiness in Him which no earthly cares or trials shall disturb—and may He at last give to both of us and to all our dear little ones, a blessed meeting in His Heavenly Kingdom.

From August 1st to the 11th, Dr. Dykes, with his wife and family, stayed at Ilkley, where his mother and sisters were still living. There he met Dr. Parry, Bishop of Barbados, and his family, who were staying at the same place for the Bishop's health. This visit was the means of establishing a friendship between the families, and many pleasant excursions were taken together. From the Bishop's daughters, in after years, Dr. Dykes received much help in his Parish.

August 5th. Set off by myself to the Latin Cross on the Keighley Road, said private prayers and Evensong, and enjoyed it much.

Aug. 10th. Walked up the moors, said Matins. Correcting Tunes for Mr. Grey's book.

Delightful walk to Nessfield, reading "From Cradle to Grave" by the way. Went to the top of the knoll above Nessfield and said private prayer there. The country looked most glorious after the rain, quite radiant and dazzling. Heard that Mr. M. had been compelled to leave Leeds. Thought much about it and think it must be some mental aberration. Lord, preserve Thy Church and the lambs of Thy flock in Leeds, from being injured by any evil report or unfaithfulness of their Pastor, and help me to keep strict watch over myself, and keep my body under, lest I be a castaway.

Durham, Aug. 16th. Received a registered letter from Southgate; found it was from E. D. and contained Twenty pounds as an offering for my church. Thank God for having put this thought into the heart of my dear cousin. May He bless her for it, and enable me to spend it, as He willed it should be spent, when He sent it.

Durham. A note from Barry, stating that he had been requested to ascertain whether I would accept the Precentorship of Westminster Abbey, in the event of its being offered to me.

Cathedral. Father Platt and Dr. Manning in the Nave; shewed them the Library and St. Cuthbert's relics. Dr. M. is a striking looking man, rather tall, spare, and ascetic looking; with an expressive and commanding forehead; but cold, ungenial, and with somewhat of a restless, uneasy, bitter expression. Couldn't say I felt drawn or prepossessed by him. He seemed uninterested, unsympathetic, unquiet, hard.

Sat., Dec. 31st. Lord, I thank Thee for the renewed care which has so tenderly watched over me and mine during the past year. For Thy many undeserved mercies. Especially for the restoration of my Church and house. Grant Thy Grace and Heavenly Benediction upon myself, my household, and my parish, for the year now commencing.

January 10th, 1865. Busy with sermon and Merbecke's "*Creed,*" which I tried to arrange more pleasingly than in Helmore.

The Diary in January and February mentions hymn-tunes composed for *The Holy Year,* at the request of Mr. Monk. This work was a Hymnal compiled by Dr. Christopher Wordsworth, who was then Archdeacon of Westminster, and afterwards Bishop of Lincoln. To it Dr. Dykes contributed six tunes.

Feb. 18th. Letter from Monk, asking me to undertake Confirmation Hymn in *The Holy Year.* Blunt stayed dinner: he wishes me to help him in an *Annotated Prayer Book* which he is about to edit for Rivingtons.

To this request Dr. Dykes consented and wrote the article on "The Manner of Performing Divine Service."

March 11th. Left our present temporary abode for Vicarage House.

Mar. 20th. Kempe[5] came. Lord Jesus, bless him to me, and me to him, and both to the good of the Parish, and to Thy Honour and Glory. Amen.

---

5. Rev. J. W. Kempe, University College, Durham, who now settled in St. Oswald's parish, as curate with Dr. Dykes.

> *June* 24th. A note of invitation from Committee of Norwich Church Congress, to read a paper on Church Music there, on October 5th. I felt much perplexed what answer I ought to give.
>
> *Jun.* 28th. After much hesitation, wrote to Norwich, to accept invitation to the Congress. Lord, do Thou Who has ordered that the invitation should be sent me, be pleased in mercy to teach me what Thou wouldest have me to say.
>
> *August* 3rd: *Durham*. Heard the pleasing information that John Davidson had promised to give an East Window to St. Oswald's. (Thank God for Jesus' sake): may He direct us all in the matters of design, Artist, etc. May He bless the donor and overrule the gift to His Honour and Glory.
>
> *Aug.* 18th. Sent off a tune for "O God most High, Creator King" to Lady Georgiana.[6]
>
> *Aug.* 29th: *Leeds*. Began writing out a tune for "Lead, kindly Light."

On the subject of this Tune, "*Lux Benigna*," which was wedded to Cardinal Newman's beautiful words, Dr. Dykes' cousin (the Rev. George Huntington, Rector of Tenby) gives the following details:

> I had been paying Cardinal Newman a visit . . . I happened to mention his well-known Hymn "Lead, kindly Light,"—which he said he wrote when a very young man, as he was becalmed on the Mediterranean, for a week, in 1832. I ventured to say, "It must be a great pleasure to you to know that you have written a Hymn treasured wherever English-speaking Christians are to be found; and where are they not to be found?"
>
> He was silent for some moments and then said with emotion, "Yes, deeply thankful, and more than thankful:" then, after another pause, "But you see it is not the Hymn, but the *Tune*, that has gained the popularity! The Tune is Dykes" and Dr. Dykes was a great Master."[7]

In contrast to the account which Cardinal Newman gives of the origin of his hymn, Dr. Dykes' friends remember his telling them that the *tune* to "Lead, kindly Light," came into his head while walking through the Strand, in London. This is not unlikely, as he had been in London, and, while there, to St. Paul's, before his visit to Leeds—when he notes in his Diary that he was writing the tune.

---

6. First wife of the Rev. the Hon. John Grey.
7. "Random Recollections" by the Rev. George Huntington, Rector of Tenby.

Thus the hymn, inspired while the poet was becalmed on the still waters of the Mediterranean Sea, became wedded to the melody rising from the heart of the musician, as he walked through the noisy, crowded thoroughfare of the great city.

The Diary alludes to a Retreat at Horbury in September 1865, conducted by Father Benson, and to a lecture at Norwich in October.

> *Sep. 21st*. Concluding address at ten. "Bless the Lord, O my soul, and all that is within me bless His Holy Name." God grant that I may never forget the feelings and resolutions, which He has put into my heart, at this "House of Mercy."
>
> *Oct. 5th*. Set to work to prepare for evening, feeling exhausted, nervous, and anxious. St. Andrew's Hall crammed. Tried humbly to seek for and trust in God's help, and did not find it fail me. Got through my paper so much better than I had dared to hope. The music, too, was very nicely done, though the choir, (especially for the unison parts) was too small and delicate for the room. Was glad to hear from Mr. Cadge and others that I was distinctly heard. Thank God! for all His mercies.
>
> *Oct. 7th*. Letter from Novello proposing to me to write a simple *Te Deum*.
>
> *Oct. 9th*. Pleased to discover the Sarum *Te Deum* was the original source of Merbecke's—(apparently).
>
> *Oct. 29th, Twentieth Sunday after Trinity*. Had Evensong with Gerty, Carry, Ethel and Mabel [his daughters], dear little things. The little girls said the prayers and lessons, and sang the Hymns and Canticles, and I said the Absolution.
>
> *Oct. 31st*. Letters from Mr. Grey wishing me to send six fresh, *old* tunes, to Mozeley. Decidedly better, (D.G.).
>
> *Nov. 4th*. Up at one but did not leave my bedroom all day. Wife had a nice kind letter from Mr. Brinton, containing a ten-pound note towards Vicarage restoration (D.G.).
>
> Mr. and Mrs. Oakeley called, and announced the success of Herbert S. Oakeley as candidate for the musical professorship of Edinburgh.
>
> *Nov. 15th*. In the afternoon, being a bright, beautiful day, took a long walk,—the first I had taken since my illness—very delightful. Passed my time during it, in prayer and Psalms.
>
> *Dec. 25: Christmas Day*. We used our beautiful new Altar candlesticks, lighted, for the first time. Also Mr. H.'s offertory bags. Church beautiful,—surplices for the first time.

6

Church Music
1866–1869

Te Deum for Novello—*Dies Irae*—Retreat at Wykeham—*Service in F*—Death of his Mother—Birmingham Festival—Tenbury—Appendix to *Hymns Ancient and Modern*—Lecture on "Church Music"—*Hymns for Infant Children*—*The Hymnary*—Burial Service

THE first important note in the Diary for 1866, and the letter which follows, show the spirit by which Dr. Dykes was actuated in making changes in the ritual of St. Oswald's Church, and illustrate his anxiety not to force innovations upon his parishioners.

> *January 27*th, *1866*. Violet stoles presented to the church by Kempe [the curate]. Rather sorry, as I was not anxious for further changes at present.

Gradually, as people learned to know and trust him, they thankfully accepted the improvements which he suggested; and, though far behind his ideal of what they ought to be, the services became more worthy of Him to Whom should be offered the very best in music, architecture, and ritual.

The following letter was written to his cousin, the Rev. E. B. Wawn, who was Theological Master in Cheltenham College, and had been obliged to resign his post in consequence of illness:

St. Oswald's, Durham
1st *Thursday in Lent: Feb. 15, 1866*

... First and foremost, I was sorry to learn from your letter, that you had been compelled to resign your post in the Cheltenham College. I am sorry for the sake of the College, and also on your own account. I can well imagine you must feel it no small trial to be condemned to, (what appears to our short-sighted view) an inactive life. How comforting it is to repose in the assured conviction, that God knows far better how to make use of us, than we ourselves: and that He loves us each too well, and takes too deep a personal interest in the welfare and progress of His Church, to allow any one of us to lead a *really* useless life—if we only have the will to work for Him, and in *His* way.

If you are not working for Him exactly in the way which *you* would choose, depend upon it, you are doing so in a far better and more fruitful (because *His*) way. I have myself become a thoroughly broken-winded old horse, and can, at present, take very small share of duty. I have only preached twice for several months, and am beginning, I confess, to feel rather anxious about the future.

However, thank God, we have nothing to do with the future.

...

I am more and more convinced, however, that I have done *right* in endeavouring to improve the Church and the services, and to render them altogether more attractive. We are surrounded by a heathen population. An ugly Church and dull service will never bring them back. We *must* make use of externals. We must fearlessly and trustfully employ the various appliances of Worship, Musical, Ritual, and Architectural, which the Church allows, and of which God Himself has signified His approval—in the full confidence that, in so doing, we are not only not doing *wrong*, but simply doing what our duty to God and man requires at our hands.

It is really comparatively little use preaching Doctrine if you do not *act* Doctrine's outward and visible expression in Ritual.

I am becoming more and more convinced of this. The Church has made, in these latter days a grand mistake, (*i.e.*) in the neglect of the externals of worship, and the sooner she sets herself to work to correct her error on this head, the better.

> I enjoyed the Norwich Congress exceedingly. It was a most interesting gathering. I rather think I did my voice a little harm there—speaking for nearly an hour and ¾ in that immense room, crammed full of people.
>
> God bless you and yours. Kindest love to Lizzie. Believe me, dear Ned,
>
> Ever your affectionate old chum,
> John B. Dykes

He was now, as his Diary shows, busy with the composition of a *Te Deum*.

> *Durham, April 23rd*. Began to copy out for Novello my new *Te Deum*, which he has asked me to contribute to his cheap series.
>
> *May 5th*. Novello sent back my *Te Deum* to alter "Hosts" into "Sabaoth," and offer me fifteen guineas if I would finish the whole Service—make it complete for Morning, Evening, and Holy Communion. May the Chief Musician show me what to do!

Another musical composition is noticed in the following extract:

> *June 24th*. Preached at Evensong and played my new "*Dies Irae!*"[1] alluding to the death of poor G. Wilkinson.

On July 9th Dr. Dykes left Durham for a Retreat held at Wykeham near Scarborough.

> *Wykeham, July 12th*. Early Celebration at 7. Nice time with Benson, talk to him about suffering, and the desire for it. He seems to think that we ought absolutely to *desire* it. He argues that, inasmuch as we must desire holiness, and as suffering is an indispensable subordinate agent, in the acquisition of that—in order that we may sincerely desire the end, we must honestly desire the means.
>
> Should not our aim rather be to desire neither *this* nor *that*, but simply the fulfilment in us of *God's* Will?—loving—not suffering, in itself, but the ever-varying expression of the Loving Will of God; seeking now in *this* way, now in *that*, to conform us to the Divine Image?
>
> There would seem to be a great fear lest the attempt to cherish a desire for suffering should produce unreality of the Christian character, and many practical difficulties—at least in the case of ordinary Christians. Benson gave me his Blessing.

---

1. *Hymns Ancient and Modern*, 398.

Thank God for the Retreat. May He Who has granted me the means of grace, be pleased in Mercy to enable me to acquire, and retain, and improve the grace He wills to bestow upon me.

The year 1867 brought with it a heavy blow in the death of his mother. It was not, indeed, without warning. Three months before the end came, in the midst of notes on his musical or parochial work, occurs the following entry in his Diary:

March 10th. Letter from F., wishing me happy returns, and giving a poor account of dear Mater. I fear she may have to undergo a severe trial before her earthly course is run. Lord Jesu! support her through her trials and pour Thy choicest blessings upon Her.

April 6th. Doing a Tune for "Father, I know that all my life."

May 18th. Received parcel of services from Novello; my *Service in F.*

May 19th. Note from Novello, with cheque for £15. 15/ for *Service*.

May 20th. Sent off Tunes to Nisbet.

May 30th. Received a letter from Nisbet containing cheque for £10 (D.G.).

June 9th: *Whitsunday.* Erny, Minnie, Miss Money and Sarah Dunn [servant], besides many of the newly confirmed, received their first Communion. May our loving Lord and Master bless and keep these Lambs of His flock, shield them from all evil, and guide and preserve them in the way that leads to Everlasting Life.

Jun. 14th. Letter from Ted, giving me bad tidings of dear Mater, stating that she had fallen into an apoplectic fit last night (Lord have mercy on her!). Visited all my evening Communion class; packed up and went by 2 o'clock to Leeds; arrived there at 5.40; drove up to the house and was shocked and overcome at seeing the blinds down. I at once understood! Dearest Mother died at three this afternoon, having never recovered consciousness after her seizure of last night. Went to see her, so calm, and sweet, and beautiful, as though in a quiet sleep. Everlasting Rest, and Eternal Peace and Light be with her. Remained in prayer some time in the room. Oh that my last end, and that of all I love, may be such as hers. Mary, Eliza, Fred, Fanny, Lucy, and Emmie here. Went to the station to meet Tom.

Jun. 16th. St. John's School room, at 7.30, for Holy Communion (the Church being restored). Tom walked with me as far as St. Ann's, where he went in to say Mass. Fred came; he and I took a charming walk to Meanwood Church. Nice service.

> Afternoon, Fred, Tom and I had a long Theological discussion. Evening, Parish Church.
>
> *Jun. 17th*. Uncle George, and William Huntington came. Went up to bid dear Mother a long and last adieu, for *this* world—before the coffin was finally closed. Oh! how sweet and placid she looks! Good-bye, dearest, dearest Mother. We shall meet again. Oh yes! Grant it Lord Jesu!
>
> *Jun. 18th*. At 9, all drove to the station and started off for Ilkley. Walked in procession to the Church, preceded by the coffin and its bearers. Mr. Snowdon read the service; after which, we all returned to the Church for prayers, and rest. She was laid by the side of dear Father.
>
> The ladies went to the Vicarage, and we out on the moors. Country beautiful. Nice quiet chat in the Vicarage garden, then returned to Leeds.

On the return journey from Leeds to Durham, he travelled with Canon Liddon, who, as the next entry in the Diary shows, promised to preach for him at St. Oswald's. That promise, however, Liddon found himself unable to fulfil, owing to the attitude which the Bishop of Durham had assumed at Houghton-le-Spring, where he had refused to license a curate unless the Rector abandoned the use of the "Invocation" before the sermon. He, therefore, much to the disappointment of Dr. Dykes, but with characteristic tact, determined not to preach. The incident is not unimportant as the first sign of coming troubles.

> *June 26th*. Called on Canon Liddon, who kindly consented to preach for me on Sunday.
>
> *Jun. 29th*. To Dr. Farrar's to see Liddon. He thinks it better not to preach, as he could not do so without omitting the Invocation, which would be like a reflection on myself, and he should not like to use it, as being a reflection on the Bishop. Mitchinson[2] came to the vestry and offered to preach twice.

At the end of August Dr. Dykes left Durham to be present at the Birmingham Festival.

> *Aug. 28th*. Drove to Town Hall. Capital places in front of side Gallery. Hall crammed. Sterndale Bennett's *Woman of Samaria*. Nothing very striking about it, but it is a charmingly written work, full of beautiful music; seems unfinished and fragmentary, but will doubtless grow upon hearing. Glorious

---

2. Afterwards Bishop of Barbados.

performance. Evening—Benedict's *Lay of St. Cecilia*. A lovely Cantata, rather dull in the early parts, but increases in interest as it proceeds, and ends most bewitchingly.

*Aug, 30*th. Heard Gounod's *Mass*. Most delicious music. Nilsson sang her part most reverently and admirably. The "*Gloria*," "*Et Incarnatus*," and "*Vitam Venturi*," most thrilling. Then *Israel in Egypt*. We were rather too near for those heavy magnificent Choruses. The treble by no means perfect, once nearly coming to a breakdown. Great, but exciting treat. Evensong.

Evening, *St. Paul*. In front gallery. Enjoyed the performance immensely, having never heard *St. Paul* straight through since I had come to "years of musical discretion."

*Durham, Sep. 19*th. Cathedral service at 8 in consequence of the Choir Festival...

Building crammed; looked very beautiful. Began punctually at four, with *Lauda Sion*, as procession of Clergy was walking in. I conducted. On the whole a great success (thank God). The Dean was much moved and pleased, and said he would not have missed it for a thousand pounds.

On September 25th Dr. Dykes went to Tenbury to stay with Sir Frederic Ouseley, and preach there on St. Michael's Day.

*Friday, Sep. 27*th. Train to Ludlow: much struck with the Tower of the Church; while asking my way to Mr. Welling's house, who should come up but himself! and while discussing with him how we should see the organ, who should come up but the organist himself! Verily my Guardian Angel has smoothed away difficulties for me. Went to church; exceedingly struck with its grandeur and beauty. Had a glorious play on the organ.

*Oct. 1*st. While writing letters, in Ouseley's study, was suddenly rushed in upon by Sir Henry Baker, who expressed his delight at seeing, at last, my face in the flesh. Quite a different style of man to what I had anticipated.

The following letters to his wife contain an account of the Services for St. Michael's Festival.

Tenbury
Oct. 1, 1867

... Sir Frederic and I met at the Tenbury station, he having come from Worcester, and I from Ludlow, so we walked together over the fields to the College, and had a little quiet Friday dinner together, and then went to Evensong. Yesterday afternoon, I had a lovely walk to a village called Little Hereford, where there is an interesting old Norman Church. In coming back, I missed my road; it was approaching 6 o'clock, and time for Evensong: and I ought to have been back at the College. But I suddenly discovered I was wrong; I heard in the dim distance the College bell ringing for prayers—then I lost it. At last I recovered my path and made the best of my way home. But I was too late to go into the choir, so I went into the nave of the church, and very glad I was that I had done so, for I had no idea until then what a charming church St. Michael's was. It was all vested in its festal costume. There is a very high simple gilded metal Rood screen, and some large lighted candles on the top of it. The Altar has a large Baldacchino over it. Candles were arranged at intervals, on the top. There was a lovely white Altar frontal, and the whole effect was delightful.

I saw a grave old gentleman sitting a few seats before me; I suddenly discovered it was the Bishop of Oxford, who had arrived during my absence, and had preferred to sit in the nave, and see the church. We were formally introduced afterwards. Poor man, he was in sad distress when we first saw him; he had heard of the sudden, (and he fears, fatal seizure) of Archdeacon Randall, his favourite Archdeacon, and right hand man, who, he says, "will be an irreparable loss to myself and the church." Dr. Jebb, also, and many others, joined us, and we had "high dinner" in Sir F.'s own dining room at 7.30. The Bishop of Oxford, when he had recovered himself, was most amusing. He talked a good deal about the Ritual Commission, and the Pan Anglican Synod. He says that the latter has been a decided success. They have published an encyclical letter, which they all signed. The Synod is still not over, and he seems to anticipate that great good may come of it.

He is one of the most fascinating men I have ever met. I preached this morning, and he preaches at night. At dinner, to-day, there was only one toast proposed, and to my horror it was "The preachers." And the Bishop of Oxford prefaced his reply with—"I beg to premise that I am not going to speak for Dr. Dykes, only for myself." (I, of course, had stood up.) So when he had finished his charming little speech, we both sat down. "No, no," he said, "that won't do." So, he got up again with a twinkle in his eye, and said that he was quite sure that, after my admirable sermon of this morning, it would be desired that I should return thanks and speak for myself. So I was compelled to get up, and stammer forth a very miserable reply.

He says the American and other Bishops are most indignant at the Bishop of Durham and other Bishops of the Northern Province, for holding aloof from the Synod.

St. Michael's, Tenbury
Oct. 1, 1867

… The Bells are ringing for our grand commemoration service: I must put on my surplice in a few minutes … The Bishop of Oxford left us yesterday. He was so nice and pleasant, and kind, and amusing. He preached a beautiful sermon on Sunday night on the Ministry of the Holy Angels. He intoned the Absolution and Benediction so well. I reminded him of the old friendship between my Grandfather and his Father.[3] He seemed pleased to have it recalled to him. When we parted yesterday, he said, with his pleasant smile, "Goodbye, goodbye. I am so glad to meet the old name once more," and he also gave me his photograph, which, of course, I shall prize.

During the next few months we have several notices of meetings, in connection with *Hymns Ancient and Modern*. The Appendix was now under consideration, and Dr. Dykes felt it his duty and privilege to render all the assistance he could towards perfecting this increasingly popular Hymnal.

Nov. 20. Harley Street, London, with Dr. Quain. Sir H. Baker called for me; went with him to Monk's (Glebefield, Stoke Newington). Set to work with the Appendix to *Hymns A. and M.* By and by we were joined by Murray, Williams, and Hungerford. Busy with Tunes; dinner at 2. At it again till 6. Went with Sir H. B. as far as "The Angel" into Islington, then to Freemasons' Hall. E. C. U. Meeting. Dr. Pusey spoke. Earnest, animated debate.

Durham, December 1. Advent Sunday. Gave notice this day of the establishment of daily Matins and Thursday Celebration. (D.G.)

Dec. 25th. Christmas Day. Wore Vestments at St. Oswald's for the first time (white linen chasuble). (D.G.)

Dec. 31st. Choirboys to tea. Dear wife and I, when the choir boys had gone, prayed the old year out, and the new in. Another year passed away. "A day's march nearer Home." (O God, may it be so.)

January 10th, *1868.* Received printed copies of Merbecke's "*Credo*," and 51st Psalm to a Hebrew Chant, from Novello. Visited

---

3. The Rev. Thomas Dykes of St. John's Church, Hull, and William Wilberforce.

Hannah Clayton. Determined to administer Holy Communion to her, to-day, if possible. She has never yet been fit to receive it, being too prostrate. Found her sitting up, evidently prepared to receive the Holy Sacrament. She and I received it alone.

Jan. 12th. Visited Hannah Clayton. Surprised when I went to see her, bed all white. Found she had died during the night. Felt so thankful I had at last been able to give her Holy Communion. She had roused up just before her death, and told her Father that she must dress herself, as she was going to a very beautiful place that she had just seen. R. I. P.

Jan. 13th. To Leeds for Lecture on Church Music.

Jan. 19th. The room was full. The Lecture went off very well indeed (D.G.). The Leeds boys sang beautifully, only they made a little hitch in Purcell—"Thou knowest, Lord." We did "The Lord bless Thee." Solo and Chorus "Ut queant laxis" (two boys), Merbecke's "*Credo*," "If ye love Me," Tallis, "Thou knowest Lord," Purcell, "If we believe," Goss, "Blessed be the God and Father," Wesley, "Abide with me," Monk. Thank God that it got so nicely over—but my voice was tired. I had never spoken for so long a time since the Norwich Congress.

Durham, Friday. I have so many things to think of. Sermon for Sunday, and also for the E. C. U. And preparation for the latter. My first Catechising on Sunday. Also, my Tunes, my sick and well. What must I do? What leave undone? Lord teach me ... To Church, to seek for direction.

Sat. 25th. Finished sermon and began Letter to "Spectator." God has indeed graciously helped me.

Sunday 26th. Catechising and Litany: very satisfactory service. Thank God for directing me to begin this. Evening. Preached from Isa. 56–57, "I will bring thee to My Holy Mount." The sermon, which I thought I should never have time to write—had been blessed; and was asked to publish it.

In February 1868 Dr. Dykes spent a week with Dr. Quain in London, where he had several hymn-tune meetings with Sir Henry Baker and Mr. Monk.

Sat. 15th. St. Andrew's, Wells Street. Service admirably done! Choir large, fine jubilant Anthem by Mendelssohn, "Let there be Light."

Sunday 16th. St. Albans at 11. High Celebration and sermon from Father Stanton. Felt rather done to death with the Gregorian Music (so called).

> *Feb. 19th*. E. C. U. Meeting. Celebration at 7 at St. Barnabas. High Celebration. Service too long; too much music, and the music altogether too slow. Sermon nearly an hour by Mackonochie.
>
> *Feb. 20th. Durham, Ash Wednesday.* Sang *Miserere* to the new Jewish Chant (very nice). Ashwell preached a beautiful sermon on Patience. The Patience of Activity.

Again in May Dr. Dykes went up to London for meetings on *Hymns Ancient and Modern,* with Sir H. Baker and Mr. Monk. On this visit he also discussed with Mr. Masters the publication of a musical edition of a small collection of twenty Children's Hymns edited by himself—thirteen of the tunes being his own composition: the rest by his brother Arthur, Sir Frederic Ouseley, Dr. Flowers, and the Rev. E. Greatorex. They were originally written for his own children, nephews and nieces. The "Hymns for Infant Children," which became very popular with the children, from the simplicity of the words and the melodious tunes, is not, perhaps, hardly so widely known as it should be. The Sunday nights at St. Oswald's Vicarage were, to the children, and the friends who joined them, the happiest part of the week. The work of the day was done, and after the evening meal the whole party assembled round the drawing-room piano. Here the newest tunes were sung over, and freely criticised. Dr. Dykes thought much of this "august tribunal," as he called it, and if the tune did not "take" with the children, he nearly always altered it, or re-wrote it.

From June 17th to the 25th, Dr. Dykes, Sir H. Baker, and Mr. Monk were daily hard at work with the Appendix to *Hymns Ancient and Modern.*

> *Aug. 28th.* Durham. Received proofs of my "*Ecce Panis.*"
>
> *Aug. 30th.* Anxious to get my old "O Paradise," in A♭ substituted, in the Appendix, for my late one.
>
> *Sep. 3rd.* Monk decidedly prefers my last Tune, so sent him a revise of it. I think improved!

In his letters to Mr. Monk, Dr. Dykes writes:

> I suppose the difficulty in arriving at a satisfactory Tune for "O Paradise" must remind one that Paradise itself is not to be attained without a struggle.

The Editors of *Hymns Ancient and Modern,* as the following letter from Sir H. Baker shows, warmly appreciated the value of Dr. Dykes' assistance, rendered, as it had been, without thought of other reward than the provision of a hymn-book worthy be used in the services of the Church.

Monkland, Leominster
February 5, 1869

I am delighted to have to tell you that, at our yearly meeting, my co-compilers voted that you be asked to accept the enclosed cheque with our most grateful thanks to you.

I am sure you will believe that we do not send this as any "payment" for the work you have so generously and heartily and ably done for us—you have not worked for, nor wished for payment—but only as a small token of our own sense of what *Hymns A. and M.* owes to you, and of our personal regard and esteem for you.

As such, pray accept it, and believe me

Most sincerely yours,
H.W. Baker

February. 6th, 1869: Durham. Found a letter from Sir Henry Baker, containing cheque for £100, in consideration of my *Hymns A. and M.* help (D.G.). How very good of them!

Mar. 19th. Dear Gerty's preparation for Holy Communion [his second daughter]. God bless the dear girl, and ever keep her humble and pure and Christlike.

Mar. 21st. Dear Gerty communicated for the first time; may God's richest blessings descend and rest upon her. May He keep her in His Love, and use her for His Glory, and preserve her to His Heavenly Kingdom.

A new hymn and tune book was about to be published by Novello (*The Hymnary*). The compilers much desired that Dr. Dykes should write tunes for it. He, on his part, felt that a new hymnbook was not needed, and though at all times willing to help in any way he could, he thought that it would hardly be right, after the interest he had taken in *Hymns Ancient and Modern,* and the kindness he had received from the committee, to forward the publication of a new hymn-book, brought out in apparent rivalry.

April. 21st. Long letter from Pollock on *Hymns A. and M.* question; also from Littleton, stating that Barnby should call on me on Friday about it. Lord, teach me what to do.

Apr. 23rd. Short time with sermon, till Barnby from Novello and Co. arrived. He entered into the question of Littleton's proposed new Hymnal. I said I could not help in it! but yet, if they would bring out simply a new Tune book, called Novello's Tune book, I would gladly help in this. Barnby seemed to approve of the proposal. I do hope (please God) that it may be so arranged that there be no Hymnal quarrelling. Thank God for helping me through this interview, which I rather dreaded.

Notwithstanding this suggestion, *The Hymnary* was published. Dr. Dykes felt it his duty not to write any *new* tunes for it, but gave his consent that any already published, which could be obtained from other sources, might be used.

*Apr. 24*th. Went with wife and bairns to Grammar School sports. We were just too late for Erny's high jump, which had been very good. By and by came the great steeplechase, which Erny won well and easily. He got one or two other lesser prizes.

*June 11*th. Training College Commemoration. [The Training College for Schoolmasters, of which his friend, Mr. Ashwell, was Principal.] Had to return thanks for the preacher in his absence and propose success to the Institution. Felt desperately nervous but was thankful I did not break down. Oh! that I had more readiness of utterance, and self-possession. I feel like a perfect fool when I have to make a speech. Never mind, God may yet help me to improve.

*July 20*th. Heard Cathedral bell tolling, announcing the death of the Dean [Waddington].

*July 24*th. Preparation for the Dean's funeral . . . At 11.30 all met in procession, Choristers, Clergy, Bishop, in the East alley of the cloisters, starting from the Dean's door. We sang the introductory sentences, (to my music) along the East and North alleys of the cloisters, then entered the S.W. door of the Cathedral and finished in procession up the Nave. But the music was ended too soon! The last sentence should have been repeated. A great crowd of people; Chevalier read the lesson, the Bishop the service at the grave. (My music, with Purcell's "Thou knowest.")

The *Burial Service*, sung on this occasion for the first time, has not yet been published, but is used in Durham Cathedral. Dr. Dykes originally intended to write music to those portions only of the *Burial Service* left incomplete in Croft's setting. But he felt the difference between his style and Croft's so much that he eventually composed music for the entire service.

Heard of the new appointment to the Deanery—W.C. Lake. God grant that he may faithfully discharge the duties of his twofold office, and that he may prove a help and benefit to the city of Durham.

In September, Dr. Dykes went to Worcester for the Musical Festival.

> *Sep. 6*th. Down to College Hall. Rehearsal of service music under Sullivan. Was introduced to him. Then to Cathedral. "Hymn of Praise" being performed. Then Rossini's *Mass*. Enjoyed the last much. Madame Sherrington allowed me to look over her copy. Sullivan also joined us. Music showy and interesting, rather deficient in religious sentiment. Rehearsal of *The Prodigal Son* (Sullivan). The introductory movements are charming.
>
> *Sep. 7*th. Early Celebration. Cathedral. Had charming place; never enjoyed an *Elijah* performance so much before.
>
> *Sep. 8*th. *The Prodigal Son.* Enjoyed it much more than on Monday and think highly of it. It falls off in interest towards the end—but the first part is very interesting and beautiful. The instrumentation wonderful!
>
> *Sep. 9*th. Cathedral. Rossini's *Mass*. It contains frivolities and objectionable movements, but on the whole, I was charmed with it; especially the *"Kyrie," "Gloria," "Crucifixus,"* and conclusion of the *"Credo."* A magnificent performance of the *Hymn of Praise,* the first time of my hearing it entire with orchestra! Wonderful treat.
>
> *Sep. 10*th. Cathedral. Glorious performance of the *Messiah*. Sat next to Hullah, during the whole of the first part. Oh how I enjoyed it. His intelligent remarks on the music much enhanced my pleasure. At the beginning of the second part of "the *Messiah*" went round with Randegger into the Lady Chapel; joined there by Oakeley, Cattley, and Madame Patey.
>
> Stood in the Pulpit and heard wonderfully distinctly. At "Thou shalt dash them" came round, heard the "Hallelujah" and "I know that my Redeemer" under the organ; then went to my old place for "Worthy is the Lamb."
>
> Stood up with Hullah, exactly in the middle—the best place. Glorious!

On October 4th Dr. Dykes went to a Retreat at Cowley, Oxford. These yearly Retreats were the greatest rest and comfort to him. The quiet time for instruction, meditation, and help in the spiritual life, was much appreciated by him in the midst of the manifold occupations of his daily life.

> *Oct. 9*th: *Oxford*. Rule of silence the whole time. Went into Mr. Carter's room before going to introduce myself to him, thank him, and ask for his Blessing! which he most affectionately gave me. Bade my kind hostess farewell, and may God remember her for good for her kindness to me.

7

In Memoriam M. H. D.
1870–1873

Tunes for *The People's Hymnal* and *The Hymnal Companion*—Scarlet Fever—Death of his daughter Mabel—Tune, "Tender Shepherd"—Christmas Carols—*Anglican Hymn-Book*—Monkland—Patterdale—Nottingham Church Congress—Bishop of Lincoln's Hymn—More hymn-tunes

MENTION has already been made of a lecture on Church Music, delivered by Dr. Dykes at Leeds in January 1869. A similar lecture, illustrated by a different selection of music, was given in January 1870, at Wakefield, and repeated in February at Hereford. On his way to Wakefield, he was, as his Diary shows, at work in the train on a musical composition.

> Jan. 17th. Long wait at Normanton, (en route for Wakefield). Busy thinking over the music of *Te Deum*.
> Jan. 18th. Morning chiefly with *Te Deum*, putting down my railway thoughts.
> Jan. 19th. Finishing draft of *Te Deum*.

On the 20th he gave his lecture—the illustrations, which he notes in his Diary, being

1. 51st Psalm, Hebrew Chant
2. "The Lord bless thee" etc.

3. "O give thanks," Palestrina
4. *Benedictus* and *Agnus*. Merbecke. *Burial Office*
5. "If ye love Me," Tallis
6. "Thou knowest, Lord," Purcell
7. "If we believe," Goss
8. "O Lord, my God," Wesley
9. "Hark the sound," J. B. D.

On February 3rd he delivered at Hereford the same Lecture on Church Music which he had given in Wakefield, with nearly the same selection of music; his own tune to the beautiful hymn, "Christian, dost thou see them?" being sung. He says:

> The lecture went off really most successfully—much better than in Wakefield. My voice was much better, the singing was better, the singers better arranged, and the Harmonium better. There were some enthusiastic expressions of thanks afterwards;—especially from an old clergyman—Canon Powell. My hymn went admirably. Sir Henry read it over before it was sung and gave an explanation of its character. The greater part of the Hereford men are *clerics*, or preparing for Holy Orders, so that I had a nice, appreciative body of singers.

In the introduction of changes in the worship at St. Oswald's he still pursues the same cautious and gradual policy.

> *Jan. 8th*. Call from Kempe,[1] during the evening, who wishes us to use coloured stoles always. I do not quite think that the time has yet come.

The following extract shows another side of his work as a parish priest:

> *Durham, Feb. 15th*. Visited Mr. S.; shocked to discover he is still unbaptized (being brought up a Quaker). Tried to urge upon him the necessity for Holy Baptism; but he seems rather determined on the subject; and also, too weak to argue. Evening, visited Mr. S. again, but he was too ill and disturbed to pay attention.
> *Feb. 16th*. Visited Mr. S. Was told by Mrs. M. that he begged I might not be admitted again and was in a very excited state.

---

1. The curate, the Rev. J. W. Kempe.

However, I went up and prayed with him. He seemed annoyed, but was calm and quiet.

*Feb. 18*th. [After two more visits.] Most painful visit to Mr. S. A fearful struggle is going on in him. He seems almost determined to resist all the overtures of God's grace, and he is evidently dying. Home. Bed. A little before 2, awaked by a rap at the door, and a message that I was to go down to Mr. S. I went down with a heavy heart, pondering how I was to assist a man who had willfully refused Baptism and opposed God's grace in his last agony. To my surprise and delight, I found, when I got there, that he was anxious for Baptism. I questioned him whether he believed the Creed, etc., and found he was really desirous of being baptized; and then performed the Office. Used an abbreviation of the public office. Much struck. Read about the Ruler of the Jews coming to Jesus by night. After I had administered it, poor S. beckoned to A., and whispered how beautiful the Prayers were. Thanks be to God. Went home with a lighter heart.

Feb. 19th. Visited Mr. S. Calm and placid. Much weaker (in afternoon, still weaker).

Feb. 20th. Heard of the death of poor Mr. S.

Feb. 25th. Dear Carry's birthday. Call from Foster, who sang through several of my songs, and sings "*Excelsior*" better than anyone I have ever heard attempt it.

A few extracts from his Diary and letters will best illustrate the number of applications which he received for hymn-tunes, and the generosity and promptitude with which he responded to the appeals.

March 15th. Received Cheque for £10 from Mr. Cooke[2] for two tunes. (D.G.)

At this time Dr. Littledale wrote to Dr. Dykes for tunes for *The People's Hymnal.*

May 25th. Received copy of *The Village Organist* containing my little composition.

May 27th. Tunes for Whitburn, and going through *The Village Organist.*

June 4th. Received copy of Bickersteth's *Hymnal Companion.* Looking over it . . . Puzzled with Tunes and letters. I have an accumulation of both, awaiting attention.

---

2. Dr. W. M. Cooke, Editor of *Congregational Church Music.* To this Hymnal Dr. Dykes contributed seven tunes.

Jun. 8th. Letter from Mr. Monk, about his *Anglican Hymn-Book Tunes*.

Jun. 9th. Received copy of Ely Book, with kind note from the Secretary.

Jun. 16th. Received Eucharistic Hymn from Walsham How, who wants a Tune to it.

This tune, to the words, "Great and glorious Father, humbly we adore Thee," was written, and sent off, within a few days.

Jun. 21st. Doing tunes for Mr. Monk.

July 22nd. Note from Dr. Cooke, with remittance from him (D.G.) and from Mr. Bickersteth, with a copy of his poem, "Yesterday, to-day, and for ever."

Later.—Reading Bickersteth's poem:—very beautiful.

The subject of the present Bishop of Exeter's poem was one that interested Dr. Dykes intensely, and it is continually referred to in letters and Diary at this time. To the author, he writes:

> Last, but not least, I must not neglect to give you my warm thanks for the copy of your Poem. The subjects of which it treats, are subjects of profoundest interest, and which have, for many years, occupied my thoughts. And although, possibly, on certain matters in the realm of unfulfilled prophecy, I may not have arrived exactly at your own conclusion, I not the less anticipate much pleasure and profit from the perusal of your poem. I was much moved, last night, when reading the inexpressibly touching account of the Seer's death, in the first book.

At this time Dr. Dykes was occupied with *The Hymnal Companion*, for which he wrote six new tunes. Of these one was the tune. "*Irene,*" to Mr. Bickersteth's Marriage Hymn,

> Rest in the Lord, From harps above,
> The music seems to thrill;
> Rest in His everlasting love,
> Rest and be still.

In sending the suggested tune, Dr. Dykes wrote to Mr. Bickersteth a letter, from which the following is an extract:

St. Oswald's Vicarage, Durham
July 23, 1870

... I confess I do not like adaptations, but I see no objection, at all, to the Tune for your Hymn (without absolutely repeating) *suggesting* the melody—"O rest in the Lord." I have had great pleasure in writing you a little Tune based upon that air, without being a real adaptation from it. The Rhythm, and general accent, of the words seemed to demand that it should be written in triple time.

Probably, however, you may have a tune already provided for those words: if so, you can put mine into the waste paper basket...

The tune was not, however, consigned to the waste paper basket. It was, on the contrary, received with delight.

Pray accept my heartiest thanks [writes Mr. Bickersteth in reply], not only for your prompt consent to our use of the "*Hosanna*" Tune—but also for your great kindness in writing the very beautiful one you enclosed for my Marriage Hymn. It was unanimously and gratefully accepted, by our Musical Committee, last night.

We think of calling it *"Irene"* if you had not thought of any other name and should gladly avail ourselves of your offer to revise the proof.

Your brotherly postscript, that I was not to hesitate to write, if we were in difficulty about any other tunes, makes me at least name our two chief remaining wants. They are for that noble Ascension Hymn (No. 157, in my Hymnal), "Thou art gone up on high," and for a Holy Communion Hymn—"Lord, when before Thy Throne we meet."

The tunes asked for were promptly sent, and gratefully accepted.

Christ Ch. Vicarage, Hampstead
17 Aug., 1870

Dear Dr. Dykes,

I do not know how to thank you, as I ought, for your most beautiful Tune. The one to "Thou art gone up on high" seems to me to breathe the very language of the Hymn, in music, and reminds me of Tennyson's lines on Woman. "Till at the last she set herself to man, Like perfect music unto noble words." And the others I like very much, especially the last two lines, and I believe many hearts, in the use of it, will rise to the loftiest privilege of Praise.

You named the *first* "*Ascension*"!—There is a tune of that name in the S.P.C.K. collection, which they kindly gave us for "Christ is gone up with a joyful sound," which Hymn stands immediately before "Thou art gone up on High," in my Hymnal. It would be confusing to have two tunes of the same name, side by side, so we have ventured to christen yours *Olivet*, but if you prefer any other name shall trust to you to let me know. And so with the second, which you did not name, and which we have called "*Eucharist*."

It is such a peculiar pleasure to me that *you* like my Poem, and I cannot but hope that on my return from America, you will be able to come and spend a few days under our roof. We should all so heartily welcome you, and it would be a great pleasure to talk over some of those hopes which Prophecy opens out to us. If songs in the house of the Pilgrimage are sweet—what will the Anthems of Home be? I take our completed MS. of the Musical Edition to the printers to-day . . . With the united cordial thanks of our Committee. Believe me,

Yours very gratefully,
E. H. Bickersteth

The Rectory, Tenby, S. Wales
August 19, 1870

My Dear Mr. Bickersteth,

I beg to thank you sincerely for your kind and friendly letter which I received last night. It is a great satisfaction to me that you like the tunes which I have had the pleasure of sending you.

I like the suggestion of "*Olivet*" much, and shall be glad to appropriate it, as the name for the Ascension Tune. Also I like the name "*Eucharist*" (if it has not yet been adopted by others) for the Communion hymn.

Accept my best thanks for your kind proposal that I should come to see you on your return from America . . .

I should indeed like to have a little quiet conversation with you, on some of those mysterious subjects on which you seem to have thought so deeply.

Wishing you most heartily a pleasant and profitable journey, and a happy return home.

Believe me,
Most truly yours,
John B. Dykes

The following letter from Dr. Dykes closes the correspondence on *The Hymnal Companion:*

> St. Oswald's Vicarage
> Durham
> *Nov. 11, 1871*
>
> My Dear Mr. Bickersteth,
>
> While venturing to send a few suggestions for the consideration of your Musical Editor, in reference to certain harmonies in your book—and also to certain of the tunes—I deem it only right to add, that I have gone through the book with *real* pleasure, that I think the *general* selection of tunes very happy, and the book as a whole thoroughly interesting and good, and a valuable addition to our existing Hymnals.
>
> Believe me,
> Yours most sincerely,
> John B. Dykes
>
> P.S. I ought to add that I think the Collection of Hymns, in the main, a very charming one; rendered doubly interesting by the valuable and discriminating little notices of the several hymns added in the Appendix.

In the late summer of 1870 a time of great trial and anxiety came upon Dr. and Mrs. Dykes. The account of this trouble is best told in his own words.

> *August 22nd. Tenby.* Letter from dear wife, in which she tells me darling Mab[3] has caught the scarlet fever. (May God soon restore her and keep the other bairns from catching the infection.)
>
> *Aug. 25th.* This morning received a letter from dear wife, saying that Gertie was in the fever, as well as Mab. This afternoon I received a second, stating that dear little Jack, who had been sent to Leeds, had broken out in it there. (Lord Jesu! have mercy upon us, and our dear little children.)
>
> *Aug. 26th.* Left Tenby for Leeds. On arriving at Cromer Terrace,[4] was startled by being told by Fanny that, instead of staying there all night, I must be off at once to Durham, as dear Gerty was worse: so rushed down to train with a heavy heart, having first seen my dear little Jack, who seems very weak and

---

3. Mabel, the youngest daughter.
4. The house of his brother, Mr. E. O. Dykes.

ill, but going on favourably. Had a nice, calm, though sad journey home;—arrived at the Vicarage a little after one. Was much relieved by meeting dear Susan, who opened the door, and finding that darling Gertie was yet alive, and that there were hopes of her recovery.

Aug. 27th. *Saturday.* There was an early Celebration for dear Gerty's recovery. Said prayers with dear bairns, who seem going on satisfactorily. Called at Mrs. Robson's, where the children (Erny, Carrie, Ethel,) are staying.

Each day of this sad, anxious time, in the midst of his Parish work, and visiting the sick, dying, and impenitent, come the entries: "Office with dear bairns"—often two or three times a day. And the walk with the other children, who were staying in lodgings, to be out of the way of infection, was never omitted. So far, the great anxiety had been for the elder of the two invalids—Gertrude—a girl of sixteen; but on August 30th, the younger, Mabel, a child of ten, took a turn for the worse. She had always been a gentle and affectionate child, specially devoted to her sister Ethel, who was scarcely a year older than herself. But one little playmate was to be parted from the other, by that veil which separates the seen from the unseen world.

The Diary continues:

September 1st, *Thursday.* Darling Mab has had another very bad night and seems no better this morning . . . She has now got inflammation on the windpipe . . . Came home from post (11 p.m.), was reading the war news, when I heard my dear wife calling. Hastened upstairs, and at once saw that our little darling was very near her end. Said the commendatory prayer, etc., and in a very few moments her happy spirit had taken its flight, and she had sunk into the cold, calm sleep of Death. It was a stunning blow to us all. "Lord Jesu, receive her soul." "Eternal rest be with her." Mr. Stoker [the doctor] came, but too late. He gently carried the little sleeper out of Gertie's room into Lawrence's empty room. Had prayers with wife and Gertie. Bed at 2. "The Lord gave: the Lord hath taken away. Blessed be the Name of the Lord!"

Sep. 2nd, *Friday.* Up at 7:45. Went to see our little darling. Called on my dear children at the lodgings and had prayers with them. Home. Said Office with Gertie and wife. Letters. Took dear wife to see our little sleeper. Letters. Sext. Dinner. Study. Writing tune for "Gentle Shepherd." Arranging service for funeral. At 7:45 called on dear children at lodgings and took them for a walk. Gertie not quite so well to-day.

Sep. 3rd, Saturday. Dear Gertie a little better to-day—(D.G.) . . . I went to the Churchyard to fix a spot for darling Mab and the rest of us. (God grant that all of us who are laid there may "lay us down in Peace.") . . . H. and his men came to photograph our little sleeping Mab. Spent most of the afternoon with dear Gertie. Took walk with Erny, Carry, and Ethel. Lovely moonlight night.

Sep. 4th, 12th Sun. after Trinity. I went to Holy Communion, but put on no surplice, and knelt in the Chancel. Comforting service. Breakfast. Study. Copied out my tune for "Gentle Shepherd." Matins in Gertie's room, with household . . . At 7:15 I went to Mrs. Robson's and said evensong with dear bairns; then we took a walk together. Compline with Gertie. She is a little better to-day (D.G.).

Sep. 5th, Monday. H. Com. at 8. *Missa pro defunctis!* Collect from Burial Office, Epistle and Gospel from Edward VI.'s 1st P. Bk. 21 communicants. Darling wife, Erny, Carry, and Ethel there, and many kind and sympathetic friends. Went with dear wife and bid our last goodbye to all that is earthly and mortal of dear, sweet Mab. Then, at 10, the funeral. The morning had been rainy; it was now bright. All the Choir assisted. They sang the sentences, etc., and the Hymn, "Gentle Shepherd," to my new tune. Service very sweet. After the service at the grave, they sang "O heavenly Jerusalem," and then each of them threw into the grave the little bouquets of flowers which Susan had sent for. Dear wife much affected—also poor little bereaved Ethel. Home. Office with dear Gerty.

Sep. 6th, Tuesday. Beautiful morning. Writing a tune for "O Lord, to Whom the spirits live." Office with dear Gertie, who is rather better to-day. Account of darling Jack not quite so good to-day. Walk with dear bairns. Made rough draft of music for "Reproaches."

A word must be said about the two hymn-tunes written during this sad week. The first was that sung at his daughter's funeral[5] to the words of the hymn translated by Miss Winkworth from the German of Meinhold.

> Tender Shepherd, Thou has stilled
> Now Thy little lamb's brief weeping:
> Oh how peaceful, pale and mild
> In its narrow bed 'tis sleeping;
> And no sigh of anguish sore
> Heaves that little bosom more.[6]

---

5. "In memoriam M. H. D."

6. In the first edition of *Hymns Ancient and Modern,* this is translated "*Gentle Shepherd,* Thou hast stilled."

Both words and tune were written under similar circumstances. In Meinhold's *Poems* the hymn is headed: "Sung in four parts beside the body of my little fifteen months old son, Johannes Ladislaus." Dr. Dykes had long wished to write a tune for it, and now the inspiration seemed to come to him, at the time of his own child's death—as it had done to the author of the words.

The other tune, composed the day *after* the funeral, was written to the beautiful hymn, number 301 in *The People's Hymnal*:

> O Lord, to Whom the spirits live
> Of all the faithful passed away,
> Upon their path that brightness give
> Which shineth to the perfect day.
> Light eternal, Jesu blest,
> Shine on them, and grant them rest.

A few days after the death of his daughter he is busy with a Christmas Carol, written by his sister, Mrs. Alderson, and afterwards published in Stainer and Bramley's collection. In a letter to his sister, dated September 17th, he says:

> I was so busy yesterday that I had barely time even to glance at your Carol, still less to think about it. This morning I have read it carefully through, and I like it very much indeed. I have also written down a rough copy of a musical setting which has come into my head, and which I will think over when I get a little time. I feel pretty sure it will come out nicely and make a charming and most appropriate Christmas Song.

The original Carol, as sent to him, was:

> Infant of days, yet Lord of life,
> Sweet Prince of Peace, all hail!
> Oh, we are weary of the strife,
> The din with which earth's fields are rife,
> And we would list the tale
> That chimes its Christmas news for us:
> *In terra Pax hominibus.*
>
> "Peace I leave with you" was again
> Thy legacy to earth;
> Sweet echo of the lingering strain,
> Of Angel choirs the glad refrain,
> That heralded Thy birth—

> The Tidings by heaven hymned forth to us:
> *In terra Pax hominibus.*
>
> O Olive Branch, O Dove of Peace,
> Brooding o'er stormy waters,
> When shall the flood of woe descrease?
> When shall the dreary conflict cease?
> And earth's worn sons and daughters
> Hail with glad hearts thy word to us:
> *In terra Pax hominibus.*
>
> Thy torn and sorrowing Church, dear Lord,
> This blessed gift imploreth.
> Be it according to Thy word,
> Be heavenly unity restored.
> Long as the moon endureth,
> Pour down the abundance of Thy peace on us:
> *In terra Pax hominibus.*

The letter continues:

> The only verse which does not quite satisfy me is the last. I do not like the words "*imploreth*" and "*endureth*" rhyming together, and I do not think the last two lines quite happy. I see you want to introduce the "abundance of peace so long as the moon endureth." But I do not think it comes in very happily. Could you get in some reference to our Lord's Reign of Peace, and then (beyond that) to Eternal Peace? How would these few verbal alterations in the last verse do?
>
> > O hear thy struggling Church, dear Lord,
> > This blessed gift imploring.
> > Be it according to Thy word,
> > Be Heavenly Un
>
> No! that won't do. Try again.
>
> > O heal Thy riven Church, dear Lord,
> > This blessed gift imploring.
> > Be it according to Thy Word,
> > Make her once more 'of one accord,'
> > Heaven's Peace on earth restoring,
> > And Peace Eternal grant to us.
> > *In terra Pax hominibus—*
>
> or

> Hear Thy rent Church, with one accord,
> This Blessed Gift imploring.
> Be it according to Thy Word.
> Thy Reign of Peace bring in, dear Lord.
> Heaven's Peace to earth restoring.
> And Peace Eternal grant to us.
> *In terra,* etc.

However, you will just think it over.

I think the 2nd and 3rd verses are best as they are, and not transposed as you are half disposed to suggest.

Evening. Dear Gerty has had a very good day (thank God)—the best she has had. She is still frightfully weak, but there has been a real improvement to-day. Just drop me a line and say whether you have sent the words to Bramley; and, if not, whether I shall send them with the music; and if so, whether you propose to alter your last verse. As it is a Godly *Sunday* hymn, you may send me the verse tomorrow. Then I can, if necessary, send the music off on Monday—for since I wrote this morning I have got it (I think) to my mind.

If their contributions are all *in* (several were in print, some time ago), and yours is not wanted, it will do for your Bazaar. But give them the chance of refusing. I think it would be a nice one to finish their book. I set two for them: one to words by Professor Bright, and one to some rather merry words by Professor Morris. And now, Peace be with *thee* and good night.

P.S. Would the second verse be at all improved by being written thus:

> "Peace I leave with you" was again
> Thy dying gift to earth;
> Sweet echo of the lingering strain
> Of Christmas morn—the glad refrain
> Of music at Thy Birth,
> When Angel choirs hymned forth to us,
> *In terra Pax,* etc.

Next day, the 14th Sunday after Trinity, he writes:

It has struck me that, by way of introducing a pleasing change into the refrain of your Carol, and bringing it to a better close, it would be very nice to utilise the beautiful variation of the Angels' Song, which S. Luke gives, ch. xix. 38. It is very interesting to observe, (and not generally noticed,) that whereas Angels, at our

Lord's Birth, sing "Peace on Earth," just before our Lord's Death, Earth echoes back the strain, and sings "Peace in Heaven."

How would it do to apply this response to *our* longing for Peace in heaven, as the consummation of the "*in terra pax*" of Christmas Day: and so, (quoting S. Luke's words and concluding with a grand sonorous line) to bring the Carol to an end thus:

> For Peace Eternal, Lord, we pray,
> *In Caelo Pax: et in Excelsis Gloria.*

I think this would make a very nice and appropriate finish and give a somewhat new meaning to the Gloria in Excelsis of Christmas Day—at least combining it with the thought of our own future glorification and exaltation.

This will also involve a pleasing variation in the Music.

Write a line tomorrow and tell me what you think about it. I will wait for your ultimatum till Tuesday morning, and then shall be able, probably, (if necessary) to send music and words off to Bramley by the early post that day.

Darling Gertie has not had a good day. She is very, very weak. This continued prostration makes one very anxious. Kindest love.

Your ever loving brother,
John

The carol, in its altered state, was sent off on September 20th; the second and fourth verses standing:

> "Peace I leave with you" was again
> Thy dying gift to earth;
> Sweet echo of the lingering strain
> Of Christmas morn—the glad refrain
> Of anthems at Thy Birth,
> When Angel choirs hymned forth to us,
> *In terra Pax hominibus*

> O hear Thy Church, with one accord,
> Her long-lost Peace imploring.
> Be it according to Thy Word:
> Thy Reign of Peace bring in, dear Lord;
> Heaven's Peace to earth restoring.
> And Peace Eternal, Jesu, grant, we pray,
> *In Caelo Pax, et in Excelsis Gloria.*

In Memoriam M. H. D.

A carol tune had also been written for the same collection, to the words, "Once again, O blessed time," by Dr. Bright, and sent up to Dr. Stainer; but this, apparently, did not satisfy the composer, for, on October 18th, we find an entry in his Diary:

> Began to think of new setting for words of Dr. Bright's Carol, "Once again." Had the proof of the one I had already written; but a little out of heart about it. Had played it over to wife and Kempe [the curate] on Sunday; but they both thought it like some other things I had written. I thought so, too: so started with it afresh.
> Wrote to Stainer, telling him about fresh setting.
> *Oct, 19*th. Finished my new Carol and sent it off by post; with letter to Stainer.

The quaint carol by William Morris, "From far away I come to you," with its "nonsense burden" "The snow in the street, and the wind on the floor," etc. was also set to music by Dr. Dykes during this year.

As the Diary shows, all through the busy round of parish visiting and hymn-tune writing, the loving father never missed the daily Office (generally morning and evening) by his sick child's bedside. In the late autumn she was able to be moved, with her mother and sisters, to Redcar. It was close upon Christmas before the whole family were assembled again in the house. During this trying period of bereavement and suspense Dr. Dykes received many touching proofs of the kind sympathy of friends. To him the following letter from the Rev. and Hon. Francis Grey was probably peculiarly gratifying, because it showed how the music which he had written to express the mingled joy and sorrow of a mourner should suggest to friends the thought of his own trouble.

Castle Howard, York
Sep. 29, 1870

My Dear Dykes,

I was in York Minster yesterday afternoon, when I heard your most beautiful Anthem, "These are they which came out of great tribulation." I cannot refrain from telling you that almost the one thought of my heart was for you and Mrs. Dykes, who have been called to pass through so much tribulation lately, and of your precious child, who has indeed "come out" of it—and what a wonderful thing it was to think of what the end of all these tribulations *must* be, if we only use them aright. Every word of these glorious promises, and every note of that touching music spoke with a loving force which they never had before; and I prayed that for you and yours these waters of affliction might indeed prove "living fountains of waters"—and that God's comforts might refresh your soul. When I first heard of your sorrow, a little more than a week ago, I shrank from intruding upon it—but after hearing that anthem yesterday, I could refrain no longer. Pray forgive me if I have been officious; and pray do not think of answering this letter.

Very affectionately yours,
Francis R. Grey

During this year, Dr. Dykes wrote, for Mr. Monk, for *The Anglican Hymn-Book*, the tunes:

1. "Angels, roll the rock away" (*Resurrection*)
2. "Jesu, to Thy table led" (*Panis Vivus*)
3. "Jesu, my Lord, my God, my All" (*Amplius*)
4. "Awake! awake! Put on Thy strength" (*Exsurge*)

The tunes "O day of rest and gladness" (*Dies Dominica*), and "Hark the sound of holy voices" (*Sanctuary*),[7] were also composed during this year, and they appeared first in *The Anglican Hymn-Book*. Hymn-tunes, as the entry for September 23rd shows, were also written for Mr. Minton Taylor's *Parish Church Hymnal*. Other entries made in the autumn illustrate the amount and variety of his musical work.

> *Sept. 23rd*. Sent off "Bound upon the accursèd tree" to Mr. Taylor. Also wrote a Harvest Tune.
> *Oct. 25th*. Sent off "The foe behind"
> *Oct. 27th*. Tune for "My God, my Father"
> *Nov. 24th*. Writing a Tune for Fred
> *Nov. 25th*. Doing "*Hora Novissima*"
> *Jan. 29th, 1871*. 4th Sunday after Epiphany. Set off to walk to Chester-le-Street. At Evensong, I preached from "My Beloved is gone down into His garden." (Had been requested to preach on state of the departed after Lady Durham's death.) After sermon I accompanied "O Paradise."
> *Feb. 24th, Friday*. Read the dreadful Purchas Judgment; may God have mercy on His poor Church, and direct us what to do.

---

7. This tune was written for Dr. Camidge, now Bishop of Bathurst, then Vicar of Hedon, near Hull.

In Easter week Dr. Dykes went to Leeds, for the opening of the new organ in St. John's Church, his brother, Mr. E. O. Dykes, being the honorary choirmaster. He preached and played the organ on the evening of Low Sunday, when he makes this entry in his Diary:

We sang my "O day of rest and gladness": had not heard it before.

This tune had been written at his brother's request, for St. John's Choir.

The tune to the words "At the Cross her station keeping," a translation of part of the old hymn "*Stabat Mater*," was written for the same choir, a year later, and afterwards published in *Hymns Ancient and Modern*.

On August 2nd Dr. Dykes went to Monkland, near Leominster, to stay with Sir Henry Baker, and arrange about tunes for *Hymns Ancient and Modern*. While there, an old servant of Sir Henry's—a great favourite of the family, and a most excellent woman—died. The account of the visit is best given in Dr. Dykes' own words.

August 2nd. It was the Children's Festival day. They all returned from Church. The children came into the garden singing: Monk there, Sir H. and Miss Baker, Mr. Maturin[8] and Miss Maturin, (curate of Dr. Jebb), all adjourned to field for children's tea and games. Sir H. tells me that his maid Elizabeth, who used to sing in the Choir, is dying.

Aug. 6th. 9th Sunday after Trinity. Feast of the Transfiguration. To Church by 7.30. At 8, first service. I celebrated, Monk served. Sir H. B. had given Holy Communion privately to Elizabeth during the early morning. Most lovely day. At Matins I preached on "Our Conversation is in Heaven": On the Transfiguration, the Festival, and the sick servant. A message came to the Church that Elizabeth was worse. Sir H. B. hurried home. Monk and I followed. When we arrived, we went into Elizabeth's room; she had a little revived. Sir H. asked me to pray with her, which I did. Evensong at 7.30. Sir H. said he thought Elizabeth worse, and so would not go. Accordingly, I took whole service, and preached from 2nd lesson, "After the fire a still, small voice." I alluded to our poor invalid. We had "Abide with me" after sermon, Monk bringing out emphatically the closing words: "In life, in death, O Lord, abide with me." Just as all was over we heard that her happy spirit had fled—she died during Evensong. R. I. P. Thank God for the blessings and mercies of this day.

Aug. 8th, Tuesday. At 10.15 started our work with Stainer (who, with Mr. Huntingford, had come the previous day) going

---

8. Now Father Maturin, who was three years curate with Dr. Jebb.

carefully through each Tune from the beginning of the book—till one o'clock. Afternoon, Tunes again.

*Aug. 10*th, *Thursday.* At 8, Celebration in the oratory. The coffin there, some kneeling outside in the garden. At 10.30, Funeral at Church. Stainer at Organ. We sang introductory sentences in unison; except the last one, which we sang with organ accompaniment, in Church. Hymn, "Christ shall gather in His own"; Antiphon, "Eternal rest grant unto her," etc. Sentences at grave, all in unison, except the last, "Blessed are the dead." Then hymn, "Brief life is here our portion." Leaving the grave, we sang "Nunc dimittis." Then in Church, as a conclusion, Psalm 150. (D.G.)

*Aug.11*th, *Friday.* At 10, set to work. Energetic discussion on "Miles Lane." [This old favourite Dr. Dykes was anxious to retain in the *Hymnal,* while some of his colleagues objected.] Finished. (D.G.)

Thank God for all His mercies to me during my visit. May He bless all my kind friends and prosper our work.

The following letter from Sir Henry Baker was received on Dr. Dykes' arrival in Durham:

Monkland
Saturday

My Dear Dykes,

May I drop the Dr.? This budget will reach you when at Durham again, in safety, I hope, and not really done up with all you have had to do here. I shall never forget your kind help and sympathy, which were so great a comfort to me, and to that dear soul. Our good Lord comfort *you*, on your dying bed, and grant us a place together in His Heavenly Home is indeed the prayer of

Your affectionate friend,
Henry W. Baker

The Rev. J. W. Kempe, who had been the assistant priest at St. Oswald's since 1865, was about to leave Durham. It was a compensation for his loss when Dr. Dykes' old friend, the Rev. W. M. Wray, who had, of late years, been a naval chaplain, consented to become his fellow-worker. The change is thus recorded in the Diary for the 16th of August:

*Aug, 16*th. Went to meet W. M. Wray. Glad to see the dear fellow. God bless our meeting together, and, (if it be His Will,) our working together, to His glory, and our mutual benefit.

*Aug. 31*st. On this night, just a year ago, darling Mab fell asleep in Jesu. Everlasting Rest, and Peace, be with her!

On September 4th Dr. Dykes joined, for ten days, a party of brothers, sisters, and friends, at Patterdale, on the Lake of Ullswater. He had been very anxious about the ways and means of sending his eldest son to College, and writes:

> *Sep. 8*th. A letter from C. D. Waited until after breakfast, and then read it on my knees. They agree to contribute £300 towards Erny's University expenses. (God bless and reward them!) Rowed to Glencoin. Walked to Gobarrow Park, and Aira Force. The rainbow on the waterfall most vivid. After reading there some time, we walked above the Fell to Dockwray; then along the road to the Wood, in which is a fine view. Thence, along the hillside, on a little grass path, to Glencoin. This is a most superb walk. I think the finest Lake views in the whole district.
>
> *Sep. 11*th. All started off, in a brake, to Keswick. Splendid day. Drove to Friar's Crag. Dear old Lake looked lovely as ever. Then rowed up to Lodore. Climbed up nearly to the top of the waterfall. Then walked to Grange, and had tea in the open air, near a cottage, where our kettle was boiled, and ham broiled. Then took a delightful walk, by Catbells. The Lake looked quite exquisite. Round by Portinscale to Keswick. Whom should I see but Sir H. Baker gesticulating to me. Had a lively chat with him and learnt that he was coming to pay me a visit in Durham.
>
> *Sep. 25*th. Finally entered dear Erny at Jesus College. Lord Jesu, watch in mercy over my dear lad, associated with a Society under Thy Holy Invocation. Give Thine elect Angels charge over him and keep him.

On October 9th Dr. Dykes went to Nottingham for the Church Congress, and on the 12th read a paper on Church Music.

> *Oct. 12*th. Congress Hall. Lord Nelson first, with an admirable paper, then Bickersteth, with a nice warmhearted interesting paper, then dear old Higgins, then self. I accompanied my own things on the organ: to wit, *Miserere*, Merbecke's "*Benedictus*" and "*Agnus Dei*," and "Hark! the sound of holy voices." Was just about 50 or 55 minutes altogether. Then Dr. Gauntlett, with a most amusing rambling colloquial address. Then the Bishop with a nice finish but referring unfairly to *Hymns A. and M.* about his Almsgiving Hymn.[9] Had a little private talk with him afterwards on the subject.

---

9. "O Lord of heaven, and earth, and sea."

The Bishop of Lincoln's complaints against the compilers of *Hymns Ancient and Modern* were twofold. First, that two verses of his hymn on Almsgiving had been omitted, and second, that the refrain at the end of each verse had been altered in some verses to suit the music. The complaints seemed just, until the reasons for the alterations had been explained; and in defence of the Compilers, it was stated that the proof of the hymn had been submitted to the Bishop before it was published, and that he had returned it without comment, not having observed the omissions; they therefore concluded he approved of the alterations.

The following letter, written by Dr. Dykes to Sir H. Baker, gives an account of his conversation with the Bishop, and the next letter the Bishop's generous acceptance of the proposed alterations in his hymn:

> St. Oswald's, Durham
> *Nov. 4, 1871*
>
> There can be no doubt that the correspondence ought to be published, and at once, before people forget all about the Congress. The Bishop's speech must have created a very unfavourable impression in many minds, in reference to *Hymns A. & M.* An impression is made, people forget *how* it was made, but it *remains* . . . I told the Bishop that I was not one of the Word Committee, and had nothing to do with the curtailment of his Hymn, and moreover that, not having been conscious of the abridgment of it till I heard of it in his public speech at Nottingham, I had no idea what the reasons of the Compilers were which induced them to omit the verses in question.
>
> I told him, however, that I must honestly say that the Hymn seemed to me on the whole *better* as a Hymn, with its verses 4 and 5 (as they stand in "Holy Year") omitted. Verse 5 is a beautiful one, but it must go if verse 4 goes, and verse 4 is spoiled by its conclusion.[10]

10. The verses run thus:
Verse 4
Thou did'st not spare Thine only Son,
But gav'st Him for a world undone;
And e'en that gift Thou did'st outrun
And gave us all.

Verse 5
Thou gav'st the Spirit's blessèd dower,
Spirit of Life, and Love, and Power,
And dost His sevenfold graces shower
Upon us all.

In Memoriam M. H. D.

I told him that the word "outrun" struck me as being by no means a felicitous one, and might suggest an utterly wrong meaning. People commonly understand it in the sense of "Outstrip," or "Overpass."

In that verse it might seem to teach that God, after giving His Only Son, surpassed, and exceeded *that* Gift, by giving something still *better*, expressed by the word "*All.*"

The Bishop quotes in his note Rom. viii, 32. But as I reminded him—St. Paul's argument, and his own argument (as it appears on the surface) are quite different.

St. Paul argues that He Who gave the greater and all inclusive Gift, cannot, and will not, withhold the lesser dependent Gifts.

The Bishop's language *seems* almost to intimate (on the other hand) that the lesser Gift, the Only Son, came *first*, and the Greater,—the "ALL," in the donation of which the Bountiful Donor out-ran Himself, came, and comes, afterwards.

And I then quoted to the Bishop that important statement of Courtier Biggs (which I think so true) that one single ambiguous expression will often entirely paralyze the devotional power of a Hymn; and therefore that, inasmuch as the teaching of verses 4 and 5 was virtually included in verse 6, I thought it safer that they should go.

I told him that I thought, had the punctuation been different, and instead of a full stop at the end of verse 4 there had been a *colon* thus (:—) leading on to the next verse and directly associating the Gifts there specified with the "*All*" of the preceding verse, there would have been less objection to the verses: still I thought the language required reconsideration. He must write verse 4 again, for your new and revised edition. I suggested to him that he might perpetuate the Hymn in its permanent shape *there*.

With regard to the refrain, of course I told the Bishop that it was impossible for a musical phrase, with one definite accentuation, to suit equally well "Giver *of* all" and "Who givest all."

Have either—but not both.

The following is the Bishop of Lincoln's answer to the suggested alteration in his hymn:

Riseholme, Lincoln
Nov. 14, 1871

My Dear Sir,

Though I have only a few moments now to do it in, I cannot resist thanking you for your letter. Your criticism on the word "*outrun*" in the Hymn which you have honoured with a beautiful tune, is just. I would read the two stanzas thus:

> Thou did'st not spare Thine only Son,
> But gav'st Him for a world undone,
> And freely, with that Blessèd One,
> Thou givest all.
>
> Thou giv'st the Holy Spirit's dower,
> Spirit of Life, and Love, and Power,
> And dost His sevenfold graces shower
> Upon us all.

If the hymn is reprinted I should be thankful to have it circulated in this form, *with your tune.*

Yours sincerely,
C. Lincoln

In the next edition of *Hymns Ancient and Modern* the entire hymn was published, in its altered form. In the preparation of successive editions of that work, Dr. Dykes had been much thrown with Dr. Stainer. The following letter, written in January 1872 to his brother, Frederic Dykes, shows his pleasure at the promotion of the distinguished organist.

> I suppose you have seen that Stainer is appointed to S. Paul's in the room of Goss—an admirable appointment. As a Churchman and a musician, he is the very man for the post. Really, the changes that have come over S. Paul's, of late years, are quite miraculous. I have just been writing to Stainer, to congratulate him. He will be much missed in Oxford. Our Church looks very pretty this Christmas, and our services have been bright and hearty. We have started a processional Cross this Christmastide—a beautiful one of 14th century workmanship, presented to the Church by an old parishioner.

During January 1872, notices are entered in the Diary of several new hymn-tunes. Dr. Dykes wrote tunes for Welsh and American hymnbooks, and (for Bishop Tozer), tunes for Swahili words. There was great difficulty about these last tunes, as the Swahili language did not lend itself well to musical rhythm.

On February 22nd he wrote a tune for the marriage of a friend, to the words, "The voice that breathed o'er Eden."

His advice was also asked, a few weeks later, about an anonymous hymn, sent him by his brother Frederic. It was to be used as a processional for a Choir Festival at the Wakefield Parish Church, and sung to the grand chorale, "*Ein feste Burg.*" Dr. Dykes afterwards discovered that the Hymn had been written by his brother. The following are the words:

> Thou art the Christ, the Son of God,
> The one alone foundation;
> On this, on Thee, is built Thy Church,
> The Rock of our Salvation
> A City builded fair!
> Thy saints her bulwark are,
> And Thou has chosen it,
> A holy dwelling fit,
> Thy Spirit's habitation.
>
> Here all Thy chosen ones are fed,
> With blessed Food from Heaven;
> Thy very Body and Thy Blood
> To feed their souls are given.
> Here the first stain of earth
> Is cleansed by second birth.
> Thy pure Blood healing gave
> To the baptismal wave
> When Thy dear Side was riven.
>
> Here on Thy flock His sevenfold gifts
> Thy Holy Spirit showers;
> Anoints Thy Priests, and sin-sick souls
> With Grace renewing dowers.
> Here joins He loving hands
> In Holy Wedlock's bands,
> Here on the heart of death
> He breathes His living breath—
> Death dies with all its powers.

> Here prayers are daily offered up
> Like clouds from censers swinging;
> Here praises rise to greet Thine ear
> With melody and singing;
> And here before the eye
> Of Thy dread Majesty,
> On Thy dear Love intent
> In awful worship bent
> Our souls to Thee are clinging.
>
> And hence Thine armies have marched forth
> Through dangers, never doubting,
> Raising the banner of the Cross
> And "Christ" their war-cry shouting.
> Who trembles at the strife?
> Death is the gate of life!
> Thus onward still they go,
> Marching against the foe,
> The hosts of Satan routing.
>
> Oh! joy of those we mourn for here!
> Oh! bliss all words excelling!
> The saintly vanguard of Thy host
> Has reached Thy Holy dwelling.
> And here amid the din,
> The turmoil, care, and sin,
> Like music in the night
> From those pure worlds of light
> We hear their Anthem swelling.
>
> From that dear Lord Who bought them now
> Naught can their souls dissever;
> Safe in His bosom now they rest,
> And harm can reach them never.
> Praise to the Three in One,
> To Father, Spirit, Son.
> All might, all glory, be
> To Thee, blest Trinity,
> For ever and for ever, *Amen*.

On this hymn Dr. Dykes writes to his brother, in ignorance of its authorship:

S. Oswald's
May 25, 1872

It is Saturday night, and I am in the birth-pangs of a Discourse. I have only time, therefore, for a very hasty line in answer to yours.

I don't know who your amateur Hymnodist is, but I think he has written a capital and very useful Hymn. I see your difficulty about the 3rd verse. The mistake, however, is this: not that he has omitted all mention of Confirmation, but that he has limited the donation of the sevenfold gifts of the Spirit to the Priests.

Now at Confirmation, *all* Christians receive the sevenfold gifts of the Spirit. The grace of "Orders," which Priests receive to qualify them for their work, is something special, and over and above the great sevenfold endowment, which is the heritage of all members of Christ, who receive the imposition of hands. I should suggest some such alteration as the following:

> Here on Thy flock. His sevenfold gifts
> Thy Holy Spirit showers;
> Anoints Thy Priests, and sin-sick souls
> With Grace renewing dowers.[11]

I don't think I quite like the 4th verse—about "our souls themselves are flinging"—but I am not sure. Anyhow, I think that, for a Hymn made to order, it is a great success. You cannot get a better arrangement of "*Ein feste Burg*" than that in A. and M. It is almost entirely Bach. It is not given entirely in the Huguenots—only scraps of it—and not so well arranged. That will do for your vocal arrangements. You must leave your organist to do what he pleases with his unison verses.

It has been already mentioned that Dr. Dykes had written hymn-tunes for the Rev. E. H. Bickersteth. The peculiar circumstances in which the request contained in the following letter was made, show how warmly Mr. Bickersteth appreciated the power which Dr. Dykes possessed of expressing the sentiment of words in music that, as it were, gave living force to written language.

---

11. The third verse was originally written:
Here on Thy *Priests* Thy sevenfold gifts
The Holy Spirit showers;
Here the sad soul that mourns for sin
With Grace renewing dowers, etc.

Christ Ch. Vicarage, Hampstead
11 June, 1872

Dear Dr. Dykes,

... I have another great request. Could you, would you, write me a tune for the enclosed beautiful Hymn, which is, I believe, by some American author—"We would see Jesus"—which I might print in my magazine *Evening Hours*. The Publishers would pay liberally for any contribution from your pen. And I cannot but think that this Hymn, if only wedded to a tune that breathed its longing, would be an added wealth for ever to our Hymnody. I have loved the hymn for years, but never knew a tune for it—and now it speaks to my heart as never before; for the Master has come and is calling to Himself my third daughter—a lovely girl of 18. She is gently sinking in consumption; but her happy trust and love have been without a cloud. She has so been the sunshine of our home circle; we can hardly venture to anticipate what it will be without her. Forgive my writing so freely—but your former kindness makes me bold.

Yours ever gratefully,
E. H. Bickersteth

St. Oswald's Vic., Durham
June 14, 1872

My dear Mr. Bickersteth,

Thank you for the sweet words, "We would see Jesus." As soon as I had read them, the tune for them seemed at once to come into my head. I wrote it out, but have let it wait a day or so, to see if I liked it on second thoughts. As I do not think I shall improve upon it, I send it. Sometimes first impressions are the best. I am sorry to learn the *cause* of the special interest you take in the words now. And yet I am sure you will feel more deeply than any words can express, that "all is well," well for you, and well for your dear child. May she, even now, in her time of weakness, be gladdened with the vision of Jesus—and may she soon see Him face to face, and be eternally satisfied with the joy of His countenance.

Believe me,
Very sincerely yours,
John B. Dykes

To Dr. Dykes

... I will send a proof of your tune "We would see Jesus" in two or three days. I have added to the receipt "Copyright secured to Author"—as we have done with all the music printed in "Evening Hours." ...

Ever most gratefully yours,
E. H. Bickersteth

About this time, the Almsgiving Hymn, "Lord of Glory, Who hast brought us" was sent to the Committee of *Hymns Ancient and Modern,* with the condition that, if accepted, an old friend of the authoress, Dr. Dykes, should compose a tune for it. It was accepted and sent to Dr. Dykes; and to his surprise, he found it was written by his sister, Mrs. Alderson. The first four verses formed the original hymn, which ended with the lines

> Lest that Face of Love and Pity
> Turn from us another day.

This Dr. Dykes thought too sad an ending for a hymn intended to encourage cheerful almsgiving; and he suggested that a fifth verse should be added, by repeating the first half of the first verse, and adding the lines, which he himself composed—

> Give us faith to trust Thee boldly,
> Hope to stay our souls on Thee,
> But, O best of all Thy graces,
> Give us Thine own charity.

The tune he named *"Charitas."*

On this, as on other occasions, Dr. Dykes rendered considerable assistance to the *word committee* of *Hymns Ancient and Modern,* suggesting alterations which he thought necessary to perfect a hymn. He had poetic as well as musical talent and could often see where a doctrine could be stated more definitely, or a vague line made clear.

The following letter, to his sister, Mrs. Alderson, refers to her Almsgiving Hymn:

St. Oswald's Vic., Durham
July 3, 1872

I must send you a line, to thank you for your note, and its enclosure. You have improved your hymn very much. It is a charming hymn, now; and I shall have great pleasure in trying my hand at a tune for it as soon as the Spirit moves me in that direction! at present I have my head and hands pretty well filled. I shall be writing to Sir H. W. B. shortly and will send the revised Hymn.

Dr. Stainer sent me rather a beautiful hymn lately, of a very strange metre, which I have just set for him. He is poet as well as musician. Your letter threw a new light upon the hymn lately sent me in MS. by Fred. I have no doubt it is his own. And a capital one it is. I think he rather spoiled part of it by toning down the doctrine. But I must have it in its best Catholic dress to send to Sir H. B. It would be a most useful hymn to that grand tune.

If you can knock off, (no: I don't mean that: for a Hymn should be in the 1st place suggested, or inspired from above, and then *carefully* perfected—well, if you are moved to write) any Saint's Day Hymns, by all means do so. Also, I am not sure if a good modern Eucharistic Hymn might not be a great boon. It will be nice employment for you, by the "sad sea waves." I do not wonder at your feeling somewhat anxious about this appointment; but as you truly say, if it is best for you and your family that you should get it—you will. And if it is not for your real good, you are far better and happier without it. It is a happy thought that whatever the magistrates *do*, or neglect to do, there is One above them all, Who will look after your best interests, and with Whom, really, the appointment lies. "Man proposes, God disposes."

I suppose you have heard that Erny's boat at Henley got the honours not only from Eton, but from Oxford and Cambridge. He is now staying at Weybridge. Our united best love to you all.

Some idea of the variety and quantity of his musical work during the latter part of the year 1872 may be gathered from the following extracts from the Diary:

Durham, Jun. 22nd. Writing Anthem, "The Lord is my Shepherd."

Aug. 4th, *Sunday*. Sang over my new Anthem, "The Lord is my Shepherd."

Aug. 5th. Finished my Anthem on this—St. Oswald's day. Laus Deo, per D. N. J. C.

Aug. 7th. Feast of Holy Name. Sent off Anthem to post, and began *Service in E flat*, both on feast of the Holy Name. May they both be under that sacred Invocation.

Durham, Aug. 12th, Monday. At 6:15, Erny and I started off to drive to station. At Barnard Castle we changed, and, while I was looking into what carriage Erny had got, the train started off. He went on, and I was left behind. It was a little after 8, and there was no train till 1.40. Felt wonderfully vexed, but soon recovered myself, and determined to make the best of it. So went, by a charming wood, into the town. Visited the church, walked by the riverside. Then into the wood again, where I wrote sketch of "*Benedictus*" and "*Agnus Dei*," for my new service. At last was off again to Tebay and so to Windermere. Then, by coach, to Grasmere, where I arrived a little past 7.

Aug. 14th. Erny's birthday, twenty-one! God bless him. Sweet walk to Colwith Force, a most picturesque and beautiful waterfall. While the girls were drawing, I was making a sketch for my *Service in E.*

Aug. 17th. Finished a fair copy of my new *Te Deum.* Reached Durham at 7. Proof of my little Anthem, "I am the Way."

Aug. 19th, Scarborough. To St. Martin's for practice. Most glorious looking organ; delicate and charming.

Aug. 20th. Opening of St. Martin's Organ. I played in the evening (Dr. Sloman in the morning).

Aug. 22nd. To North Cliff. Studying subject for another short Anthem for Mr. Allon. Bathe; was never more nearly drowned in my life. Another half minute, and I do not think I could have recovered myself, the tide so strong. Thank God for all His mercies!

Sunday, Aug 25th. Played and preached at St. Martin's.

Sep. 7th. To Worcester. Wrote part of the Jubilate on my road. Studying the Passion Music.

Dr. Dykes stayed with his friend Canon Cattley for the musical festival.

Sep. 8th. Talking to Cattley about his bells. Wrote a bell tune for him.

This tune is still to be heard in the Worcester chimes.

Sep. 9th. Rehearsal. All through the Passion Music. Music most touching and divine. A new revelation to me.

*Sep. 12*th. Passion Music. Sat by Whinfield, and had full German score. Most delightful—Lloyd's singing perfection. *Lobgesang.* Glorious performance.

*Sep. 13*th. Heard part of *Messiah.* Off by 3:35 train. Wrote a short *Te Deum* on my journey.

*Sep. 22*nd. Tried my little Anthem, "*Unto Him that loved us.*"

Besides the compositions mentioned in these extracts, at the suggestion of his brother Edward he wrote an "*Agnus Dei,*" and a hymn-tune to the words, "*At the Cross her station keeping.*" A song, "*Too late,*" was also composed, and shortly before Christmas a new hymn-tune to "*Hark! the herald angels sing.*"

8

The Trial
1873–1874

"The Lord is my Shepherd"—"The Song of Praise"—Bishop Baring refuses license Mr. Peake—Correspondence with the Archbishop of York—Monkland and Malvern—Legal Proceedings—Birnam—*Hymns Ancient and Modern, Revised Edition*—The Trial; Court of Queen's Bench

THE storm was now beginning to gather, which, before it dispersed, clouded the closing years of the useful life of Dr. Dykes. The entries of the Diary for 1873 begin in their usual quiet way. But before six months were passed, the genial atmosphere of love and peace in which Dr. Dykes loved to live and labour, was suddenly changed for the fierce heat of controversy. Dr. Dykes never recovered the shock. It is not too much to say that it killed him.

> *Durham, Jan. 4*th. Writing long letter with reference to a children's service, for which I had been finishing some Litany Tunes.
> *Jan. 11*th. Composed a set of chants for the *Te Deum*.
> *Jan. 27*th. Writing a Tune for the Manchester Jail.

This tune was written at the request of the Rev. R. Tomlins, who was then Chaplain of the Manchester Jail. It was called "St. Leonards," and was entitled, "The Invitation to Rest: 'Come unto Me.'" We give the first verse:

> And is it Thy voice, Patient Saviour, yet calling?
> And is it Thy sad, earnest features, I see?
> And is it Thine Arm strech'd to save me from falling?
> And dost Thou yet bid me draw nigh unto Thee?

In a letter to Dr. Dykes' nephew, Mr. N. D. Levett, Mr. Tomlins writes:

> The Tune was sung at Lichfield Cathedral, three or four years ago, at a Diocesan meeting of the Lichfield Choirs. How it got there, I do not know, nor did the authorities at Lichfield know; but they afterwards wrote me, apologizing for using it. It found its way somewhat widely to the churches and chapels at Manchester. It has been greatly admired.

> Apr. 27th, *Durham.* Letter from the commissioners, undertaking to pay two complete curates' stipends of £120 (D.G.), besides the £45 for the house rent for one.
>
> May 9th. Finished new Tunes for "The roseate hues" and "The night is gone."
>
> May 14th. New Tune for "Sweet Saviour."
>
> May 25th, 28th, 29th. Letter from Skeffington; he wants both my sermons . . . Sermon finished and taken to the post. Lord bless it to Thy honour and glory. Began to copy out another sermon for Skeffington: "The fruits of the Spirit."
>
> June 4th and 5th. Doncaster for Choral Festival. High Matins 11.30. Between five [hundred] and six hundred choristers; but only 250 surpliced. Heavy selection of music. I preached from 2 Chron. xx. Felt I could not fill that large church with its lantern towers. Thank God for helping me through my dreaded sermon.
>
> Jun. 6th. Called on Rogers [Dr.], tried his two magnificent pianos: then to church. He helped me with the organ stops, so that I got on better. Most noble organ.

About this time Dr. Dykes also wrote tunes to the hymns "For ever, beatific word," and "Lord, I hear of showers of blessing."

To His Brother Fred

St. Oswald's, Durham
June 30, 1873

I have not yet received any proof sheets of the Anthem.[1] I suppose I shall be having some fragments by and by.

---

1. "The Lord is my Shepherd"

> Erny is at Henley—staying with some friends at a charming spot on the Thames. Their boat has again been victorious.
>
> Dublin beat Oxford—but Erny's boat beat Dublin—after a fearful race. Erny had to be carried out of the boat. Jack won a silver medal the other day, for steering the Grammar School in a victorious race.
>
> Both [of his two sons] seem to have a taste for aquatic pursuits.

On May 20th Lady Victoria Evans Freke wrote to Dr. Dykes from Belmont, Bournemouth, to ask his assistance for a tune-book she was compiling, as a companion volume to the Rev. Edward Harland's [A] *Church Psalter and Hymnal*. This book, afterwards much enlarged, is known as *The Song of Praise*. Dr. Dykes consented, and wrote eleven new tunes for the work, the enlarged edition of which contains, in all, forty-three of his tunes, new and old. The demands on his time were increasing more and more, for, besides his parochial work, his counsel and advice were much sought after, both by Clergy and laity, and requests for his hymn-tunes came from all parts. These requests he looked upon as calls from God, as much as any other work. Meanwhile he had also been greatly occupied in changes arising out of the enlargement of the parish of St. Oswald's, which had a population of about four thousand when Dr. Dykes first took charge of it, and had been recently increased by the addition of a pit village near Durham. It was therefore to him a great delight to receive an offer from the Ecclesiastical Commissioners to pay the complete stipends of two curates as well as to pay the house rent for one. Yet, almost simultaneously with this offer came the news that he must lose his friend and curate, Mr. Wray.

> *May* 12th. Answering letters about Curacy. Wray told me he had had an offer of the living of Ovingham, and should probably be leaving. Oh Lord Jesu, send me a good fellow-worker, if I lose my present one.
>
> *May* 15th. Hear that Wray has accepted the living of Ovingham. God's Will be done!
>
> *May* 20th. Estimate from Novello for printing Anthem ["The Lord is my Shepherd"]. Appalled at the expense! More applications for the Curacy, but the real man hardly seems to have applied yet. Lord, who is it?

At last the fit man was found in the Rev. G. E. F. Peake, of whom Dr. Dykes had received a most satisfactory account from his late Vicar, the Rev. and Hon. Francis Grey.

> *Jun.* 10th. Call from Peake, applying for Curacy. *"Domine dirige me."*
>
> *Jun.* 12th. Received this morning a very nice letter about Peake. Our prayers were specially asked at Celebration this morning for the appointment of two faithful Priests for this parish. Is this letter some token that God has heard our prayers? and an earnest that He will direct me? as I *know* He will.

He was still in search of a second Curate, and eagerly looking forward to the increase of the staff which the offer of the Ecclesiastical Commissioners enabled him to make, when he received the following letter from the Bishop of Durham:

Auckland Castle, Bishop Auckland
July 4, 1873

My dear Sir,

. . . I must require of an Incumbent, on his nomination of a Curate, that he give me his written pledge, that he will not require of such Curate:

1st. That he wear coloured Stoles.

2nd. That he take part in, or be present at the burning of Incense.

3rd. That he turn his back to the congregation during the celebration of the Holy Communion, except when "ordering the bread."

I must also require of a Curate a written promise that he will offend in none of these things . . .

Yours truly,
C. Dunelm

His own feelings on receiving this letter, and in sending a reply, are jotted down in his Diary in the following words:

> *Jul.* 5th. Startled by receiving a letter from the Bishop, in which he refuses to license any Curate, except Incumbent and Curate will give a written pledge that:
>
> 1st. "The latter shall never wear a coloured Stole."

2ⁿᵈ. "Never have anything to do with Incense."[2]

3ʳᵈ. "Shall never stand with his back to the Congregation" (at the H. Eucharist) "except when ordering the Bread." Alas! alas! Lord, teach me what to do . . .Finished letter, in which I declined to sign any such document as the Bishop wishes me to sign. Lord forgive me if I am acting wrongly.

Were he to sign it, he knew it would stop much good work in the Diocese, just as a revival of Church Life was beginning, for no High Churchman would be allowed a Curate, except under conditions to which he could not conscientiously submit. Already the Bishop had refused to license a Curate for the Rev. the Hon. Francis Grey, Rector of Morpeth, unless he promised to give up using the Invocation before the sermon. Now on Dr. Dykes the Bishop sought to impose a new set of conditions. With all his loyalty to the Bishop, he felt it to be his duty to resist.[3]

On all sides Dr. Dykes was entreated to resist these illegal conditions. Bishop Baring, on the other hand, believed, with so many other like-minded Christians, that he was not only doing right, but bound by his official position to act as he did. In perfect sincerity he feared the "inroads of Popery." But he had forgotten that, while the world lasts, and men are differently constituted, there must be difference of opinion as to lawful modes of worship. To some, a high ritual is a great help; to others, it may be a great hindrance. Only let the Love of God fill the heart, and all such differences disappear.

> *Durham, Jul. 13*ᵗʰ. Preached on "Sanctify the Lord God in your hearts"; alluding to my present difficulties with the Bishop.
> *Jul. 14*ᵗʰ. Beginning a letter to the Bishop. Lord help me!
> *Jul. 15*ᵗʰ. Restless and desponding about the Bishop's conduct, and the prospect for the Parish.
> *Jul. 16*ᵗʰ. Going on heavily with the letter. Cathedral. Then charming walk up Crossgate Moor. Sweet time of comfort, meditation, and private prayer. Thank God for His loving-kindness.
> *Jul. 20*ᵗʰ. Letters from the Bishop. Opened on my knees, after prayer for acceptance of God's Will and guidance. The Bishop will not license Peake. *"Fiat voluntas Tua."*

The Bishop writes:

---

2. Incense was not used in any church in the Diocese, and Dr. Dykes had no wish to introduce it into St. Oswald's.

3. For his reasons, see his correspondence with the Bishop, printed in Appendix 1.

I regret that I must decline to license the Rev. G. E. F. Peake to the Curacy of St. Oswald's, Durham.

Yours faithfully,
C. Dunelm
To the Rev. J. B. Dykes

Dr. Dykes was the last man to desire to make a martyr of himself; his only wish was to see and know God's will, and to do it.

> *Jul.* 20th. In Church from 5 to 6, asking for Light and Guidance. Ashwell came. I read over to him the last of the letters of the Bishop. He recommended me to publish it. Oh Lord, teach me whether it is for Thy Glory, and the good of Thy Church!
>
> *Jul.* 21st. Heard the sad news of the death of the Bishop of Winchester! A mighty Prince has fallen. R. I. P.
>
> Francis Grey came; he agrees the letter had better be published. Lord, overrule the publishing to the good of Thy Church.
>
> *Jul.* 24th. A Reception, to meet the new Bishop of Barbados [Mitchinson]. Had some talk with him; he does not recommend my yielding.

In his trouble it was a relief to him to leave Durham for a few days, and on July 20th he wrote the following letter to Sir Henry Baker:

> Just a line to say it would give me sincere pleasure to come over to Monkland on Monday, 28th, for the inside of a week.
>
> I am in great perplexity. I want two Curates; and the Bishop won't license any, except I and they give a written pledge beforehand that the Curate shall never "stand with his back to the congregation" at the Celebration, except when just "ordering the Bread," shall never wear a coloured Stole, etc.
>
> I have refused to sign, or ask a Curate to sign, any such document whatever; so he refuses to license. And there we are.
>
> Please remember me sometimes in this difficulty, in your prayers—that I may be guided to do what is *right* and according to God's Will—avoiding alike the Scylla of cowardice and the Charybdis of rebellion.

On July 28th he went to Monkland to stay with Sir Henry Baker, for *Hymns Ancient and Modern* committee work.

> *Jul.* 30th. Heaps of letters—one from the Archbishop of York, kind and clever, but unsatisfactory . . . Finished my reply to the Archbishop. Lord help me, and teach me what to do.

The two following letters are to his wife:

Monkland
July 31, 1873

... I have just been writing to those excellent Lawyers;—no sooner does one get fairly disposed of Tunes, for the day, than one has to set to and write letters. I fear it is a case of "Christian, seek not yet repose." However, Sir H. W. B. begs me to assure you he is doing his best to take care of me ... On Monday, if all be well, Monk, Sir Henry, and I are going to take a run on the Malvern Hills; and we are to stop the night at the Hotel, and return on Tuesday. I shall be glad to do this, as I have never seen Malvern, and want a breeze of good fresh air.

—

The letters I receive make me quite thankful that I am, through God's Providence, just at the present moment, away from Durham. It is plain that nothing definite can be done, until Counsel's opinion has been had, so I am rather rejoicing in being out of the fray. It would only have kept me nervous and excited to have been in Durham. And now, having disposed of Tunes and letters, I shall be off on the tramp. God bless you all.

Another, written on the same visit, is to his brother Frederic:

Monkland, Nr. Leominster
August 4, 1873

What is to be the upshot of it God only knows. I do not wish to be willful and headstrong—I can only hope and pray that God would teach me what I ought to do, and give me Grace and Strength to do it.

I have had a long and kind letter from the Archbishop of York. Of course he counsels submission, and tries to dissuade me from appealing to himself judicially. On the other hand George Anthony Denison, and *many* others write earnestly urging me to stand firm.

At present, through the kindness of Beresford Hope, Counsel's Opinion is being taken in London, as to the legal right of the Bishop has to exact these pledges before licensing.

I have just been writing to the lawyers, who are preparing the case, and expect to hear the result in a few days. I have been most thankful to get a few quiet days of Hymn-work. We are just off for a couple of days to Malvern. I return to the North this week.

Letters now came from all parts, both from friends and strangers, entreating Dr. Dykes not to give way to the Bishop's demands. Amongst the very many which were sent, we select two letters from Archdeacon Denison, from which the two following quotations are made:—

East Brent, Highbridge
July 31, 1873

Dear Dr. Dykes,

I received yesterday an extract from *The Standard* giving an account of your Bishop's dealings with you. Nobody can be surprised . . . to find that the only weapon practically remaining to them [the Bishops] in their contest with the Catholic revival is eagerly used. But the lack of all equity and fairness, and the manifest tyranny of this use—must, I believe, in the end, work out the remedy. Meantime, in individual cases, there is much difficulty and suffering—your own case is a special example—mine is another, and I believe that the cases are likely to be multiplied by the Bishops.

I see nothing to be done (unless the law can be brought to interfere) but to say that, Licensed Curates being refused, it only remains to reserve the ordained hand, in a Parish, so suffering, for such things *only* as require an ordained hand, and to throw EVERYTHING else into lay hands.

All my knowledge of the Clergy forbids the supposition that they are going to succumb to the tyrannous exercise of Power, entrusted to the Bishops for a wholly different purpose.

If any is to blame in a parish it is the Incumbent and not the Curates. If the Incumbent can be restrained and is content to remain Incumbent—being restrained, that is for each one to say, in his own case. But if he cannot be restrained, then I am much mistaken if the law will allow him to be punished INDIRECTLY, through Curates. If this be law, it is high time that it be no longer law.

But I am persuaded that it is not law, and I hope I may see the matter tested. I must see if I cannot force the point in at the Bath Congress.

Yours always in Christ,
George A. Denison

Aug. 1873

. . . Extreme tyranny is best met by passive resistance. When the congregation see what the Bishop forces matters to—there may be a prospect of compelling even the Bishop of Durham to recede.

But if you were to give way one hair's breadth now, a precedent of the most disastrous kind would be established . . .

We are embarked in a great struggle. We must be prepared to *carry it out*—suffer individually as we may. It may very possibly be, that upon the moral courage and steadfastness of the men, in this particular time, hangs the whole future character of the Church of England. There are those, I fear, who are playing at these things: *but we may not play at them.*

Yours always in Christ,
George A. Denison

By August 17th he was back at Durham.

Aug. 17th. Wray preached a nice touching sermon—"Brethren, pray for us"—his farewell sermon; asking their prayers for me, also for himself.

Aug. 20th. Heard from "Few and Co." Counsel's Opinion to be given on the 29th.

The one thing Dr. Dykes would have wished to avoid was, going to law. He was a man of peace, and hated party disputes; but all his friends agreed in thinking that no other course was open. He had offers of help on all sides, and the English Church Union undertook to share the legal expenses. A fund was also raised, through the kindness of Mr. Shaw-Stewart, in conjunction with Mr. Beresford-Hope and Canon Cooke of Exeter, entitled "The Dykes Defence Fund." He was advised that an appeal would be made to the Court of Queen's Bench.

The following is a letter to his brother Frederic:

St. Oswald's, Durham
Aug. 25, 1873

. . . Matters remain *in statu quo* as regards the Bishop. Counsel cannot meet until the 29th of this month, when the Attorney General, Dr. Stephens, and Mr. Bowen, will hold a consultation and record their opinion. I have been asked to be present if I am in town, but as I shall *not* be in town, I shall wait quietly for the issue. The Lawyers who have drawn up the case are sanguine.

One good result has followed already. Wray left me, last week, so last Sunday I discontinued, and gave notice that I should hereafter discontinue, the use of "Table Prayers," as they are profanely called. I shall say all the Eucharistic Service or none. So, on the Sundays when I have not a second Celebration, I shall only have Matins, Litany, and Sermon.

Aug. 21st. Received "These are they" from Novello. They have purchased Ouseley's book from Cox and Co., and are about to reprint it. Started, with knapsack, to walk to Houghton-le-Spring. Charming walk.

Aug 22nd. Wrote out tune for "Thy way, not mine, O Lord" which had come into my head during yesterday's walk.

Aug. 25th. Call from Lowe. He proposed the establishment of a Sisterhood. No sooner had he gone than Major Wilkinson called, and proposed the same thing. Informed me that his sister would subscribe £10, and he £20 a year towards it. He also offered to help in any way. Thank God for Jesus Christ's sake! Felt most grateful; surely it seems as if it were God's Will that I should do something towards the establishment of a Sisterhood here. Wrote to Sister Jane and asked for information respecting Sisters. Lord, give my letter good success. Wrote draft of a tune to "Hail, Gladdening Light!"

Aug. 27th. Letter from Few, informing me that the Bishop had sent to retain Dr. Stephens, but that the Dr. (together with the Attorney General) is already retained on our side.

Aug. 28th. Letter from Sister Jane: they cannot send us a Sister from St.Thomas's. I must try elsewhere. Wrote to Clewer.

Aug. 30th. Letter from Few, telling me that the "Opinion" is in my favour. (D.G.) Also a letter from Professor Stewart. [This was in reference to tunes for *The Irish Hymnal*.]

Aug. 31st. C. H. Fowler promised me £10 a year towards Sisterhood. Heard from Clewer; they cannot help me.

Sep. 2nd. Letter from Few, consenting to my proposal that *I* should send "the Opinion" with a private letter to the Bishop.

Sep. 6th. Letter from the Bishop, directing me to his Lawyers; by the same post received copy of "Opinion." (D.G.)

The following is the letter from Messrs. Few and Co., of August 29th, enclosing the opinion of counsel on the case which they had submitted to them:

2, Henrietta Street, Covent Garden
29 Aug., 1873

My Dear Sir,

As no doubt you will be anxious to learn the result of our consultation of to-day, I send you a line, in anticipation of the Opinion; which I may not have before tomorrow or Monday.

The consultation was an extremely good one and lasted a full hour. All the bearings of the case were regarded and pulled to pieces in a very searching and satisfactory mode. The result is that Counsel are decidedly of opinion that these requirements of the Bishop are illegal; and that a mandamus will be granted, requiring the Bishop to issue his licence without any such special declaration.

The course to be adopted, therefore, will be that we personally address a letter to the Bishop, on behalf of yourself and Mr. Peake, calling upon his Lordship to forthwith grant the required license, failing which it will be our duty to apply to the Court for a mandamus to his Lordship in enforcement of the application.

I was somewhat amused to hear from Mr. Stephens, at the end of the consultation, that he finds it is a very general practice throughout the Diocese of Durham—that the Celebrant turns his back upon the congregation, at the consecration of the Elements; and he has advised that when the application for a mandamus be made, should the Bishop not give way, an affidavit of this practice should be presented, with the other affidavits to be then used. I cannot help entertaining a strong belief that the Bishop will not show fight, but will give way, more especially now that we have secured the advocacy of Dr. Stephens.

Believe me to be
Yours very faithfully,
R. Few

Copy of Opinion

Has the Bishop any right to enforce as against either Dr. Dykes or Mr. Peake, the requirements set forth in his letter to Dr. Dykes, dated 4 July, 1873, or any and which of them?

If the Bishop has no such right, what steps can and should be taken by Dr. Dykes or Mr. Peake to obtain the desired License to Mr. Peake to act as curate to Dr. Dykes?

And generally to advise what should be done to get rid of this objectionable declaration.

> 1st. We are of opinion that the Bishop has no such right.
>
> 2nd. We think that the proper course to be pursued is, for Dr. Dykes and Mr. Peake to apply at the commencement of the ensuing Term to the Court of Queen's Bench for a rule, calling upon the Bishop to show cause why a writ of mandamus should not issue against him. The granting of a writ of mandamus is to some extent a matter of discretion, but we are of opinion that the Court of Queen's Bench would grant a mandamus under the circumstances, compelling the Bishop to license Mr. Peake.
>
> (*Signed*) John Duke Coleridge
> A. J. Stephens
> Charles Bowen
> 3rd *September, 1873*

In September a brief holiday was spent with his family at Birnam, near Dunkeld.

> *Sep. 16th*. To Church (close at hand) for Matins. Lovely morning; liked the look of the place, though rather closed in with hills. Charming walk to Rumbling Bridge, and the falls of the Braan. Then to the Hermitage Bridge, and lower falls. Then to the grounds of the Duchess of Athol. Saw the desecrated Cathedral.
>
> *Sep. 23rd*. Birnam Hill. Stayed at the top of the over-hanging Peak, and thence through the heather to the walk which leads to the top. Exquisite views, and soft golden evening. May such be the evening of our life!
>
> *Sep. 25th*. Off to Pitlochry—then made the ascent of Ben-y-Vrackie. On the road, wrote music to "*Anima Christi*"—also during the day wrote several chants. Delightful walk. Views grand but hazy. The little streams and pools in the bog looked like innumerable mirrors, shining through the mist.

Part of October was spent in revising a new anthem, the words of which, "The Lord is my Shepherd," were suggested to Dr. Dykes by his brother Frederic, who was then honorary choirmaster of the Wakefield Parish Church (now the Cathedral). It had been written for more than a year, but, finding the cost of printing so great, Dr. Dykes did not at first feel justified in publishing it. However, as part of the expenses were guaranteed, the publication was now no longer delayed. It is a beautiful anthem, but rather long for an ordinary service. Dr. Dykes, however, arranged a plan for shortening it. The two following passages, quoted from letters to his brother Frederic, refer to this Anthem:

St. Oswald's, Durham
Oct. 21st, 1873

I think I should prefer the dedication of the Anthem should remain as it is, if you and your worthy Choir have no objection. The first idea of writing the Anthem came from yourself. I have had no time hitherto to correct the proofs, so I am taking a turn at it tonight, to have the luxury of a little bit of leisure.

We had Father Page (one of the Cowley Fathers) stopping with us last night. He is just off to Bombay, with another member of their order, to start a Missionary brotherhood in India.

St. Oswald's, Durham
Feb. 3rd, 1874

As soon as you have decided on the number of copies you will want for your Choir, please let me know . . . E. D. sent a copy to Sir George Elvey;—he says he thinks it "very fine," and will be glad to introduce it at St. George's, Windsor, as soon as he can hear where he may cut it, so as to reduce it more to the usual Anthem length—as he fears it would be rather too long as it is. I see I shall have to face this difficulty, but I think I shall be able to manage it.

On November 17th Dr. Dykes was again called up to London on business connected with hymn music and the preparation of his case against the Bishop.

Nov. 20th. To Few and Co. going through affidavit. Then to Novello and sold Copyright of Anthem "These are they."

Jan. 6th, 1874. Shocked to hear of the death of D. B. Mitchell of Dundee, for whom I have been just writing a "*Benedictus*" and "*Agnus Dei.*" [Jesu, mercy.] Wrote to Mrs. Mitchell.

Mr. Mitchell, an excellent, energetic layman, who acted as honorary choirmaster at the parish church, Dundee, had written to ask Dr. Dykes for permission to use the tune *Oswestry*. In his answer Dr. Dykes writes:

The Tune you mention in your last note, you are quite welcome to. The words are by the Rev. Walsham How,[4] Whittington Rectory; to whom you had better send a line for permission to use the words.[5] He sent them to me some time ago, and asked me to set them to a very simple tune, which might be sung in unison

---

4. The late Bishop of Wakefield.
5. "Great and glorious Father, humbly we adore Thee." No. 208, *Church Hymns*.

or harmony; so, if you use it, you had better mark one or two verses to be sung in harmony. With regard to the *"Benedictus"* and *"Agnus Dei,"* I shall be glad to try them. You say they are to be simple; I presume also short. Let me know how soon they will be wanted.

Before these were sent to Mr. Mitchell, Dr. Dykes heard the sad news of his sudden death, and wrote to his widow:

> I have been reading the Bishop of Brechin's touching and beautiful sermon lately; (on the death of Mr. Mitchell). It must be a deep gratification to you, in your sorrow, to possess such a testimony of the worth of him whom God has taken from you. The Bishop comes to Durham at the end of this week and preaches at the Cathedral on Sunday. I shall be so glad to see him, for I have never yet fully heard the circumstances of your husband's death.
>
> I am hoping to publish shortly the little *"Benedictus"* and *"Agnus Dei"* which I wrote at his request. I will send you them (in case I do so)—as soon as they come out.

The following letter, to his brother Frederic, is also on the same subject:

> St. Oswald's
> *Sunday, Eve of Purification, Feb. 1, 1874*
>
> . . . I am just going to publish the little *"Benedictus"* and *"Agnus Dei"* (supplementary to my *Service in F*) which I wrote for poor Mitchell and was about to send to him the very morning I heard of his death. It will be a small *In Memoriam*. Have you seen the Bishop of Brechin's sermon?
>
> I have been alone all day, to-day *i.e.* I have done all my services single-handed.—Organ as well—except that a good layman, C. H. Fowler, read the lessons; and my son Jack played the voluntaries.[6]
>
> Did you see the article in the Saturday Review yesterday week, entitled "Bishops and Curates"? It was upon my case in Queen's Bench and was very good.

Unfortunately, the *"Benedictus"* and *"Agnus Dei,"* here alluded to, which were to complete Dr. Dykes' *Service in F*, appear to have been lost. On searching for them, to arrange for publication, they could not be

---

6. His youngest son, who was then nine years old, is now on the staff of the Royal College of Music.

found, and they never have been found. Hoping they would "turn up," Dr. Dykes did not re-write them, and thus his Service remains incomplete.

In January 1874 Dr. Dykes went to London, as his approaching action required him to be in the neighbourhood of the Law Courts.

> *Jan. 13th, London.* Went with Sir H. Baker to Dr. Stainer's. Tunes till dinner. To St. Paul's; Liddon preached—most interesting service. They began with "Lead, kindly Light." Then the address on the Life of St. Paul, a short office with canticle—another Hymn. To Langham; writing "Hail, gladdening Light!"
>
> *Jan. 15th.* To Sion College; a lecture from Stainer on the Ecclesiastical style in Music. Discussion, and, to my annoyance, was called upon to speak. Managed very badly. Lord, Jesu! to Thee I offer my incapacity. Busy with "Hail, gladdening Light!"
>
> *Jan. 19th.* To Westminster Hall,—then to Queen's Bench. Small Court, full of Barristers; Judges Blackburn, Archibald, Quain. My case soon came on, but it was obvious, from the very first, that the Judges determined not to interfere. So, after Dr. Stephens had tried to get out his argument, for about three quarters of an hour, with perpetual interruptions from the Bench, he gave up; ostensibly with a view of ascertaining whether there are any precedents for Queen's Bench interfering with the discretionary powers claimed by a Bishop, in granting or withdrawing licences, the Judges altogether ignoring the force of the Clerical Subscription Act, Sect. 9. The affidavits were not read. Well! *"Fiat voluntas Tua."* Went to Few's, who seemed much surprised at the collapse of my case. So ends my first appeal, and I hope my last, to the Court of Queen's Bench.
>
> *Durham, Jan. 25th.* Preached on "Lord, what wilt Thou have me to do?" Made a new tune to "Sun of my Soul."

In a letter to his son Ernest[7] he tells the story of the action and its result.

Firgrove Lodge, Weybridge
Jan. 19, 1874

> I am sure you will be sorry to hear that I have lost my case—at least, to all practical purposes. The Judges absolutely refusing to interfere with the discretionary powers which the Bishop may have, or may claim, in the matter of granting licences to Curates.
>
> As soon as the case was opened, I saw at once that the Judges *intended* to take this line. The affidavits were not read.

---

7. Now the Rev. E. H. Dykes, Vicar of St. James' Church, Barrow-in-Furness.

Dr. Stephens began them but was soon stopped. The line which the Judges took was, that whatever power of discretion a Bishop had, *before* the passing of the Clerical Subscription Act in 1865—that power he still possesses. Whereas it appears obvious that the act, which definitely decreed that certain documents and certain documents *only* should be exacted of Curates seeking licences—did circumscribe and define the Bishop's power, and at least renders it illegal for him to demand, (what he might have demanded before the Act was passed) additional subscriptions and declarations, others than those there specified.

However, the Judges would not see this. Dr. Stephens tried to hammer it into them, but they had so plainly made up their minds *ab initio*, that there was no chance for Counsel. Although I am bound to say that Dr. Stephens rather disappointed me— there seemed to me several points which he might have made; and which he failed to make.

Well, well, God's Will be done! I need not say that I feel surprised and disappointed, and somewhat anxious about the future. But I cannot but feel confident that somehow or other, (perhaps in a way which I cannot now see)—all will be overruled for good.

I have seen Mr. Few the lawyer; he was entirely unprepared for the result. I shall see Dr. Stephens tomorrow. By way of a little pleasing variety after the unsatisfactory termination of my *own* case, I succeeded in getting over the policeman in charge, and finding my way into the large court where the famous Tichborne case is dragging its long length along. I got at last a capital seat, and heard Hawkins finish the first division of his speech, in which he undertakes to prove that the defendant is none other than Arthur Orton—some parts of his speech were very telling. It is certainly difficult to see that huge mountain of flesh—every inch the Butcher, and mistake him for a gentleman.

Henry has come for the letters, so I must finish. I can only trust that the "kindly light" will "lead me on" to do what is right in this matter.

God bless you all.

The decision of the Judges did not affect the opinion of the counsel, the most learned ecclesiastical lawyer of the day.

"I retain," writes Dr. Stephens, on January 23rd, 1874, "my opinion; that no Bishop has a right to require any subscription from a Stipendiary Curate, other than those that are required by the Clerical Subscription Act, 1865.

"I was glad that you were present and observed the *animus* of the Court."

The trial over, Dr. Dykes resumed his quiet, busy life.

> *Feb. 8*th. Gave notice of daily Celebration during the week, on behalf of the London Mission.
>
> *Ash Wednesday, Feb. 18*th. To Thee, good Lord, I dedicate this holy season of Lent. May it be a time of deepened penitence, of spiritual revival, and growth in holiness, for myself, and my people.
>
> *Feb. 24*th. Busy with "O Trinity, most blessed Light."
>
> *May 5*th. Received cheque from Sir Henry Baker for £100. (D.G.) Quite unexpected. Most welcome help towards dear Erny's[8] expenses.

The cheque mentioned in the preceding extract from the Diary is acknowledged by Dr. Dykes in the following letter to Sir Henry Baker.

> St. Oswald's, Durham
> *May 5, 1874*
>
> Pray accept yourself and convey to your Revd. colleagues, my warm thanks for the very handsome, and unexpected gift (£100) I have received from you this morning. It is really very good of you all, and I do feel most grateful.
>
> Nothing could have come in more opportunely. I have just received some rather heavy bills for my dear boy at Cambridge, who takes his degree this year—and I had been in a state of puzzlement how I was to manage; I was seriously considering ways and means—when this most providential help came, for which God be thanked. You are good enough to speak of the trouble I have taken. I can honestly say, that any little trouble I have had, and am likely to have, is a constant source of interest and pleasure to me. I cannot tell you what a help I have occasionally found it, in the midst of Parochial and Episcopal worries.
>
> Never was [a] letter more opportune than that you sent me a week or so ago, about "Hail, Gladdening Light!" On the very day when it came, the Bishop was over at Durham, and the important meeting of the Laity took place to present the money of the Guarantee fund (£7,000 and more), with a most offensive address about the "Romanism" and "unfaithfulness" of *certain* of the Clergy—an address responded to in a still more offensive reply on the part of the Bishop, strongly confirming and

---

8. Dr. Dyke's eldest son, who was at Jesus College, Cambridge.

repeating all the ignorant slander of the laity. The whole thing worried me much. I was therefore so very, very thankful to have *this* to think about.

So instead of troubling myself about the wretched meeting, I spent my scraps of spare time in revising, simplifying, and copying out the music for this self-same glorious Hymn—and managed to forget my troubles.

This setting of "Hail, Gladdening Light!" is still in MS., and will, it is hoped, be published with the rest of Dr. Dykes' Tunes.

9

Through Pain to Peace
1874–1876

Pamphlet, "Eucharistic Truth, and Ritual"—Hymn-tunes—Lodore—
"Inspiration Stone"—Failing health—Leeds Mission—Last Lent at St.
Oswald's—Ovingham, Folkstone, Switzerland—Tell's Platte—Return to
England—Ben Rhydding—St. Leonard's—Death—Funeral at St. Oswald's—
Last hymn-tune ("*Via Crucis*")

> *May 28*[th]. First installment of proofs of my letter. *Domine dirige me!*

THIS entry in the Diary refers to Dr. Dykes' letter, written to the Bishop of Durham, and printed as a pamphlet, under the title of "Eucharistic Truth, and Ritual." It is a powerful appeal to the Bishop from Dr. Dykes, on the treatment he had received, and on the futility of trying to stamp out the living spark, kindled by the Holy Spirit of God, by which the Church was awaking to new life, and spreading its renewed light over the length and breadth of the land.

As soon as the pamphlet was published, letters of thanks for his outspoken Sacramental teaching came to him from all parts. It was not without a struggle that Dr. Dykes compelled himself to write this letter, but, painful as it was to him to differ so widely from his Bishop, he felt that the time was come when he was called upon to witness boldly for the truth. The Diary for many weeks contains references to the letter.

> *Monday, Jun. 16th, London.* Tunes and Music H. &. M. with Sir H. Baker. Correcting proof of my letter. Royal Academy, where I met Ned and Sanderson. St. James' Hall—E. C. U. Meeting. Glorious meeting. The Lord's Prayer and Nicene Creed quite overpowering. Felt comforted by the kindly reception I received, joined with the many little circumstances of my journey. It seemed as if God had prospered my way, and that He was helping me with the letter, and that it was His Will I had come up to see about it, and receive this little encouragement.
>
> *Durham, Jun. 18th.* Dear wife had received a gratifying telegram from Erny. In the first class of Theological Special. (D.G.)
>
> *Jul. 16th.* Sent off Welsh Tunes.
>
> *Jul. 20th.* Off at 10:30 to Stoke Newington (Monk's).
>
> *Jul. 21st.* Up at 4.15 a.m. Writing till 5.15. To bed and at last fell asleep. Tunes and writing "Letter."
>
> *Jul. 22nd.* Woke at 6—so worked in bed. Stainer wrote a charming chant tune for "Hail, gladdening light!"
>
> *Jul. 23rd.* Woke at 5—got up and wrote a tune for "*Veni Creator.*" Feeling rather knocked up with the confinement and broken nights, and the double anxiety of the Tunes and my letter.
>
> *Jul. 24th.* Thank God for a refreshing sleep. We had a grand fight about the high E in "Benediction." At 5, Sir H. B. and I, after waiting a long time for a cab, were just too late for the train at King's Cross, so telegraphed to Leeds. Nice, prayerful journey. Leeds a little before 3 a.m. To Cromer Terrace.
>
> *Jul. 25th.* Pleasant journey to Durham. Harmonising and doing "letter."

This journey was taken in order that he and his wife might be together on the anniversary of their wedding-day (July 25th). During this visit he wrote for Mr. Monk, for some specially solemn occasion, a tune to a translation of the hymn "*Adoro te devote.*" Mrs. Dykes seems to have remonstrated with Sir H. Baker on her husband's worn-out appearance, on his return, and received the following reply:

> Horkesley House, Monkland
> July 29, 1874
>
> I don't wonder at your husband looking tired; he missed his train (as I suppose he told you) on Friday, and so had four hours' extra work, alone, at the Midland Station, and then travelled until

3:00 in the morning; and then after breakfast home to Durham. Besides which he was doing double work all the time he was with us, *i.e.* this grand literary brochure, as well as our *Hymns A. and M.*

But I assure you that I will do my very best to cook him up, and take care of him in every way. And as he is to be here for ten days we can get more leisure, and less work, day by day. His life *is* precious. I will do all *I* can for him.

When this letter was written, Dr. Dykes had already returned to Monkland, where he, Sir Henry Baker, and Mr. Monk, worked steadily at the new edition of *Hymns Ancient and Modern* until August 8th.

Aug. 2nd and 5th. Wrote tune to "The Son of God goes forth to war." Awake at 3:45 (a.m.). Got up to harmonise "*Vexilla Regis,*" and had not been able to sleep afterwards.

Durham, Sunday, Aug. 9th. Up at 7, having been awake since 3:45. Have been working too much at Tunes, my Pamphlet, and other things. Did the whole of the service alone.

Aug. 14th. Received first copy of my Pamphlet, also the Bishop's letter, asking for thanksgiving for his recovery.[1] So, Pamphlet out exactly at the time, and not before the time when it could with any decency be sent to the Bishop. Only one of the strange, (Providential) occurrences that have marked its course.

Aug. 20th. Received laconic note from the Bishop of Durham, acknowledging the receipt of my Pamphlet, but not referring to the friendly letter which had accompanied it.

The following letters to Mr. Monk may be of interest, because they give an account of the tunes Dr. Dykes was writing at this time for *Hymns Ancient and Modern.*

St. Oswald's Vicarage, Durham
Aug. 24, 1874

My Dear Professor,

I hope that a day of rest has restored you from the fatigues of a week's hard work, at the Hymn and Tune manufactory, Portland Place.

For myself, on leaving on Saturday I found it hard to stop; so, I worked as far as Peterborough. Then I shut up and determined to have done with Hymns and Tunes for the rest of my journey. But on my road to the station I discovered that Sir

---

1. The Bishop had been very ill.

Henry was quite right in his "who follow"! idea, and that my tune would be wonderfully improved by adopting it. So, as soon as I got into the railway, I rewrote it. I have since thought it over, and slightly modified my railway version: but I adhere to our chief's notion, and think my tune a much finer and more striking one, in consequence. I will send it to you.

But alas—alas—as soon as I had disposed of this, *another* hymn came rushing into my mind, about which I have heard Sir Henry speaking many times and about which he was expressing himself anxiously just before I left.

I mean the old Evangelical "Just as I am." I wrote a tune to this some twenty-five years ago, which was sold for the Missionaries, and which has had a run in dissenting and quasi-dissenting books. It was not bad as a tune, but the accent was unsatisfactory. I have many times tried to improve upon it, but always failed . . . At last I put it into *triple* time, in which form I showed it to you and Sir H. B. at Monkland. But it lost its character when taken from its original form, and you wisely rejected it. So, I thankfully gave it up and have been anxiously waiting for Barnby [to whom it was sent] to set the Hymn worthily. He declined. Still, I never thought of trying it again myself, because I felt I had failed, and I thought somebody coming fresh upon it would do it better. However—so wayward and capricious are we—I had no sooner finished "The Son of God goes forth to war," than—possibly as a relief from this stirring and warlike hymn—the plaintive "Just as I am" intruded itself upon me, and, at once, it set itself to music. I seized the favourable moment and put it down. I have since tried it over with my young folk at home, and slightly modified it. But I cannot help thinking it (although I am the last person who should so say) far the most satisfactory setting to the *words* that I have yet seen, and I have seen scores and scores of them, and never liked one.

This being the case, I have only thought it right to send it to you for your inspection, that, if you do not take to it, you may throw it behind the fire (if you have a fire this hot weather), and if you do, you may show it to Sir H. B., to see what he thinks of it. Only, please, do not quite make up your mind till you have sung it over *through*, with the whole *Hymn*. One cannot pronounce fairly on a tune that has any pretensions to merit, simply by playing it once over.

You will see I have adopted your excellent artifice in "Jesus is God," and lengthened the first line. For in this Hymn, it is very nice, in *some* verses to go on continuously from the end of one verse to the beginning of the next—"O Lamb of God, I come, just as I am"—and I think the little pause in the first line helpful on other grounds.

You and Stainer and Sir Henry laughed at me the other day for *apologising* for setting so many Hymns. And I really feel it still to need, if not an apology, at least an *explanation*. My explanation is simply this:—I never think of setting a Hymn that *is* worthily set, where the tune can be got. That would be mere silly caprice, or vanity, or presumption. But if a Hymn does *not* appear to me worthily set, then, I own, I am often induced, I may say, sometimes almost *compelled*, to try to do my best for it.

I know so well the teaching power of Hymns, if they are happily wedded, that I am very anxious to do my best, (as far as God is pleased to help me) to add to the number of those useful and felicitous unions. God forbid that I should make these attempts from any unworthy desire to thrust *myself* forward. I earnestly pray that this motive may never, *never* actuate me. I shall be just as thankful for your grand tune to "Jesus is God" as if I had written it myself, or for the happy settings of "The roseate hues," and "Thy Life was given for me," by Stainer and Macfarren (even though they do supersede pet tunes of my own), as if I had been fortunate enough to have *my* work wedded to those words. My one desire is this: that each hymn should be so set to music (by whomsoever God wills to select for that purpose) that its power of influencing and teaching may be best brought out. All other considerations must be subordinate to that.

Now I must finish. Please *do not* answer this. I will send "The Son of God goes forth" tomorrow if I have time.

Ever, my dear Mr. Monk,
Sincerely yours,
J. B. D.

S. Oswald's, Durham
Nov. 10, 1874

My Dear Mr. Monk,

... I seem very much in the dark as to the recent settlement of tunes to words. Therefore, I have no idea whether you have yet anything satisfactory for the touching little Hymn on the "Burial of a Child." The tune we have is a very good one: but the last two lines are more suited for a Hymn after the "Fierce raged the tempest" style, than for the calm death sleep of a little baby. The transition from the 5th to the 6th line is harsh and abrupt. [See original Edition, 358.]

At all events, if this tune is retained, I cannot but think (as I have before said) that there should be a second, more tender tune, as well.

The one I send herewith is associated with sweet and sad remembrances: having been originally written for the funeral of one of my own dear little daughters: and I know, has been found helpful and comforting.

I have removed the long endings of the lines since I showed it to you, (as I think I did at Monkland), and have thereby simplified it. However, there it is, in case a tune is needed. I had sooner it went into *Hymns A. and M.* than any other collection, and if you are not sick of my tunes, it would make a companion to the (funeral) Tune for adults. [400]

Sincerely yours,
J. B. D.

Aug. 25th. Wrote to Archbishop of York, Gladstone and Beresford-Hope, sending them copies of the Pamphlet.

Aug. 27th. P.C. from Gladstone, acknowledging with thanks receipt of Pamphlet. Copying out Coffin's new Transfiguration Hymn.

Sep. 1st. Nice letter from Dr. Newman. Sent off letters to the Archbishop, and proofs of tunes.

On September 1st Dr. Dykes joined a family excursion to the Lakes. The party consisted of his eldest son and two daughters, his sisters, a niece, and his brother Edward. The holiday was but a broken one. It was interrupted by the correspondence with the Archbishop, to which the Diary refers, and by the letter-writing to which the preparation of the new edition of *Hymns Ancient and Modern* gave rise.

[No date] Off with Erny to Darlington—then to Keswick. Was chiefly busy with letter to the Archbishop, on the journey. Lucy and Emmie met us at the station. Sent off luggage and walked to high Lodore. Mrs. Wilson's lodgings.

Sep. 8th. Busy with Archbishop's letter till breakfast. Writing it until noon. Took a turn up the hill behind the house. Charmed with the delicious and most romantic view.

Sep. 14th. Off with the girls; they drove to Seatoller. Erny, Ned, and I left the ladies at Grange and pursued our walk at the right of Castle Hill, along the Moors, until we reached Honister Pass. Eliza had written me a pretty set of words for a part-song, so I was mentally setting them during part of our journey.[2] We intended to ascend Great Gable, but the wind was so high we were obliged to beat a retreat and descended by Scarf Gap and Buttermere. All met at the Inn and walked back through the vale of Newlands, over Catbells, and so, by Grange, home.

*Sep. 15*th. Up in the rain to "Inspiration stone"—to write my part-song. The rain suddenly ceased, the clouds dispersed, the sun shone, and the effect was magically beautiful.

---

2. The words written by Mrs. Alderson for Dr. Dykes to set to music for a part-song are copied in his Diary as follows:

To the winds with thy care and trouble!
Let us climb the mountain now,
And fling them away to the breezes
That shall fan and cool thy brow,
On the springy moss and the bracken
Thy bounding step shall tread,
And we'll drink of the sparkling streamlet
As it wells from its rocky bed.

To the winds with thy care and trouble!
We will drown them in the tide
As all in the glowing evening
On the tranquil Lake we glide;
And the rocks and the wooded islets
Shall re-echo our choral lays
As we raise our voices together
In the songs of other days.

To the winds with thy care and trouble!
They shall vex thy soul no more
As we read aloud in the sunshine
Some tale of the days of yore,
Stretched 'mid the rock and heather,
And watching the shadows creep,
And the gold, and purple, and crimson,
The mountain sides that steep.

To the winds with thy care and trouble!
For here no care is found
In the glory and the beauty
So lavishly spread around.
If such be the wayside lodging
That is furnished forth for thee,
What shall the fields of Heaven,
And the many mansions, be?

This, *so-called*, "Inspiration stone" was a rock, at the top of a wooded hill behind the house, where Dr. Dykes retired when he had any special work to do.

> *Sep. 16*th. Received kind proposal from the E.C.U. to purchase copies of my Pamphlet for Members of Convocation. Started off and met our party (all but Eliza and Fanny, who were sketching) on the Lake and pulled to Keswick. Charming day: very enjoyable ascent up Skiddaw.
>
> *Sep. 17*th. Finished a long letter to Sir H. Baker on Eliza's Hymn. They had set off to Keswick by Lake. I followed and joined the party at Walla Crag. Thence to Druid's Circle—Keswick and the Lake. I pulled all the way to our landing-stage. Much enjoyed the walk and row. Writing to Sir H. B. on "Purged from sin's awful and accursèd load."
>
> *Sep. 18*th. Another letter from the Archbishop—forbidding publication. Writing all the morning, a second long letter on Our Lord's Death, to Sir Henry Baker.
>
> *Sep. 19*th. Writings to Archdeacon Denison, also the Archbishop. Just finished his letter in time. Off to Penrith. Parted with the Leeds contingent there—then to Durham.

Throughout the whole of this visit to the Lakes, Dr. Dykes was also engaged in correspondence with Sir Henry Baker on the subject of a hymn written by Mrs. Alderson, and offered by Dr. Dykes with an appropriate setting of his own composition to the editors of *Hymns Ancient and Modern*. The letters may, it is hoped, prove of interest, from the light which they throw on the jealous care that was exercised to preserve the doctrine of the hymns from any taint of error.

> *August 11, 1874*
> [Dr. Dykes to Sir Henry Baker]
>
> My sister has sent me her new Hymn (the Last "Word"), finished and revised. I think it most touching and beautiful and will send you a copy if all be well tomorrow. At present I am just off to Coatham, where I am to preach this evening. I have written a simple quiet Recitative Tune for my sister's Hymn which will make it as short as a Hymn in any ordinary short metre. It seems to me too beautiful to lose any of it.

In another letter he adds an expression of his deep sense of the value of the hymnal, and of the immense importance of bringing it, as far as possible, to perfection.

God has blessed the book so wonderfully hitherto, that I believe He still has a great work to effect through its gentle, quiet influence, and I feel strongly we ought to spare no pain and trouble and discussion to make it as perfect as possible.

To his sister, Mrs. Alderson, he makes suggestions for the alteration of the hymn, in order to meet Sir H. Baker's objections.

St. Oswald's Vicarage, Durham
10th *Sunday after Trinity*

Fanny will have told you what Sir H. B. has said about the Hymn.

He first took exception at the long, unusual metre; he thought a simpler metre would have been more suitable and simple and quiet.

I like the metre, and would not have you alter it. It will make a nice variety—and I can make a very simple Tune which would help it on. Then he does not like the sense running on unbroken in one continuous sentence, from the 2nd to the 3rd line—because there is always a musical pause at the end of the 3rd line: This is rather one practical point which distinguishes a Poem from a Hymn. However, he likes the Hymn, and thinks it will do if you make a nice ending. He says you must picture the service of the three hours' agony—and ask yourself with what sort of thoughts you would like to end it.

One of Mrs. Alexander's "Words,"[3] is very nice. I do not like the other, and both will need a good deal of touching up. In your second verse you might easily make the 2nd line, "Purged from sin's awful and accursèd load." You will have to think of the 3rd line. Perhaps, "And then Absolved, in tranquil peace commending" would hardly be understood; although I believe it to be theologically correct—and that the hyssop touch of Vinegar was really a ceremonial purgative to qualify the Divine Penitent—(the Great Absolver, Himself Absolved) for entrance into the inner Sanctuary. I made Sir Henry read your St. Matthew's Hymn over again; he says—and I quite agree with him, that you have improved it very much; and he thinks that if you had sent it originally in this form, they would never have chosen Mrs. Alexander's St. Matthew's Hymn, which the Committee has done.

I want him to use both—but he thinks they cannot afford space for two. However, I shall try again, because I honestly prefer yours to Mrs. Alexander's, and think it would be more generally useful.

---

3. "Seven Last Words."

Can you help us with an end to "Days and Moments"?

"As the tree falls," etc., is to go out. The S.P.C.K. has substituted—you will see what.

Sir Henry has made another substitution, and I another, and we are utterly undecided which to adopt. I don't like his, and he does not quite like mine. Have you ever tried St. James? or Transfiguration? They are sadly in want of a good (short) Hymn for both of those days.

Can you send me a copy of your St. John the Baptist Hymn?

The verse in Mrs. Alderson's hymn to which Sir H. Baker particularly objected originally stood thus:

> Freely Thy life Thou yieldest, 'ere its ending'
> Purged from sin's awful and accursèd load;
> The conflict o'er in perfect peace commending
> Thy Spirit to Thy Father and Thy God.

The point at issue was that Sir Henry Baker thought it not right to speak of the "load of sin" being lifted *before* our Lord's *actual* death—at the "Word" "It is finished." Dr. Dykes believing, with Dr. Bright, Mr. Carter, and many others, that "the work was finished, and so was all the suffering which it involved. The Cup had been set down empty. He had done what He came to do, He had borne what He came to bear. All was in that sense over. The series of types and prophecies had been fulfilled."[4] We give the last two letters on the subject, the first from Dr. Dykes, the second from Sir H. Baker.

St. Oswald's, Durham
September 22, 1874

Thank you much for your kind letter. Just a word or two in reply.

I will ask my sister to send two alternative lines; but at the same time I am glad that you will read what I have said to your coadjutors; because I feel more and more strongly drawn to the belief that the doctrine of the Hymn is *true*, and that what I wrote to you (I fear hurriedly and imperfectly) is true. And truth will take care of itself. Why not utilise a Hymn to teach forgotten truths?

Since coming home, I have been reading Carter on the "Passion and Temptation of our Lord." He regards the Cry "It is finished" (as I have done) as the Cry of Complete Victory. "There could be no agony" (he writes) "after this word" [but if

---

4. Dr. Bright: "Seven Sayings from the Cross." The Sixth Saying.

Sin was yet on His Heart there must have been Agony]. "Still more surely do the words that follow express the feelings of One already emerged from the terrible Conflict and beginning to enter into the Exaltation of the Divine Sonship. FATHER, into Thy Hands I commend My Spirit."

As Ellicot writes: "The Sponge of Vinegar was pressed to the parching Lips; the dying Lord received it, and with a loud Cry of *consciously completed victory* for man, and of most loving resignation to God, bowed meekly His Divine Head, and gave up the Ghost."

I am very sorry you cannot get to Durham, but *do* go to Cowley. I am sure I need a Retreat, to get my head clear and calm; and I am sure you must need it.

You will work all the better afterwards. You need it for your own sake, and for your people's sake. I will gladly give you a week anytime and anywhere, between then and Advent, and do any amount of work if it will help you . . .

I would have written a better Tune to "O Paradise," if I could, but I do not think I can. If properly sung, the present tune is very effective, and it is a great favourite here.

A Clergyman (I think) in Yorkshire told me that he had had his choir divided, and had put one portion under the belfry simply to get the proper effect of the Echo at the second "O Paradise," (which ought to be marked *pp*). He said the effect was very striking and charming.

Both the American books have adopted it (besides other books). It merely needs a slight simplification and a few expression marks to make people understand it.

Thank you for what you say about myself being "Gloriously represented" in the book. I really wish and pray to care less and less about being myself represented. But I do wish to see each and every Hymn worthily set, and this is why I have been obliged at times to press some of my own Tunes—because I felt they expressed the words more truly than the tunes (not even written for the special words) to which they were being wedded.

The following is the answer which Dr. Dykes received from Sir Henry Baker:

Monkland
Oct. 6, 1874

I withdraw all the earlier part of a long letter I had written to you.

I *cannot* go into this controversy now. I do not know one single text of Scripture which authorizes us to speak of our dear Lord "being released from the load of our sin"; but at any rate I *dare* not say so. *Never*, never, could I say so of Him *before* He had died. "At its ending"—is nearly as bad as "Ere its ending." He DIED, really DIED, for our sins: THAT is my faith. My first impulse was to give up the Hymn after reading yours to-day, but as I came back from Matins, the following verse was suggested to my mind, and I cannot but hope that *it*, or something like it, might be accepted by you on your sister's behalf—it is surely true and not out of keeping with the hymn, and avoids disputed points:

> Freely Thy life Thou yieldest, meekly bending
> E'en to the last beneath our sorrows' load;
> Yet strong in death, in perfect peace commending
> Thy Spirit to Thy Father and Thy God.

You will admit that He bore "*sorrows*" to the end, and the "Last *loud* cry that pierced His Mother's heart" (as an old Hymn says), proved Him to be *strong* in death. So this verse is beyond dispute; and surely not a bad verse. I write to-day to ask my colleagues to accept it, and to telegraph to me tomorrow—and I now ask you, my dearest friend, to do the same.

To this change Dr. Dykes and Mrs. Alderson consented, to avoid disputes; though Dr. Dykes felt that the doctrine of the disputed verse was theologically correct.

More than one instance has been quoted from the Diary in which Dr. Dykes had felt that he had been helped by Divine interposition in some moment of special difficulty. The following entry records another and a striking case of a similar kind.

> *Nov. 14*th. Rather in trouble about Reynell's bill for Pamphlet. Letter from Uncle George containing a draft for £50. (D.G.) A Godsend towards the paying of the bill.

The passage is explained in a letter to Mrs. Dykes, who was staying in Leeds, and had written to tell her husband of his uncle's death.

St. Oswald's, Durham
Nov. 16th, 1874

I cannot say I am altogether astonished at the intelligence conveyed in your note. I feel so sorry I did not see the dear old man again. God rest his soul! I have written to John Jarratt, but you must let me know where, and at what hour, the funeral is to take place.

And now about Uncle George; I suppose I had better make a clean breast of it. He *did* send me £50, the other day: *but* it has gone to my printer for that delectable Pamphlet. The bill, you know, comes to all but £60. Well, I have been most exercised about this lately. On Saturday morning, especially, I got up quite in low spirits about it. I could not get it out of my mind. But, as I was dressing, the thought came into my mind very strongly; You often say that you believe God helped you to *write* that Pamphlet, and that you were fulfilling a duty to write it. Well, if God helped you to write it, will He not help you to *pay* for it? This thought comforted me, and I went to Church and forgot my troubles.

On coming home to breakfast, after two weddings, I opened Uncle George's note, and the enclosure gave me such a start! I could hardly get on with my breakfast: it seemed such a regular Godsend. I hope to get at least half of the money back again from Masters—but I thought it better to send it at once.

I have been writing a long theological letter to the Revd. James Martineau, tonight, and a long musical one to his son.

Two days later, Dr. Dykes went to North Cave, near Hull, to stay with his father's cousin, Canon Jarratt, and attend the funeral of his uncle, Mr. Frederic Huntington.

Nov. 19th. Hull at 9:40; to George Street. Large gathering of the family. Saw dear Uncle Fred in his coffin. (R.I.P.) Funeral at Kirkella—looking at family vaults afterwards. Will was read; among other small bequests, "Fox's Book of Martyrs" for me—which caused some suppressed laughter.

This uncle (his mother's brother), Mr. Frederic Huntington (the old family doctor, and senior Surgeon at the infirmary), died in Hull, much regretted, on November 14th. With all his eccentricity, few who knew him had any idea of his constant acts of kindness in visiting the clergy, the poor, and many others, from whom he never would take payment. He divided his patients into two classes: those who could, and those who could not pay—calling the latter "Christ's patients."

Overwork and, above all, anxiety arising from the position in which he stood towards his Bishop, had told heavily on Dr. Dykes' strength. The following entry in his Diary is the beginning of the end:

> *Dec. 16th.* Offertory paper. Could not think what to write about. Desponded about my unreadiness. Could get no ideas.

His wearied, anxious mind was needing rest, and from this time his work gradually became too great a strain upon his strength. However, for the moment, the effort was made; the Offertory paper was written. It was the last he wrote.

> My dear Parishioners,
>
> In bringing before you the Offertory account for the year 1873-74;—the publication of which has, I regret, been so long delayed—I am happy to observe that our receipts exceed those of the preceding year by about twenty pounds. I think it right also to add that, independently of the offerings in money, a special offering of blankets for the use of the poor was made during the past year; which will account for the fact of a less sum than in previous years appearing in the accompanying Statement under the heading "Clothing for the Poor."
>
> The improvement of the New Cemetery is still progressing: more earth is being gradually added; and the result promises to be quite satisfactory.
>
> I think it as well to state that the new and revised edition of our Hymn Book will be ready by the beginning of February, and that I hope, if God spare me, to introduce it into the church at the opening of Lent, so that we may be able to avail ourselves of some of the new hymns for Passion and Eastertide.
>
> Having often expressed my sense of the general injury to the cause of the Church in the Parish, occasioned by the retention of our old closed pews, and the consequent general system of private appropriation by a portion of the Parish of what belongs by law and right equally to all—resulting in a virtual exclusion and perpetuated alienation of the mass of the poor from their Parish Church—I am thankful to state that a commencement has already been made to collect small weekly subscriptions, in the first place amongst the poor themselves, towards a general reseating of the Church; with a view of rendering it more what a Church should be—a place where rich and poor meet

together—a Sanctuary for the united worship of our common Father, Redeemer, and Sanctifier, Who is no respecter of persons, and in Whose House and august Presence earthly distinctions may well be, for a while, forgotten.

A system of penny weekly subscriptions may appear to some unworthy of consideration. But we have still to learn the "Power of the pence" in the Church of England: and God blesses all honest endeavour, however small. When the poor have done their part, I have no fear of those whom God has blessed with larger means, refusing to contribute to the carrying out of some properly considered plan of internal Church Restoration, of which there is so great need.

I am still left single-handed in this unwieldy Parish, with a population rapidly increasing on all sides.

How long this state of things is to last, God only knows. It is at least a satisfaction to think that the attempt to force the Purchase Judgment on the Church, by the exaction of extra-legal pledges as a condition of license on the part of Incumbents and Curates, has not spread elsewhere, and that this is the only Diocese in which the disastrous system of punishing Incumbents by cutting off the Means of Grace from the Parishioners has been adopted.

The unsettled aspect of Church affairs in the country is indeed such as to awaken grave anxiety; we cannot but be reminded of the truth of our Lord's mysterious words, "Suppose ye that I am come to give Peace on the earth? I tell you, Nay! but rather division." (S. Luke, 12, 51.) Division first, then Peace. Our Lord warns His Church that she can only gain popularity in the world by unfaithfulness to Himself. He assures us that His own career must be that of His Mystical Body; slowly winning her way through persecution and obloquy; always appearing to be worsted, and yet always rising stronger after each defeat; always bearing about the dying of her Lord, but always strong in His Immortal Life. The Eucharistic controversy, now again raging in the Church, is as old as the Church itself. *Apparently,* it has mere reference to a few minor matters of outward ceremonial: its *real* issues lie much deeper than this. It really concerns the truth of our Lord's own words, spoken on the eve of His Crucifixion, when He bequeathed His Sacrament of Love to His Church— "This is My Body; this is My Blood." The profound truth which these words involve and express was rejected, when first propounded by its Divine Author (S. John 6, 52–57, 60, 66); pious disciples as well as thoughtless worldlings were offended. So, it has ever been since: so, it will be to the end. But the Church must still hold on her way, proclaiming by word and deed, in her pulpits and at her Altars, whether men will hear or whether they will forbear, the everlasting verities she has been commissioned to teach. And Truth will win its way at the last.

But I will not enter on this great subject here, as I have expressed myself on it at length elsewhere. I would only venture to urge that in these exciting times, we should be on our guard against a hard, unloving, contentious spirit. "Mysteries are revealed unto the meek." The attitude of our souls in reference to these high and holy truths should ever be, "Lord, teach Thou me," "Lord, I believe me: help Thou mine unbelief." "O send out Thy Light and Thy Truth that they may lead me!"

May God give us all love, and wisdom, and forbearance, and of His infinite mercy "guide us into all Truth."

Your affectionate Friend and Pastor,
John B. Dykes
S. Oswald's Vicarage
Advent, 1874

Throughout the early part of 1875 may be traced the gradual failing of Dr. Dykes' health, and the sad reality is revealed that his work and grave anxieties were rapidly undermining his strength.

To Thee O Father, Son, and Holy Ghost, I humbly offer myself at the beginning of a new year. Bless me and mine, keep us in Thy Love. Use us for Thy Glory.

Jan. 3rd. Sunday. Preached on "Not My Will but Thine be done"; on the Circumcision and the New Year.

Jan. 8th. Letters about Tunes from Lady Freke, Dr. Allon, and Sir Henry Baker.

Tried to think of sermon; got perplexed and bewildered.

Jan. 9th. Long letter from the Bishop of Peterborough.

Jan. 11th. Again, utterly upset. Visiting H. and S. Gave a terrible account of the drunkennesss and vice of her son. Felt keenly that the Church is doing nothing to arrest this.

Jan. 13th. Call from Sir F. Ouseley. Disconcerted. Feel all unhinged to-day, nervous and incapable.

Jan. 15th. Awake from before 4 o'clock, feeling fagged and restless. Could get nothing done. Cathedral. Anthem, "My God, my God, why art Thou so far"—"in the night season I take no rest." Found the words very comforting.

Jan. 17th. Sir F. Ouseley helped me, and left on Monday.

Jan. 21st. Attempted a letter to the Bishop of Peterborough. Could do nothing; quite disheartened. Had a nice walk round

Farewell Hall, trying to bring my difficulties before God, and asking for light and help. Again began letter to the Bishop of Peterborough, and with God's help finished it. Nice bit of cheery talk with dear S. Thank God!

Jan. 25th. Awake since four. Tired! Tried to do a bit of sermon—could not.

On January 28th, feeling that he needed change, Dr. Dykes came to the family home in Cromer Terrace, Leeds, and attended some of the services of the Leeds Mission, then being conducted.

Jan. 27th. Parish Church: On Temptation. At 4, address from Wilkinson.[5] Solemn and beautiful children's service at St. John's. I played the organ.

Jan. 29th. Horbury (D.G.) Evening at St. John's. Very nice sermon and addresses on the Passion by Mr. Wylde and Mr. Bullock.

Jan. 30th. Parish Church. "Who is she that cometh out of the wilderness?" Addresses very beautiful. We were invited to stay in the Church afterwards and make a surrender of ourselves to God. I feebly and humbly tried to do this. Lord have mercy on me, and sustain my will. Home, Tunes, packing, nice journey. God helped me to pray then, and during the day, with fervour. Oh may He hear and answer my prayers! Shocked to hear a bad account of dear Carry. The last letter more favourable.

Dr. Dykes' third daughter (Caroline Sybil), then in Dresden, was in great danger from diphtheria. Happily she gradually, but slowly, recovered.

Jan. 31st. Awake all night.

Feb. 6th. Letter from Robinson of St. Catherine's, suggesting that I should offer myself a candidate for the Professorship of Music in Cambridge.

This, of course, Dr. Dykes felt he could not do, even if he had desired the position—his present duties were too varied, and manifold, to allow his undertaking others, to which he could not give proper attention.

Feb. 7th. Holy Communion—alone. Preached new sermon—"Jesus of Nazareth passeth by."

Feb. 8th. Trying to make a Tune but could not. "God's Will be done."

---

5. Afterwards Bishop of Truro, and now Bishop of St. Andrew's.

Feb. 21st, Sunday. Feeling fagged. Preached an old sermon. "I will not let Thee go." Thank God I got some comfort from my own sermon.

Feb. 29th. Trying to do Hoskins' Litany. All power gone!

Call from P. Wilkinson, who has been to Auckland and seen the Bishop. Felt much discomposed. He (Wilkinson) urges me to concede part of the position. Felt utterly bewildered after he had gone. How can I get on? Yet my health is breaking down. I have had very little unhappiness in my life; now it has come upon me. Lord help and teach me.

March 2nd. Woke at four, in a sort of paroxysm of sorrow, but God gave me a little sleep, else I should have been utterly crushed.

Mar. 4th. Slept better. Beautiful morning. Attempted a sermon, could do nothing. Tried to pray, could not. J. T. Fowler coming. Walked to Croxdale. Prayed all the way home (D.G.). Felt much better this evening than I have done for some time.

Mar. 7th. Mid-Lent Sunday. Slept only from 12 to 1. The most miserable night I have ever passed; up at 6.50. Dare hardly rise to celebrate. Blessed be God for the text "The Blood of Jesus Christ cleanseth from all sin." Remembered I had still a claim in that atoning Blood.

Never had such difficulty in my life in speaking. Could not articulate. Barmby preached. Again "The Blood of Jesus Christ" comforted me. Fowler assisted, Baptisms, etc. Call from Fowler; he insisted on my going to Ovingham. To Church. I preached an old sermon. The two Fowlers came in.

This was the last Sunday Dr. Dykes ministered at St. Oswald's, and here the Diary ends. In this last entry the tired soul clings to the One only source of comfort, where he had ever found peace and rest, and where all must find it, who really need true comfort and help in their times of trouble.

The struggle had been too much for him. No one who did not know Dr. Dykes can understand how great, to his loving spirit, was the trial of having to be, apparently, in open conflict with his Bishop—whom, as a man, he sincerely respected and liked. The pressing needs of his parish, too, weighed heavily on his mind. His duty had never been neglected but had been taken either by himself or the kind friends who so generously offered their help. Besides those already named, he had much assistance from the Rev. Julius C. Lowe, Minor Canon, and Chaplain at the prison, who, when his own work was done, would come to help Dr. Dykes at

St. Oswald's. Others, too, were always ready to offer help. But the future had to be faced! and at this time he seems to have been unfit for work or thought, bewildered with conflicting duties. Still, his only desire was to know and to do God's Will.

By the advice of his friends, he took a day or two's rest at Ovingham, with his friend and former curate. From Ovingham he went to Newcastle to consult a doctor; and there he wrote the following letter to his wife:

> Newcastle
> *March 9, 1875*
>
> I am writing this line at Newcastle, whither I have come over with Wray from Ovingham, to consult Dr. Embleton. He tells me that I *must* get entirely away, and have perfect rest at once. He wishes me to be off to London, thence to Switzerland, or somewhere, tomorrow. He is very urgent on the necessity of immediate action, but the thing seems to be impossible. My dear friends in Durham are most kind in volunteering help—but who is to take charge of the parish? And with whom am I to go? You may imagine I feel in great perplexity. I am very sorry to bother you with all this, but I am beginning to feel that I dare not trifle, as I am sorry to say that my sleeplessness and general incapacity seem steadily to increase. I am so much obliged to you for your dear kind notes. Pray forgive me for not having replied. I have been really anxious to report better of myself; but I fear I cannot do that as yet.
>
> My present idea is to stay at Ovingham a day or two longer, but I ought to be getting home and facing difficulties and making arrangements.
>
> God bless and direct you, my darling. Pray for me.

It now became necessary that Dr. Dykes' departure should not be delayed.

He went first to Folkestone, with his wife and his sister, Miss Dykes; then, as the doctor had recommended that he should go abroad, kind friends placed a sum of money, for travelling expenses, at his disposal. He begged that he might go to Ilkley, a place which had always suited him; but it was thought better that he should not be so near home.

From Folkestone they went to Paris, where they were joined by Mrs. and Miss Cheape. It was early summer, and Paris was too hot and noisy; after remaining there a short time, the party travelled to Switzerland, and settled in the quiet hotel at Tell's Platte, just above Tell's Chapel, on the lovely Lake of Lucerne. There it was hoped that the perfect rest and beautiful air and scenery would restore the wasted, wearied frame; for Dr. Dykes seemed stricken with a general atrophy. However, he became much worse, was entirely confined to bed, and for some time had to be fed every hour. The Swiss doctor, who was called in, recommended that he should return to England as soon as he could bear the journey.

Great was the kindness shown by many friends and visitors, both English and American, during the nine weeks spent at Tell's Platte. At last it was decided that, by easy stages, Dr. Dykes might be brought back to England. He rested a week in Thun, and then, with the help of his old friend, Mr. C. Hodgson Fowler (who had come out to him from England), he was brought slowly back again.

Dr. and Mrs. Dykes went to Ben Rhydding in Wharfedale, where he seemed to gain strength, and was even able to go to church; and hopes were entertained that he might gradually recover. But when the cold weather set in, his frame was too weak to bear it, and towards the end of December he and his wife went to St. Leonard's, in search of a warmer climate. But a more perfect rest was in store for him. His life's work was done, and the loving Master accepted it, and called him Home. On January 22nd, 1876, as his wife was reading a prayer from the service of the Visitation of the Sick—his happy spirit was taken by the angels to the blessed rest of Paradise.

At midnight, on Thursday, January 27th, his body was brought to St. Oswald's Vicarage, Durham (followed from the station by two faithful friends) and laid in the study he loved so well. Early on Friday morning it was removed into the church, where a hundred and twenty-seven worshippers received the Holy Eucharist, and joined in Communion with their dear Lord, and the spirits of those loved ones at rest in Paradise.

The following account of the funeral was written by the late Canon Ashwell, of Chichester:

> He was laid to rest, in his own Churchyard of St. Oswald's, almost under the shadow of the vast tower of his own Cathedral, on Friday, Jan. 28th. It was very touching and impressive. The Church quite full, and it is not a small one; Celebration at 8 a.m., with more than a hundred Communicants, of whom a very great part were men. At nine o'clock the funeral service began, with the 39th Psalm. Then after the Hymn, "The King of Love my Shepherd is"—to Dr. Dykes' own Tune—and the Lesson. The whole of the Congregation, joined by numbers more from

the streets, followed the procession; Clergy and Choir singing Psalm 51, to the place of interment. All quiet and orderly, showing every feeling of respect to one whose life and conversation had been known to them for seven-and-twenty years, and who, near fourteen years, had been their Vicar. The Hymn, "O Heavenly Jerusalem," was sung at the close of the burial office, and then the Clergy and Choir returned to the Church singing the Hymn "Jesus lives."

Dr. Dykes had been thirteen years Precentor of Durham Cathedral, and thirteen years Vicar of St. Oswald's. His had not been a long life; had he lived until the tenth of March, he would have been fifty-three years of age. But he had done his life's work in the time his Master had given him to do it in. He had striven earnestly to devote his talents to the glory of God and the good of his Church, so long as his strength and powers lasted.

Who that has sung his hymn-tunes does not feel that they came to him as inspirations? He rarely wrote a tune unless the words were sent or suggested to him, and then the tune seemed at once to adapt itself to the words. This is probably the secret of the success of his tunes. They came from his heart, and found their way into the hearts of others. It mattered not who applied to him for tunes, whether Churchmen or dissenters, high or low, rich or poor, the work was given, ungrudgingly, as work for God.

In numbers of cases he would receive no payment for his tunes, especially when the Clergy applied for them; and at first he devoted any money accruing from them to charity. Afterwards, when he became more widely known, and larger sums came in, he considered it a legitimate source of income, to be taxed with the rest of his money—for charity—still reserving to himself the privilege of giving his services where he felt the payment could not be afforded. His literary work, too, was much appreciated so long as he had time to devote to it; but that had to be put to one side when the claims of his parish interfered with it.

Of the cloud which hung so heavily over the later months of his life no more need be said. We will only quote the words in which the late Canon Ashwell replied to a request that he would write an obituary notice of Dr. Dykes:

Canon Lane, Chichester
Jan. 27, 1876

> It will be a labour of love, however mingled—steeped I should say—in sorrow, to do what I can in Memoriam of one so dear to me, and so reverenced also, as our lost Dr. Dykes. More, I can hardly trust myself to say or to write. But I must ask to be furnished with materials and information of whatever kind you can give me.
>
> ...
>
> I know that all words must be intrusive at such a time to poor Mrs. Dykes, for whom I grieve more than words can say. So, I must only ask you to say, that if ever occasion offers I shall feel honoured in rendering her the smallest service.
>
> If ever there was a martyr, Dr. Dykes was one; let us think now of his Crown.

To show how much Dr. Dykes' life and work had been appreciated, it is touching to record that, as soon as it was known his wife and family were poorly provided for, a fund was raised for their benefit, and the money flowed in from all parts until it reached the sum of £10,000, and was then stopped.

So far as can be ascertained, Dr. Dykes' last tune was written for Dr. Allon's *Congregational Psalmist,* to Miss Adelaide Proctor's beautiful words, entitled, "The Pilgrims." The hymn seems to harmonise so completely with his own feelings at the time the tune was written, that it forms a touching sequel to the last days of his ministry. We give the tune with the words, and also Dr. Allon's letter, written to *The Guardian* about this time.

Through Pain to Peace

Via Crucis

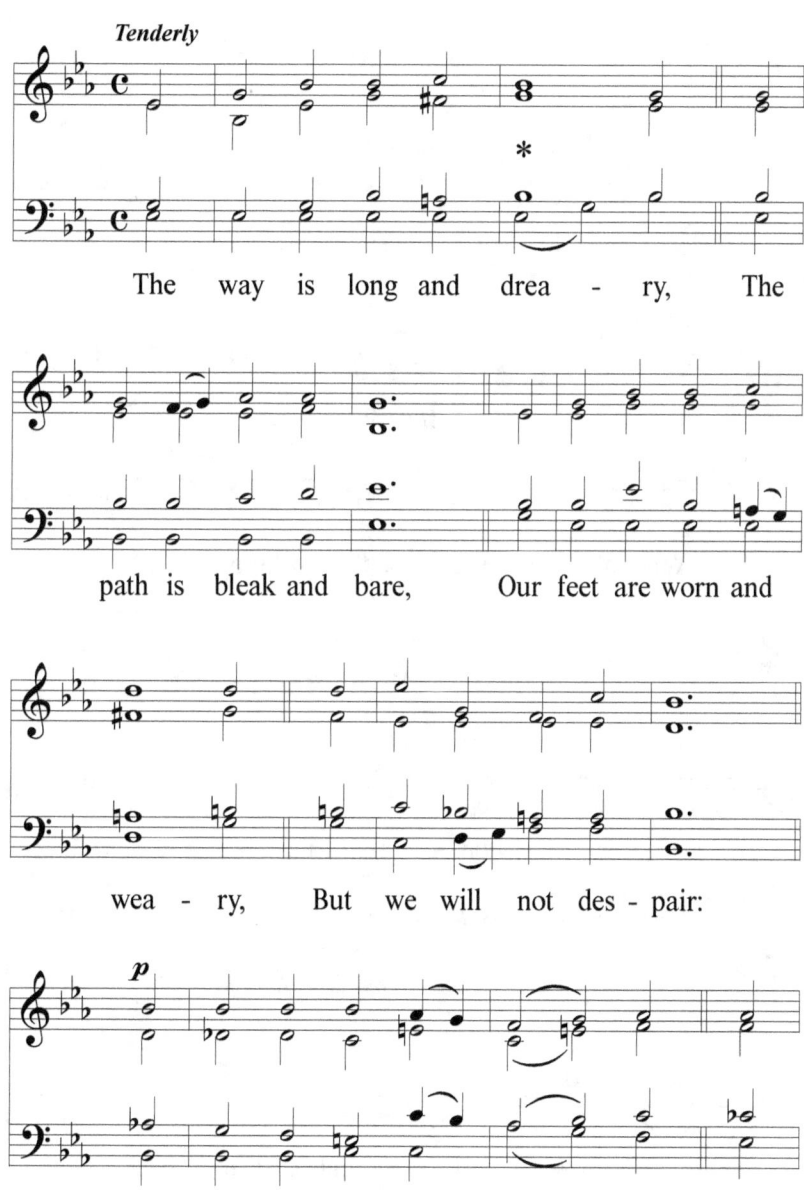

The Pilgrims

The way is long and dreary,
The path is bleak and bare;
Our feet are worn and weary,
But we will not despair.
More heavy was Thy burthen,
More desolate Thy way;—
O Lamb of God, Who takest
The sin of the world away,
Have mercy on us.

The snows lie thick around us,
In the dark and gloomy night;
And the tempest wails above us,
And the stars have hid their light;
But blacker was the darkness
Round Calvary's Cross that day;—
O Lamb of God, Who takest
The sin of the world away,
Have mercy on us.

Our hearts are faint with sorrow,
Heavy and hard to bear;
For we dread the bitter morrow,
But we will not despair:
Thou knowest all our anguish,
And Thou wilt bid it cease;—
O Lamb of God, Who takest
The sin of the world away,
Give us Thy Peace.

Adelaide Anne Proctor

The following is Dr. Allon's letter:

I shall deem it a great privilege to be permitted to contribute the enclosed.

First, as an expression of common gratitude for his rich and precious contributions to the worship song of almost all English-speaking congregations. I will not attempt to characterise or to eulogise Dr. Dykes' hymn-music further than to say that, in many instances, he has given even to some of our best hymns a devotional expression, not only far superior to all other settings of them, but far beyond their own verbal significance. I venture to say that they are valued and used as much in Nonconformist congregations as in those of his own church. I doubt whether in the kingdom there is any Nonconformist church, and certainly there are very few Nonconformist families, in which they are not sung.

And next, I should like to express my own sense of the courtesy, solicitous kindness, and singular unselfishness to which the Rev. Sir H. W. Baker testifies, and of which as a compiler of Church Music I have had large experience. Not only did he unreservedly offer for my use all his compositions over which he had retained any right of disposal, but with difficulty could he be prevailed upon to accept even the most modest pecuniary acknowledgment for them: he repeatedly returned amounts sent to him, on the ground that he had already elsewhere received a sufficient consideration for them. A little more than a year ago, when I was making some additions to the *Congregational Psalmist,* he kindly offered to write music for any hymns that I wished. I have reason to believe that an exquisite setting for congregational use of Miss Adelaide Procter's, "The way is long and dreary" which he then wrote for me, was his last musical composition. Only a few days before his last illness, he informed me that a setting of Mr. Monsell's hymn, "When I had wandered from His fold," was partly done. He was not permitted to complete it.

I, for one, feel it very much to be thus drawn in the practical sympathy of most holy feelings to one from whom, in many things, I greatly differed. Men like Lyte, Keble, Moultrie, and Dykes, with whom we hold the highest fellowship of the Christian life, do very much to make us practically realise our essential Oneness in Christ, and, therefore, to make any bitterness of necessary controversy impossible.

If the suggestion of a collection of Dr. Dykes' musical compositions is acted upon, I shall be very happy to place at the disposal of the editor the tunes he wrote for me, as also two or three anthems for congregational use of his composition.

The evening of a life of bright usefulness had been darkened by the cloud which, for the time, hid even the Light of Christ's Presence from the weary traveller.

But the pilgrim's way led through pain to peace—by the way of the Cross to the way of Light—through the garden of Gethsemane to the garden of Paradise, where the "loyal heart and true" should bask for ever in the perpetual sunshine of the Presence of that Master for Whom he had lived and worked, to Whom he had dedicated his great gift of melody, in Whose Name he had preached and written and ministered, and in Whose Cause he had suffered so patiently.

We give part of a very impressive sermon preached from Job xxix. 11, 12, and St. Matthew xvi. 27, by Dr. Lake, Dean of Durham, in the Cathedral, on the Sunday after Dr. Dykes' funeral.

> You will agree with me, my Christian friends, in feeling that it would be strange if this day were to pass away without some tribute of respect and affection to the eminent member of this Cathedral whom we have just lost, and whose memory is now, and will long continue to be, dear to many of those who hear me. When a devoted servant of that Lord whom we all so imperfectly worship, but Who loves us all, is called home by his Master to Himself, and, above all, when this is after many a labour and sorrow, our first feeling is, perhaps, that of thankfulness that he is gone to his rest and his reward; our next is that of admiration of his holy life, and an earnest prayer that we may ourselves be able to profit by his example. Both these thoughts may well be in our hearts this afternoon. We have lost an eminent Christian, a faithful servant, and consistent minister of Jesus Christ—one whose singleness of heart and will and devotion of labour none can doubt; one who has been a true witness to God in his generation, and of whom all of those who might be unable entirely to agree with him might well say: "May my soul be with his!" This is not the time for me to attempt to bring before you the character of one whom many of you knew so much better than myself. In what I have said I have already touched on those features which have endeared him to so many, and (may I add?) are of far the highest price in the sight of God. But it will not be out of place to say that, beyond his own parish, no place owes him more gratitude, or was more a witness to his zealous labours, than this Cathedral. Eminently qualified by his genius to conduct its noble services, no man could better appreciate their religious power and beauty, and no man, I am sure, regarded his office in a more religious light, or laboured more personally to make those who attended and who assisted in them feel that to sing the praise and glory of God is an essential function and part of God's worship. And surely to have thus tuned the Hymns, and (as it were) struck the key-note of adoration, is to have held no small place in the Church. How many on this day in every part of England are raising to God the strains which he was privileged to conceive, and with the

solemn and grateful thought that he to whom many owe them has returned to God! I do not say that he has not many, and perhaps higher, claims to your loving respect; for he was a man of deep theological learning, and (what is far better) earnest religious thoughts; and though I would not speak as if I agreed in all the conclusions of that thought, yet I hold it the worst heresy to imagine that man can devote earnest thought and learning to God's service without bringing down a blessing on His Church. I would enter upon no disputed matter to-day; but less than this I cannot say. If I believe the promise of the Lord that His Spirit should guide us unto truth, I cannot doubt that, in whatever way, the prayers, the studies, the labours of men like John Dykes have been an offering acceptable to God, and a great blessing to the Church of Christ.

Amongst the many letters of sympathy Mrs. Dykes received after her husband's death, the following passages may be selected as representative; the first from his most intimate friend, associated closely with him in work to which he devoted so much of his energy; the second from a friend to whom he was less well known, but who was connected with him on the literary side of his clerical life; the third from a comparative stranger, who expressed the feelings of hundreds who only knew him through his hymn-tunes.

Sir Henry Baker had been waiting for a telegram to inform him when the funeral was to be and through some mistake it had never been sent.

The following passages are extracted from two of his letters to Mrs. Dykes:

> Horkesley House,
> Monkland, Leominster
>
> *No* telegram is come yet: so, I will add a line to the very hasty one I sent you the moment I received the sad news yesterday. I cannot say how much I wish I had seen him again.
>
> How wonderful are the ways of God! I had thought what a bright sweet end of this life *his* must be. So, in truth, I trust it is. He does indeed rest from his labours, and his works must follow him,—those blessed works of making so many a Christian soul "rejoice in the Lord" in his sweet Tunes. We did indeed think of him this morning as we sang "The King of Love my Shepherd is"—to *his* tune. Oh! that we may indeed sing with him the praise of the good Shepherd within His Heavenly House—for

ever. You will yourself be comforted and drawn nearer to Christ …

I shall hope soon to hear about the funeral. I am unfeignedly sorry, and have been on the constant look out for a telegram. But perhaps it has been so ordered to spare me a very trying journey. Only I feel as if I *ought* to have followed to the grave one to whom I owe so much. If any account is printed, do try and let it be said how wholly unavoidable circumstances kept me away.

May God comfort and bless you all! and be indeed "a Father to the Fatherless and a God to the Widow"—is the true prayer of your husband's very affectionate—and your own sincere friend,

Henry W. Baker

We are going to sing *only his* tunes to every hymn all next Sunday, and the *Dies Irae* after Evensong—*for him*; followed by "Ten thousand times ten thousand."

The second passage in a letter, also written to Mrs. Dykes, is from the Rev. J. H. Blunt.[6]

Beverston Rectory,
Tetbury, Gloucestershire

Allow me to add one word of sympathy to those which you will be receiving from so many friends. Had I been within any easier reach of Durham I should have been in Church on the morning to join in the Communion that will give all who loved him another tie with him and the Land of peace, light and refreshment to which he has gone.

He has left a great blank in the Church on earth, but the work which he has done will live after him in many a grateful soul. For myself I shall always remember my friendship with him with great pleasure, and shall never think of him otherwise than one who had a saintly mind, which was doubtless trained still more for the end that has come by the suffering which has been brought upon him.

The third is from a distinguished American clergyman, the Rev. Dr. Staunton, and is addressed to Dr. Dykes' friend and generous helper in the parish of St. Oswald's, Mr. C. Hodgson Fowler.

---

6. Editor of *The Annotated Prayer Book*, etc.

713, Broadway, New York
Mar. 23, 1876

Dear Sir,

Some days before the receipt of your kind note the sad news of the death of Dr. Dykes had reached us, and I need not tell you that the loss of one whom I had learnt to reverence and love has been to me the cause of very sincere sorrow.

Several years ago, when our Church adopted *Hymns Ancient and Modern*, my attention was specially attracted to the tunes written by the Doctor, on account of certain features which indicated such a peculiar force of thought, and fervour of devotional sentiment, on the part of the writer, as to give them a charm which made its way directly into the depths of every Christian heart. I pointed these out to some musical friends, clerical and lay; and it soon became a settled point that whatever music bore the name of Dr. Dykes, might be accepted at once as the work of a master mind.

In the autumn of 1872, I spent a month or two in England, and went to Durham with two objects in view, one of which was to see the Cathedral, and the other to see Dr. Dykes. I am not sure but that the Doctor occupied a larger space in my mind than did the Cathedral. I made acquaintance with him through a general letter of introduction from the Bishop of New York; and during my stay of only two days in Durham, received from the Dr. and his family attentions for which I have ever felt grateful. Had I not been "booked" for the steamer which was soon to sail from Liverpool, I could have lingered with delight in Durham, to enjoy still more of friendly intercourse with one of the most saint-like, gifted, and attractive men that I have ever known.

. . .

Thanking you for the honour you have done me, in this recognition, as one not unknown to Dr. Dykes, and not unworthy to do some slight service to his memory, and with kindest expressions of condolence and sympathy with the bereaved family,

Believe me,
Very faithfully yours,
William Staunton

Of Dr. Dykes' work as a parish priest little has been said. In no special way did it differ from that of any other devoted clergyman. But of the spirit in which he laboured, the following incident, trifling in itself, yet rich in suggestiveness, may serve as an illustration.

"Last summer," says his friend, Mr. C. H. Fowler, "I was talking to a working man outside St. Oswald's Vicarage, as to who was to be the next vicar. The man said:

"'They will never get another gentleman like Dr. Dykes.'

"I asked, 'Do you remember him?'

"'Yes,' he said, 'and I always remember one night when I was working on the road near the Vicarage. A man came and rang the bell. Dr. Dykes put his head out of the window and asked what it was. Someone was ill. "Will you wait a minute for me?" "Yes!" said the man; and in little more than a minute Dr. Dykes was with him, running down the street; and as he went I could see that he had only slipped on his shoes, with no stockings, and had put on his cassock, he was so quick to go.'"

10

Spiritual Letters, Etc.

Some allusion must now be made to a part of Dr. Dykes' life-work which had an important and widespread influence; and this, at no small cost of labour, and mental care and anxiety to himself. This work seemed to come unsought into his hands, and was accepted by him as an opening of God's Providence; and the intense desire to work, in any way which the Master seemed to point out, made him throw into it all his energies. This work, which needs all the powers of the matured spiritual life, with all that a refined nature can supply of tact and delicacy, was, he well knew, unpopular; but that was the last reason in the world why he should shrink from supplying to other troubled spirits a medicine which he had found most beneficial to his own. He had, by instinct, a very keen insight into human nature; he always seemed to be able, at a glance, to detect the secret springs of action; and his opinion on character was highly valued, and anxiously sought, among his friends. This penetrative faculty it was which, under the guidance of God's Holy Spirit, and quickened by an ardent love of souls, fitted him, in a remarkable manner, for dealing with troubled consciences. This inborn fitness for the work soon made itself felt, without any idea, apparently, on his part, of such being the case, or any wish to add a most difficult and responsible task to his other varied labours. He could not shirk a way so evidently opened out to him by that Divine Hand Whose slightest indication he was ever on the watch to follow, wherever it might lead. The firm yet delicate touch with which he could lay bare the seat of the disease, and probe the long-forgotten wounds of the soul, made his advice and direction increasingly valued, and he found himself soon the trusty guide and counsellor of many a weary spirit, sparing no pains in administering the wholesome medicine of discipline, pouring in the oil and wine of consolation, pronouncing with intensest feeling God's absolution on the penitent. His mind had long been made up with regard to Confession, as a means of grace, and a help in the spiritual life; and this was no theoretical view, but one arrived at by slow degrees, in his own personal experience. Without entering on the vexed question of good and evil in the practice, we may fairly allow that it is those who have made use of it who may be supposed to be the best judges of its benefits; while what is good for the well-balanced mind may be hurtful to the morbid, or sentimental.

With Dr. Dykes there was no undue magnifying of the Priestly Office, no craving after spiritual dominion; he was led to the work by the real and earnest desire to be helpful to doubtful, wandering spirits, and to use what spiritual light he possessed to guide others on the road which, by his own experience, he knew to lead into green pastures and quiet resting places, where the ear is opened to hear the Shepherd's voice, and the sight quickened to behold the Hosts of God. There the soul comes to understand the meaning of the often-repeated words, "The Peace of God, which passeth all understanding." The habitual expression of his countenance told plainly enough that it was that "Peace" which kept his own heart and soul at rest, amid the turmoil that surrounded him. At times there was a glow, as if it shone with an inward light. Many of his friends, who are privileged to retain for ever in their remembrance his "Sunday evening look," can bear witness to this. And what joy was it to him, to bring others within reach of that service of consolation and gladness!

But he knew full well that, before the healing balm could be applied, sin must be felt, acknowledged, and deeply repented of. He knew that "sin unconfessed is sin unrepented of, and sin unrepented of is sin unforgiven," and he would not withhold the human help that may be given to assist in casting off the load. As the physician, who would administer the right medicine to the patient, must know the symptoms of the disease, and the patient, knowing his ailment, must be willing to disclose those symptoms, and submit to the wholesome regimen prescribed, so it is with disease of the soul. And the distinction between the use of Confession in the Roman and Anglican Church ever remains—the distinction between binding it on the conscience, as a peremptory command—a duty necessary to the soul's salvation; and recommending it as a means whereby the soul may receive help and comfort, but leaving it to the individual whether to make use of it or not.

To an Invalid, on Fasting Communion

The Rectory, Tenby, S. Wales
Sep. 28, 1869

With regard to your question respecting non-fasting Communion, I think the question admits of a ready answer. The command that you *should* communicate is absolute. It comes directly from our Blessed Lord Himself, and therefore has an unqualified demand on our obedience. The super-added counsel that we should do this fasting, though coming to us on the high authority of the Church, and therefore claiming our dutiful acceptance and observance, can never be held to be an injunction of equal coordinate obligation with that of the direct and immediate mandate of the Saviour, and must, therefore, necessarily give way, in case circumstances should arise rendering the fulfilment of both precepts impossible.

If you may not, in consequence of your health, communicate at the early Celebration, do so with a quiet conscience and thankful heart at the *late* one, even although after breakfast. You would not take so substantial a breakfast as at other times, as an expression of your willingness to obey the Church's precept, as far as you are able but do not allow yourself to be disturbed by any morbid or disquieting scruples; rest quite sure that your loving Lord, Who Himself, by the orderings of His Good Providence, hinders you from fulfilling an ordinary rule of the Church, will never let you be a loser through your involuntary non-compliance with that rule.

You will, perhaps, when the weather is fine, be able to get, occasionally, to the early Celebration (and I own I have often been surprised to find how well *seeming* invalids are able, without harm, to do this—and how often they really seem physically benefited by it, and by the invigorating influences of the early morning air). When you find you can do this, you doubtless will; but when you cannot, go peacefully, and undoubtingly, to the late Communion.

With regard to the general change in your circumstances of life, arising partly from your present failing health, and partly from your father's marriage, I have only to repeat what, I think, I said before: do not fix your thoughts on the circumstances themselves, but simply on God's Will acting and expressing itself through those circumstances.

Accept whatever change in your condition His Good Providence may bring about, thankfully and reverently; and do not allow yourself to wish that things were otherwise. Try consciously to acquiesce in, and cordially correspond with the manifestation of God's Will concerning you, in the full, unhesitating persuasion that what He orders is best, and that what you know not now, you shall know hereafter—and that certain grace of character which God longs to see in you cannot be worked in you, but by means of this peculiar conjunction of circumstances. Cherish no thought of unkindness towards her who must hereafter stand to you in relation of Mother; receive her dutifully and affectionately. Thus by not resisting in any way, but *yielding* in *all* things to God's Will, you shall find peace and happiness come to you; and come by the very means of those changes in your outward condition which you now regard with some apprehension and aversion; and God will gradually and gently lead you on to still higher grace. May His Blessing ever rest upon you.

Yours most sincerely in Christ,
John B. Dykes

On Confession

St. Oswald's Vicarage, Durham
Nov. 19, 1868

My Dear____,

In reply to your note, it appears to me that there are two dangers from which we must steer clear: the one seeking private Confession and Absolution, without any serious feeling of the need of it, and merely because we think it is the correct thing, and a mark of good Churchmanship and the like,—the other assuring ourselves that there is no need of it, just because there may not be any definite act of open sin upon our conscience to disturb it. It is so very possible that our estimate of ourselves may be altogether wrong and the unconsciousness of any special sin interposing between our Souls and God may be the result of not having examined deeply and closely enough. The Lord tells us that many who will be condemned at the Awful Bar of God, will regard themselves to the end with the utmost complacency—"Lord, Lord, have we not prophesied in Thy Name?" etc., to whom the Judge will answer, "I never knew you." "Depart from Me."

Now, one great use of occasional Confession appears to me to be this, that it is such a real help in self-examination. No serious person would go to Confession without an honest and searching self-examination beforehand—and no honest Christians will go through this process, carefully, and prayerfully, without (I fear) finding themselves very much worse than they had before imagined. Then again, the authoritative sentence of pardon pronounced on oneself individually is such an incalculable help and blessing. I am not for one moment doubting but that God does bestow His Pardon more widely than perhaps we imagine, and often independently of the regular and direct channels of conveyance which He seems to have ordained in His Church. I have no doubt also, but that the public Absolutions pronounced in His Name, in His Church, are effectual in operation in the case of those whose hearts are fully prepared to receive them. Still if we can have this Blessed Gift of Forgiveness, brought home, as it were, and applied to ourselves personally, I should be disposed to think it the safer and more humble course to avail ourselves of it. It is a help to earnestness, a help to sincerity, a help to humility, and a help against spiritual sloth and procrastination. What can be done any day, is often not done at all. Moreover, the very unpleasantness of confessing our faults before a fellow-sinner is in itself advantageous as a help to humility. If we are ashamed to let a brother know how weak and sinful we are, how can we bear the keen, all-penetrating glance of the Holy God?

Now do not misunderstand me. I do not for one moment wish you to feel in any way forced to adopt a practice of which you do not feel any need, and which you do not think would be for your soul's health. God leads us all by different ways. For myself I have found the practice most helpful, and I have seen its use in the case of others; but I *dare* not *urge* any to adopt it.

The Church of England leaves the matter open, and forces no one. She dissuades no one, but she evidently contemplates a much wider use of the Ordinance than exists at the present day.

After all, you must be guided by your own conscience. Pray to God to direct you aright. He will guide you to do what is most pleasing to Himself.

On a Boy's Enthusiasm as a Worker for Christ

Durham
1869

My Dear ____,

I have read you brother's letter with great interest. You have, I am sure, great cause to be thankful to God for the earnest, hearty, religious tone which pervades it. It is really quite refreshing to find a little enthusiasm in Christ's cause manifested in a lad; to see him anxious in his small way to do the work of an Evangelist. One would be sorry to check any fervour, or any impulses which may have been stirred up in him by the Holy Ghost, or to do anything to restrain him in his endeavours to help on his school-fellows in the right path. His letter shows one how much latent love for Christ there may be in young and innocent hearts, which merely needs to be fostered and directed, and which is too often wasted and extinguished by worldly associations and pleasures.

Still I quite agree with you that the letter is not without its indications of danger lurking in the distance, which will have to be carefully guarded against. What chiefly impressed me with a sense of possible danger was in the passage where one sees a touch of animal excitement and affection independent of the gentle fervour of the Holy Ghost. Now, of course, there must always be peril at hand, when natural excitement is in any way regarded as a proof of, or is mistaken for, Heavenly zeal. The ardour of the flesh is more palpable than the serene glow of the Spirit—and is sometimes not only a dangerous counterfeit, but even an actual hinderer and opponent, and extinguisher of it. I would recommend you quietly and gently to warn your brother against any of this demonstrative affection, also to remind him of this, that *immediate* duties must always be attended to before secondary duties, even though the latter may be in themselves higher and more holy. For instance, a boy who neglects a hard lesson for the purpose of visiting, or giving good advice to a schoolfellow, is failing in obligation to God.

God knows better than the boy what is good for him, and it is God Who has given him the uninteresting lesson to learn, and Who has a blessing in store waiting the faithful and conscientious mastery of it, which will be forfeited if the task is neglected for any self-chosen work, however attractive, and, in itself, sacred. Also I think I should advise him, as a general rule, not to set himself up, as an Evangelist, or to lay himself out for that kind of work, but only to keep himself ready to fulfil boldly and humbly any such work, if God points it out to him. He must be careful not to run where God does not call him, with the thought that he can do good—He can do nothing except God sets and enables him to do it. Therefore let him be very diligent in his own work, fulfilling to the very best of his power all his known duties, little or great, learning every lesson perfectly, being always punctual, always obedient and always prayerful, keeping his eyes perpetually fixed on Him Who has said, "Without Me, ye can do nothing." Then God may and probably will (if He thinks good) give him some definite work to do (now in one way, and now in another) for the spiritual benefit of his schoolfellows. At all events, he should remember this, that a good, consistent example is better than ten thousand sermons.

This then, I think, should be his great aim, to set a good example, or rather to do his duty in the sight of God perfectly for God's sake, not to aim directly at evangelising, but to offer himself to God to be used by Him in any way He sees best. If he is honest in his resolve, God will guide him with His Eye, and secretly and intelligibly direct him, each moment, what to do.

Wishing you and yours most heartily all the blessings of the season and a happy New Year,

Believe me
Ever yours affectionately,
John B. Dykes

On Preparation for Communion

1869

My Dear____,

With regard to your receiving Holy Communion on the first Sunday in February, as it is your regular day, I should advise you to stay and communicate as usual; you need all the help you can obtain, and you would naturally like to take this opportunity of praying our Lord to grant a special blessing on the work in which you trust to be engaged on the morrow, which you hope may be a means of drawing you more closely and more indissolubly to Himself.

I am glad that you are gradually regaining your strength. Do not make yourself anxious and uneasy about your Confession. Christ is far more ready and willing to forgive you, than you are to seek for forgiveness. Just make the best preparation which time and health admit of, and trust to His Love and Help.

Believe me ever yours affectionately,
John B. Dykes

On Retreats, etc.

St. Oswald's, Durham
1872

My Dear____,

I must send you a line in answer to your question.

As for the Retreat, I should certainly advise you to go to it; you might find it a great help. It is merely a time for quiet retirement—some good man meanwhile directing your meditation, and (to myself at least) it is always a period of great refreshment.

With regard to Confession at a Retreat, it is quite optional. The Priest who conducts the Meditation cannot hear the Confessions of all—he has not time; so some go, some do not. As for the Resolution, you must make that yourself. And I would not advise you to think much about it beforehand; except, (if you determine to go) praying God to help you to make a prudent and useful Resolution. It is best to leave those things rather to the Retreat time, and trust to the light then given you.

You ask me if it is possible to go on caring for a person who is constantly crossing and thwarting you? Do you never cross and thwart your Lord? and does He therefore cease to care for you? Moreover, how do you know that this person *is* trying to cross and thwart you? Are you not judging her, and imputing motives you have no right to impute? May not the feeling of dislike which you are secretly cherishing be due to something wrong in *yourself*, and not altogether to something wrong in her? May there not be some lurking feeling of jealousy or censoriousness, or of impatience, or selfishness on your part which ought to be vigorously assailed and uprooted, and of which this sense of dislike is but a token and result? It is very unsafe to cherish these sorts of feelings, of personal repugnance. They generally arise from some whimishness or over-sensitiveness or want of large-heartedness on our own part. To act kindly to and *think* kindly of a person against whom we are tempted to cherish unloving feelings—is a most useful Exercise of charity and humility.

I do not think there was anything necessarily wrong in your listening to the story of your friend's grievances, even although her Father and Mother were involved in it. It is sometimes an immense relief to people to "air" their troubles, and a little friendly sympathy and advice may do them a world of good.

You must not encourage any resistance to the positive and expressed will of Father or Mother. One ought to hear both sides of every question before one can offer an opinion worth listening to. The Parents must have some valid reason for withholding their consent. Is the gentleman able to keep a wife? If not he has no business to marry. Could not some mutual friend be found who would quietly talk the matter over with the parents?—for they surely are not utterly unreasonable. Meanwhile, the young lady must learn a lesson of patience, and of quiet submission to the Will of God. If God sees it best for them both that they should be united, He will in His own good time (not before) remove all hindrances. And if He does not see it to be for their good, they are a thousand times happier and better as they are. Anyhow it is *wrong* for her to fret and worry herself. God bless you.

Ever yours affectionately,
John B. Dykes

On Humility

July, 1872

My Dear____,

With regard to your spiritual besetment, it is well to be conscious of it. To know a fault is a good stage on the road towards correcting it and amending it. If, knowing it as you do, you simply take our Lord's own two practical words and act upon them—"Watch and Pray"—you will not get far wrong. People are often willing to receive humiliations coming direct from God, but not those coming from our brothers and sisters. Of course the mistake is the forgetting that all alike really come from God, only that He sends some to us through our brothers and sisters; and that we are bound to see and accept His Will, in the one case no less than the other. I suppose we see a sort of picture of the light in which God regards pride and complacency in the case of Herod. As soon as he takes to himself the credit of what belongs to God only, "He is eaten of worms"—he becomes an object of loathing and contempt. "God dwells with the humble, the proud He beholdeth afar off." If we would know how God has humbled Himself, and how He looks for, and loves to see humility in *us*, we should think of that wonderful passage in *Phil.* ii., 3—11, compared with S. John xiii., 1—17. Meditate sometimes on these passages (perhaps with your hands held out in the form of the Cross)—when you feel strongly tempted to self-laudation; or you might read on your knees *Imitation* Book i., 2; Book iii., 4, 7, 8; [Thomas à Kempis] one chapter at a time.

Only take pains and be patient with yourself, and God will give you the victory. God bless you.

Yours affectionately,
John B. Dykes

On a Rule of Fasting and Abstinence

Oct., 1872

My Dear____,

I do not see anything deceitful in your modifying your mode of keeping the Church's fasting days according to the circumstances in which you are placed. The Church orders that you are to keep certain days of Fasting or Abstinence, (as the case may be) but she does not prescribe *how* you are to keep them. This must always depend upon circumstances. It would never do for you to come into direct collision with your parents on the subject. If your Father wishes you to take meat, of course you must obey. So it is as well to act prudently, and to make as little fuss about such things as possible. There is something rather unpleasant in a daughter even appearing to be remonstrating or giving her testimony against what her Father is doing. And I am so much frightened of your doing anything to give your Father a distaste for Catholic practices, and so of your throwing him back in his steady advance in sound wholesome Churchmanship.

If you think he would take no notice of your eating, and would offer no objections, then you can do as you like; but if it would fidget him, you had almost better go without meat when you *can*, and at other times go without pudding, etc., keeping to one course, if possible. If you and he could have a quiet talk on the subject, some time, it would be the best, so that you could come to some understanding—until then, I think you had better do as I have suggested.

I am very glad you enjoyed the Retreat and trust you may derive permanent benefit from it. The carrying out of your resolution will require watchfulness; but anything is valuable which tends to make and keep us watchful. Only while trying to be watchful, beware of being morbid or self-conscious, and don't be put out if you find your resolution rather harder to keep than you at first expected. God sometimes humbles us by our failures as well as by other means. "If thou prayest for humility, expect humiliations."

Believe me yours affectionately in Jesus Christ,
John B. Dykes

On Charity

My Dear____,

Possibly the Epistles of the last two Sundays may have helped you partially to discover the cause of the loss of the sense of God's Favour and Love, which seems for a time to have come over you—although it has now passed away.

If we are cold and unloving to others, God will seem cold and unloving to us.

It is in the exercise of Love that we are able to realize God's Love.

Your notes show too many breaches of charity, I mean in the way of talking or thinking of the faults of *others*, speaking disparagingly of them, judging them, and conversely thinking too much of *Self*. Even your temporary distaste for intercessory prayer is an evidence of the same failure in *Love*: you cannot sufficiently throw yourself into or feel an interest in the needs of others. You must simply pray for a large increase of Divine Charity and watch against anything inconsistent with Love. Check at once the contemptuous thought or word, the feeling of irritation when you are a little put out of your way—the disposition to take offence at trifles. It is only by *"Loving"* that is, by practically exercising Love in all its details, that "God's Love is perfected in us."

One immediate result of the failure in Love, is a loss of *Joy*. The unloving are always joyless. The course of the Spirit's work is "Love, Joy, Peace." You are quite right in heeding any little warning or check, which the Holy Ghost may give, and trying at once to find out what there has been to cause a temporary withdrawal of the light of His Countenance.

He merely wishes to keep you vigilant and circumspect, lest old temptations should come upon you unawares, and overpower you.

May He soon cause His Face to shine upon you evermore and give you His Peace.

Yours ever in Jesus Christ,
John B. Dykes

On Character

Feb., 1874

My Dear ____,

With regard to the failing to which you refer, I do not think there is any need to allude to it. What you have to acknowledge are definite acts—not mere tendencies and predispositions. All people's characters are different. Some are rather formed to rule, some to obey. Each class has its special dangers and temptations, as well as its special uses. If your tendency is rather to hold your own, and have your own way, there is nothing abstractedly wrong in this. Some people never like to have their own way—because they never know it. They do not know their own minds, and always yield to others. God has uses for both sets of people. We must only try to keep our natural tendencies (whatever they are) in check and under control. There is no use trying to make ourselves what we are not, and what God did not intend us to be. Our business is not to *un*make the character which God has made for us—but to try and regulate it and perfect it *after its kind*. All the rest must wait till I see you.

Yours ever,
John B. Dykes

On Clouds in the Spiritual Life

My Dear____,

We shall be very glad to see you next week. I can arrange to see you any day most convenient to you. We must not lose heart because a cloud for a time seems to hide our Lord from us. It must be so! Uninterrupted sunshine is not good for the earth. It is not good for the soul. We must have our occasional dark days. But as we pray, "Through cloud and sunshine, Lord, abide with me," so we must try "through cloud" as well as "through sunshine" to abide with Him. Treasure in your heart the remembrance of this season of dryness and its passing away. It is useful to recall God's dealings with us. It may be a help to yourself in other dark days, and a help to others also . . .

On the Wedding of a Sister

Durham
Jan., 1875

My Dear____,

So the wedding is really to come off tomorrow morning! Well, I am sure I wish most heartily health and happiness, and every blessing to the young couple. I am so glad that you have been able to arrange for an early Celebration that day. It will be such a nice sobering, quieting and hallowing inauguration of the eventful proceedings. Nice for them before their union, and nice for you before your separation. For no doubt if you bear that separation patiently, and thankfully, it will prove to be a source of blessing to yourself. Of course it is hard at times to forget one's own sorrow in the joy of others: but it is very blessed to be able to do so. We are bidden to "Rejoice with them that do rejoice, and weep with them that weep." The former of these duties is generally the harder of the two. It is comparatively easy to be sorry and sympathise with the distress of others, but when you yourself are sad at heart, it is much more hard to rejoice in their joy. But our sympathising Lord will help you to exercise this grace, and also, I trust, to prove the happiness of exercising it. I cannot but feel for your dear good father; for I am sure in his quiet way he will feel the loss of ____ very much; all the more need for you, my dear child, bracing yourself up to supply the loss, and to do the duty of two single ladies rolled into one.

I am so thankful that you have already begun to view matters in rather a brighter light. My dear wife and the young people are all quite well; I cannot say I feel altogether so myself. My isolation and difficulties and responsibilities seem to have pressed upon me this Christmas, in a way which I have never experienced before. But it will never do to exhort you to be merry, and reserve to myself the gloomy privilege of being sad. So, I can only pray that the Epiphany Light may shine upon us all, and that we may all have a taste of Holy Joy. Give my kindest love to all. I shall think of you all tomorrow!

Ever yours affectionately,
J. B. D.

To an Invalid, on Keeping Lent

St. Oswald's Vicarage,
Durham
March 10, 1870

My Dear____,

I am sorry to hear that you are out of health, but if you have any sort of constitutional delicacy of chest, or lungs, I do not wonder at your finding this long continuation of cold weather, very trying. Of course, if you are under doctor's orders, you must not abstain from flesh-meat or other nutritious things, which are necessary for you during Lent. Still I think you may even yet do a little in the way of fasting, by abstaining, as far as possible, from delicacies, and trying to practise some little act of self-denial, at each meal—confining your dinner to one course, sometimes giving up butter at breakfast and tea, and sometimes sugar—if you can get milk, and it suits you, substituting it for wine or beer; but these are mere hints I throw out. You will act upon them as far as circumstances permit, and you see your way. I merely wish you to keep up the feeling of *sympathy* with our Blessed Lord in His long fast, and so to obtain that part of the blessing which flows from a sincere endeavour to imitate Him in that particular.

But of course *fasting* is a very comprehensive word, and is used by our Lord to designate mastery over the *flesh* in all particulars. Our nature is three-fold—Body, Soul, and Spirit. In each of these there is a root of sin. Our Lord, in His Sermon on the Mount, teaches us to subdue these three evil roots or tendencies, viz. by "*Fasting*," "*Almsgiving*," and "*Prayer*."

1st. When thou *fastest*. Here is the subjugation of the *Body*.

2nd. "Thou, when thou givest Alms." Here is subjugation of the longing covetous soul, which will yearn for, and desire, the world, its allurements and riches and distinctions.

3rd. "Thou, when thou *prayest*." Here is a humbling and subduing of the proud, rebellious Spirit.

Each of these words you see is very comprehensive and embraces a large sphere of duty. Fasting, chiefly, has reference to our duty to *self-Almsgiving*, our duty to our neighbour—*Prayer*, our duty to *God*. And our Lord, by His three-fold victory during the dread forty days, not only over the *Flesh*, but also over the *World* which strove to allure His Soul, and over the *Devil*, who sought to stimulate His Spirit to pride and self-consciousness—teaches us what our three great aims in Lent should be—not only (1st) to subdue the *flesh*, by self-denial for His Sake, in any way in which His Good Providence may point out; but also (2nd) to subdue worldliness and covetousness in us, by detaching ourselves more from this world, in all its forms, by acts of kindness and unselfishness; and 3rdly to subdue our Spirit by increased devotion and by humbling ourselves before God in prayer. So, while you exercise self-denial, try at the same time to practise more charity in the full sense of the word, and also more *devotion*: so as to humble your Spirit, and detach your affections more from the world, while you subdue your flesh. If self-denial is practised by itself, without increased charity, and devotion, it will soon degenerate into mere formalism, and give birth to peevishness and irritability or pride and self-complacency. So that while you are more strict with yourself, be very sure to try to be more kind to others, and more devout and humbled before God.

Let me recommend you two little tasks for this Lent. Commit to memory—

1st, The brief description of charity contained in I Cor. xiii., 4–7, praying and meditating on it, and examining yourself by it; and

2nd, The seven Penitential Psalms. You will probably not be able to enter at once into the full meaning of them, or experimentally realise these deep and strong penitential utterances. Still I think you will find it useful to commit them to memory and to use them devotionally, asking God to enlighten you as to their meaning and to help you in the personal application of them. As they have been the penitential utterances of the whole Church of God in Jewish as well as Christian times—yes, and of the Great Head of the Church Himself, we are sure that their solemn words must in some deep and real way be suitable to ourselves also—and that we shall do well to ponder them, again and again, by night and by day—at all times, so as to make them our own and enter more fully into their spirit.

Our Lord's prompt and effectual use of the written word in His Temptation shows us how needful it is to have the mind and memory stored with its sacred utterances.

And now—may God give you a fruitful and happy Lent. Especially pray that you may be helped in reference to your conduct towards your dear and afflicted Mother. Think little of self and much of God. And now goodbye and God bless you.

Believe me
Ever yours affectionately,
John B. Dykes

On Temper

St. Oswald's Vicarage,
Durham
Nov. 10, 1870

My Dear____,

I am really much grieved to hear the accounts you give me of your recent outbursts of temper. But if this is a form of temptation to which you have in former times given way, you must not be surprised if the Devil plies you with it, when perhaps you least expect it. At present, if you have not already done so, seek the first opportunity of expressing your regret to____for your hastiness and ask her to forgive it and do the same also with your own sister. Don't be ashamed to acknowledge yourself in the wrong to your sister. If you were not ashamed to do the wrong, you must not be ashamed to confess it. Then having made such reparation as you can in the way of asking forgiveness—of those who were the immediate objects of your temper—and, of course, having also humbly sought forgiveness of God—put the sin away, note it down against your next Confession. But do not let it meanwhile keep you from Holy Communion. Make your next Communion bear a special reference to this fall, recalling the circumstances once again. At God's Altar, renewing your prayer for pardon, and making fresh resolutions against this sin. Do not doubt that God will forgive you; and His forgiveness will be formally ratified and confirmed in your next special Absolution.

Also try to get good out of this lapse. Let it make you more humble, and also more vigilant. Watch the first rising of ill temper, dread it more, hate it more, pray against it more earnestly.

Thank God more fervently for His great mercy in not allowing you to be overcome in past times by this sin, and to be led into any dreadful crime by it, and for having given you grace to get a considerable mastery over it. Surely this is an earnest and pledge that He intends you to gain a complete victory over it.

Let what He *has* done encourage you for the future, and seek to be more loving and gentle and yielding.

I think perhaps this time you had better wait quietly until your regular time of Confession comes round. It is sometimes more sobering, and in the end more healing to the soul, to have to wait awhile for the absolute certainty of forgiveness, than have all cause for anxiety at once removed. Still do not for a moment doubt God's forgiving Mercy.

May God bless you and keep you. Believe me

Yours most sincerely in our Blessed Lord,
John B. Dykes

On Carelessness in Prayer

The Vicarage, Hebden Bridge
Near Manchester
June 14, 1871

My Dear____,

Your note only reached me last night, just as I was going down to an E.C.U. meeting, so I had no time to answer it before post. Do not lose heart because you find temptations coming thick upon you. All the more cause why you should not relax your struggles. Beware of the first beginnings of irregularity, or carelessness; beware of curtailing prayer, or self-examination—force yourself to pray and try to secure the early morning for it.

The Devil almost always begins with this: making us careless in prayer. He takes care that we do not fortify ourselves against his assaults, and do not definitely invoke and cherish the indwelling Presence of the Holy Ghost, and then he comes upon us, and finds us unable to resist him.

Never relax your vigilance. Never think you can do without earnest prayer. You may at times be in heaviness through many temptations—but struggle on. You will overcome at last.

Believe me yours very sincerely in our Blessed Lord,
John B. Dykes

On a Rule of Life

St. Oswald's Vicarage, Durham
Nov. 24, 1873

My Dear____,

Since the reception of your letter, I have had to pay a visit to London, and the interruptions in my work, caused thereby, have thrown me back in my correspondence.

I trust your Confirmation has passed off satisfactorily. I very much liked the preparation you were making for the day itself, and am thankful to learn that ___is throwing himself so well into the work. May God crown it all with His Blessing. But it will be a grievous thing, my dear child, if you allow your work for God to be a means of drawing you *from* God. To bring about this is one of the favourite artifices of Satan.

If you let self come into it so much that you are apt to become jealous or impatient at the interference of others, or if you allow the work itself so to engross you, and occupy your time, that you have neither heart nor leisure for your devotional exercises, you may be sure you are getting wrong, and that "the things that should have been for your health, are become an occasion of falling." You may give *all* your goods, all your energies and thoughts and time to help God's "poor" and ignorant—and yet if you lose "Charity" thereby, if you allow envious or angry feelings to arise towards any sister in Christ, or if you so far lose the warmth of your affection for Him, that your Communion with Him becomes irregular, cold, and unreal—then be sure your work is becoming full of danger.

It is a most subtle form of Idolatry, when work is loved and worshipped for its own sake.

You have no business whatever to undertake more work, of any kind, than you can engage in consistently with the full discharge of your devotional obligations to our Blessed Lord.

If you are driven to go to bed late, *i.e.* too late for your health and calmness of mind, to get up late, so that your prayers have to be tossed slovenly about into any place, said after breakfast, or said with weariness and inattention—then you are doing more than God wishes you to do, or than is good for your soul's health.

You *must* live by *rule*, you must make a rule of life for yourself, *and keep it*. Modify it, week by week, as you like; only when made keep to it. It does not do to be living by impulse and at random.

Christ's soldiers, and servants, and fellow-workers, must be under discipline, they must *feel* the pressure of His "Gentle yoke and light burden."

You will work with tenfold success and blessing, if you will undertake less (it may be), but do what you undertake more devotionally and calmly and lovingly, and thankfully and recollectedly, and in a more orderly and punctual manner. You should aim, as a matter of religious obligation, to acquire a gentle, tranquil, self-controlled *outward* deportment. All rudeness and impetuosity of demeanour, you should avoid as un-Christlike and *sinful*.

It is no excuse to say that your work makes you excitable; if it does your work itself is wrong. Your only safeguard is to look to Jesus habitually in your work—to take your orders, as it were direct from Him, to combine the Mary with the Martha, to do all your work with the simple view of pleasing, not yourself, but Him, with His Peace resting in your bosom. May that Peace which passeth all understanding ever remain with you.

Believe me,
Affectionately yours in Him,
J. B. Dykes

On Temptation

My Dear____,

The effect of the Temptation to which you have been lately subject, should be to deepen humility and thankfulness—to show you how weak you are in yourself, and how much you owe to God's restraining grace. How frequently such assaults prove the truth of St. Paul's words, "Let him that thinketh he standeth take heed lest he fall," and show us the Divine tenderness and wisdom of our Lord's reiterated exhortation to watchfulness.

The advice given by Goulburn to which you refer, is, I believe, sound and good. Temptations of this character have a peculiarity of their own, that they must not be parleyed with, or even deliberately resisted, but fled from. If assailed by such thoughts during prayer or meditation (says one of our great spiritual writers) do not even turn from your prayer to repel them, but go on as if they did not belong to you; pursue your prayer with all possible intensity. However, the other method that you have found useful, must always be a safe and blessed one,—to tell your difficulty in plain unvarnished words to your Loving Lord Who says "Come unto Me all ye that travail and are heavy laden" (with the burden of temptation)—" and I will give you rest." If your temptation (should it assail you again) has this result, to draw you to Jesus, it will just frustrate the end for which the Devil sent it—to draw you *from Him*. He will have over-reached himself and will let alone a mode of assault which has issues so different from what he hoped and expected.

You ask if it is wrong to use the fear of the shame of Confession, as a help in resisting sin? Certainly not. Such a motive is often most useful and salutary, just as a temporary and immediate check at times when higher motives might not at once have effect, and as a sort of stop-gap, until the higher motives (the Love and Fear of God etc.), have time to come into play.

This is, in fact, one of the great practical uses of confession. Fear to offend and grieve an earthly parent is a good and proper motive as far as it goes. May God help you now and ever to overcome, and may all good Whitsuntide blessings rest upon you.

Yours in our Blessed Lord,
John B. Dykes

On the Value of Obedience in the Spiritual Life

My Dear____,

I received this morning the enclosed note from Sister ___ in reference to yourself, in which you see she consents to receive you for a time as a visitor.

This, I think, is the most satisfactory arrangement that can at present be made. I see by your kind letter which arrived here this evening, that you do not altogether relish the idea of entering as a visitor. But it seems obvious that you can only be received, at present, in that capacity; therefore settle it in your mind that it is best it should be so—and be very thankful to God for providing so satisfactorily for your immediate needs, spiritual and temporal. You must check that repining spirit to which you are allowing yourself, far too much, to give way. You *must*, for it is finding fault with God . . . it is a virtual telling Him that He does not know what is best for you, that He is either unwise or unloving, or both, and thus it cannot fail to be very displeasing to Him.

I fear by the tone of Sister ___'s thoroughly good Christian note to you, that you have been representing yourself to her rather *too much* in the light of a martyr.

Now, my dear child, you must let me be very honest with you. You must remember that such a representation of your present state, is only *half* true. There are two sides to the picture. I have myself tried to see *both* sides, and after seriously and prayerfully endeavouring to weigh what you, on the one hand, have told ___, and on the other hand have told me, I cannot feel otherwise than morally convinced, that you have *not* been a loving dutiful daughter, that you have failed very seriously in your observance of the letter and spirit of the 5th Commandment, and also of the New Commandment, as applied to those of your own kindred and household.

Now God has seen, and noticed this, and *because* He loves you, *because* He sees in you yearnings after a better love and obedience to Himself—He wishes gently to correct this deep fundamental fault of your life.

He sees that your Love, as yet, is irregular, undisciplined, and has too much of self about it. So He wishes to draw you out of self, and creature love, to the Love of Himself; and then He wishes you to love the creature *in* Himself and for Himself, and according to the rules of His most Holy Fear and Love. Now do accept all God's loving discipline. Accept it as a penance—if you will—and yet as a penance given by the very wisest and tenderest of all Directors; and do not tell to others more than is absolutely necessary about your home troubles.

There is something sweet and soothing in eliciting human sympathy by an enumeration of one's own grievances; but this is dangerous, it helps to foster self-love, and to kill humility.

Humble yourself under the Mighty Hand of God, that *He* may exalt you in due time. It is plain to see that there have been faults on both sides. The only way for ultimate reconciliation is for all to forgive and forget.

What God has in store for you ultimately we none of us know. "Man proposes—God disposes." Leave yourself placidly and trustfully in His Hands; look for His "kindly light" to lead you on step by step. Don't care or wish to look beyond the present step. Day by Day seek His daily Guidance and daily Bread. You will find His clear, soft Light, much better than your own fitful sparks. He will bring you to Himself, where alone you will find true Peace. "The heart is restless," says St. Augustine, "till it rests in Thee."

Believe me
Ever yours most affectionately in Christ,
John B. Dykes

P.S. I fully believe that our friends departed in Christ do continue to take a deep interest in our welfare and aid us by their prayers. If you want a verse on which to meditate, I will suggest avery short and very familiar one—the 5th Petition of the Lord's Prayer. "Forgive us," etc.

On Keeping Lent

Sexagesima Sunday, 1871

Of course, you would prefer to be at St. ___ during Lent, to being with your old friends; but perhaps that *may be* one reason why God prefers that you should go elsewhere.

He is just as able to give you all things needful for body and soul, in one place, as in the other.

Our Lord spent His Lent in the Wilderness, apart from *all* means of Grace, but the Angels came and ministered unto Him. If you follow His steps in lowliness, meekness, and obedience—

> Round *you* too shall Angels shine
> Such as ministered to Him.

About the future I cannot speak. "Sufficient unto the day is the evil thereof." "One step enough for" you.

Submission to God's Will

Sep. 1, 1871

You have yet to learn, my dear ____, the meaning of your daily prayer, "THY Will be done," You say it with your lips constantly, but you do not *mean* it. Your real prayer is, "*My* will be done. I wish, dear Lord, to come back to ___, therefore grant me *my* will, whether it be *Thine* or not." But this will never do. You are losing Grace, throwing away Peace and Comfort and grieving God's Holy Spirit by so doing. You see you have already made the attempt, coming back before it was God's time for you to come. And no permanent good has resulted from it—you have had to go away again, and probably to render more distant the time of your permitted return.

Therefore, do not try any more to *tease* God on this point. God says to you as He did to Moses, "Speak no more to Me of this matter." He knows without your telling Him of your secret wish to return to ___, therefore leave it to Him to bring about *when* and how He thinks best.

He has a work to do in you. He has lessons to teach you, which at present can best be carried on away from ___. He sees certain radical failings of character, which He knows are keeping you back from progress and peace and real holiness, and which He wants gently to correct and remove—if only you will let Him have His own way with you.

Now be a good child, and do not perversely thwart Him or mar His work.

Durham
Feast of St. Michael and All Angels

Your kind note of last night made me feel very thankful. May God in mercy help you to carry into practice the suggestion which His Holy Spirit has put into you. Only follow the leadings of God's Will and try to crush and trample on your own lower and rebellious will (as St. Michael trampled on the Dragon) and you shall have comfort and Peace.

I enclose the Hymn for which you ask.

On Fasting Communion

St. Oswald's Vicarage, Durham
May 8, 1873

My Dear Miss____,

Thank you for your letter. To enter into the whole "*Vexata quaestio*" of Fasting Communion, I have neither time nor inclination now. Your own mind seems clear on the point—therefore act up to your own convictions. But do not seek eagerly to press your own views on the consciences of others.

What the rule of the Early Church was, and what the ordinary rule of Christendom at the present day is, everyone knows. But there is this great fact before us:—The English church to which we immediately owe our allegiance, and which stands to us in the place of the Catholic Church—our Spiritual Mother—she, under the wise and over-ruling Providence of God, has not thought fit to press this matter upon her children. She has nowhere reaffirmed the old law.

Neither her Synods nor Bishops have ever attempted to enforce it. So that the law remains among us—not as an active energetic law, the slightest breach of which requires special dispensation; but as a passive Law, a Law most useful to *guide* consciences, but not rigorously to *bind* them.

You may see this point (as to the necessity of Fasting Communion) very clearly for your own guidance. Well: be it so. But you have no right to seek to put a yoke on the necks of others, and to fetter their consciences. I know well that some of our modern leaders of the younger generation express themselves very stiffly and strongly on this question—write merrily about "the cup of tea heresy," and speak of even the swallow of a drop of water before Communion as a mortal sin, etc.

It must be remembered, however, that older spiritual guides, certainly not their inferiors, in wisdom, learning, devotion, and true Catholic instinct (I may mention such names as Pusey, Keble, Neale, Carter, etc.) have arrived at altogether different conclusions, as to the positive binding nature of the antient canons on us in the English Church in the present day. Dr. Bright very truly reminds us that "The Antient Church *never* celebrated on Sunday, in the middle of the day, as the Modern Church does. The sayings therefore of the Fathers on Fasting Communion were sayings of men before whom the question of persons who have no access to early Communion, and cannot go through a long Sunday forenoon service, without having broken their fast—had not been brought.

In St. Chrysostom's time it was considered quite as irregular and wrong to administer or receive Baptism unfasting, as to administer or receive Holy Communion. This antient mark of Reverence to the earlier Sacrament has entirely died out now. Our Prayer Book very truly says, "It is not necessary that traditions and ceremonies be in all places one and utterly alike, for, at all times, they have been divers, and may be changed, according to the diversities of countries, times, and men's manners; so that nothing be ordained against God's Word."

...

How do you think our Blessed Lord Himself would legislate on these points? Is there any single thing in His whole teaching to lead one to imagine that He Himself would fence His Mysteries round with hard technical rules of discipline, such as those on which some among us are trying to re-impose?

Do you think He Himself would have been agitated and excited the other morning at the cup of tea, as you were? Doubtless it was out of a feeling for His Honour that you were thus disturbed. Still, I think, "you disquieted yourself in vain."

In a question of this kind on which our Spiritual Mother is silent, and has refrained from laying down any positive law, and on which our own guides are by no means agreed, it does not become any of us to dogmatise too positively. An earnest desire to conform our own practice to that of the whole Catholic Church, wherever ascertainable, will be sufficient to influence our own individual conduct! But with regard to others, we make seek gently to influence them so far as we legitimately can: but we must not seek to force our own convictions on them, or to compel them to see with our eyes. May God bless you and guide you.

Ever yours affectionately in our Blessed Lord,
John B. Dykes

Spiritual and Sacramental Communion

St. Oswald's Vicarage, Durham
April 25, 1870

My Dear____,

You have done quite right in consulting Mr. P. if you felt any conscientious scruple in taking food before a late Communion.

When you mentioned the circumstances to me, I could only give you my own opinion, and give utterance to the convictions which I confess I still strongly hold.

I cannot but think it must be detrimental to the spiritual health of any soul to go on so long as you appear to have been doing without actual participation in that which our Lord declares to be our very Meat and Drink, and indispensable to our vitality and growth in Grace (except indeed you were absolutely out of reach of this Holy Sacrament).

I confess I cannot look upon an act of "Spiritual Communion" in any way as a substitute for the Real Gift, which our Blessed Lord has ordained to give in one way only, viz.: through actual Sacramental participation.

Nor can I look upon the theory of the equivalence of "Spiritual" and Sacramental Communion, but as a dangerous, though specious, artifice of the Enemy of Souls, under colour of reverence and devotion, to keep us from real living and abiding fellowship with the true Source of our Life, and from that Holy Mystery in which our life is ever and anon renewed and reinforced by the Communication of His Own. Every Christian certainly must wish to receive the Holy Communion before all other food in the day.

But if it comes to be a question, whether to forego Sacramental Communion with Christ, or to take such little food beforehand as is *needful* for the sustenance of the body, whether in fact to give the precedence to a positive command of Christ Himself, or to an Ecclesiastical regulation—however venerable—I cannot but think we must be compelled to act on the principle embodied in the Apostle's words, "We must obey God rather than man." But I not the less respect and feel your difficulty. Wishing you all good Easter Blessings, Believe me

Ever yours most sincerely in Christ,
John B. Dykes

The Fruits of the Spirit

S. Oswald's, Durham
May 26, 1870

My Dear Miss____,

I am sorry you did not call when in Durham. I should have been glad to have talked over with you the subject referred to in your note.

In reference to the proposition that you should go for a while, and undertake the teaching of your sister's children, I almost think, by the way in which you yourself represent the reasons for and against, that you realize that the *higher*, and therefore the wisest and best course of the two to adopt, is to undertake the responsibility. The reasons why you should *not*, merely centre in yourself and your own need; the reasons why you *should*, relate to others as well as yourself, and involve the good of the children.

I think you might very well, for a time, and as you have no special engagement to prevent you, engage in this work. If you recognise God's Voice in it and set about it with the simple wish to carry out His Will, in reference to yourself and your little charge, you will find it full of blessing to yourself and to them.

If you know beforehand that it is a position calculated to try you in the matter of *irritability* and *contempt*, be doubly watchful in these particulars; and thank God for giving you an opportunity of disciplining yourself, and mastering certain tendencies, which you know to be wrong.

With regard to Gal. v. 22, 23, I advise you, three times a week, for the next month, to *say* the passage, recounting the fruits of the Spirit, on your knees before God: and each time, to dwell for a few minutes on *one* of the fruits, taking them in order, trying also to keep *that* particular grace specially in your mind till the next meditation—and also trying to *practise* it. Thus you will go over the nine in three weeks. The fourth week, you might take three at each meditation. I merely wish you to impress this passage firmly upon your mind, at this particular time, when we are thinking of our Lord's Ascension, and the consequent Mission of the Spirit.

1. You see how, first of all, comes Love—the first and best and most difficult of all graces: and of which all the rest of the nine graces mentioned are manifestations under different conditions.

Love is *self-giving*. Self-sacrifice in its very essence. Selfishness its greatest enemy.

2. Then comes *joy*—the inevitable result of self-giving:—giving joy and therefore joyful.

3. Then *peace*. Outward brightness and joy, deepening into calm, inward peace. This is the first triplet. Then we have Love under trial from coldness and misunderstanding. So here comes—

4. *Long-suffering*. Love gently and bravely, enduring contradiction. Then—

5. *Gentleness*. This is the central word of the whole group. It expresses the outward deportment of the Christian. The word signifies suavity, urbanity, gentle courtesy, approachableness. So that Love's trials do not make it fretful, but kind and gentle and affable.

6. And next comes *goodness*: indicating that this gentleness is not the result of mere weakness of character, but of deep, solid goodness. And this ends the second triplet.

Lastly we have Love under the severe testings which come through *God*, through *man*, and through *self*.

7. God may seem to hide His Face—but love can never lose confidence in Him, even under the most afflictive Dispensation. "Though He slay me, yet will I trust in Him." Hence we have, as a next fruit of the Spirit, *Faith* in God.

8. *Man* may oppose himself, thwart and injure us. But love never loses *meekness* towards those that oppose themselves. It is ever, like the Great Example, "humble and *meek*," yielding, not fighting, vanquishing by submitting.

9. And lastly, *self*. The unruly flesh may oppose itself. Love keeps the body under, and brings it into subjection. This *temperance*, which is the last fruit of the Spirit enumerated, signifies entire self-control, perfect self-mastery, a grace perhaps acquired the last and hardest of all.

Now, test yourself in all these one by one: and *try* and pray to acquire them.

I am very glad you have made the resolution in reference to the *unloving feeling* which you were allowing to lodge and do mischief in your bosom. God help you to keep it.

This letter has had to be written amid many engagements, and rather against time. I hope it is legible, and that you will excuse any want of clearness.

May God evermore bless and keep you.

Believe me
Yours most sincerely in the Lord,
John B. Dykes

On Nursing, and on Dealing with Dissenters

St. Oswald's Vicarage, Durham
Sep. 1, 1870

My Dear Miss C____,

Your first letter did not reach me till some days after it was written. I was in South Wales when you wrote it: but was hastily summoned home, in consequence of the scarlet fever having broken amongst my dear children. Two of them caught the fever in Durham. The rest were sent off to Leeds to escape infection, but hardly had the youngest of them (a little boy of about five) got out of the railway carriage, then he was seized and is now laid up in Leeds.

So the others had to be sent back again to Durham, and are now in lodgings. This you may be sure makes us very anxious, especially as the fever (in the case of one especially) has been of a most malignant type. The doctor considered her case all but hopeless; but through God's great mercy she seems to have got over the crisis and to be progressing favourably: although another who had had the fever less severely—after getting well over the crisis—has fallen back and is now in a most critical state.

May I trust that you will kindly remember us in your prayers?

I am so glad to hear that you like your present work. It is one of great interest and importance. For it is impossible to tell what amount of indirect influence for good a kindly sympathising and religious-minded nurse may have.

In visiting the sick, you will find hymns very useful. Often an invalid is better reached by a hymn than by any other means.

Under the circumstances you mention, I should certainly not shrink from your promise of occasionally relieving the poor woman in her attendance on her sister, and thus allowing her to go to a place of worship, even if it is a Methodist Chapel. Times of trouble are not times for controversy, and then people require to be very gently and tenderly dealt with. Probably all the religion, all the love for Christ they have, has come to them through Methodist channels. They are quite right in standing up for, and not hastily repudiating a system from which they have received real benefit; and to which they owe a debt of real gratitude . . .

Had the Church done her duty, there would have been no dissent.

These dissenting agencies have in many places been the only means of keeping the people from absolute heathenism—and we owe a debt of gratitude to God that by such instrumentalities, however imperfect in themselves, He has kept, and does keep, so many in His Fear and Love, and from falling from Him.

I don't wonder at the Wesleyans loving and refusing to give up their class meetings, and spiritual Conferences, when they can get nothing of the kind in the Church of England. So I would rather try (at least, until you can command your friend's perfect confidence) to find out how many points of agreement you have, than to cause them to distrust you, by dwelling on matters in which you do not agree. In learning wound-dressing, and going through your necessary experiences, I would advise you as much as possible to associate them in your own mind with the wounds of the soul—of which they are God's own picture. There are numerous passages in the Psalms which speak of sins under this image. "My wounds stink and are corrupt through my foolishness." "There is no whole part in my body." And also of course let them remind you of those Adorable and Blessed Wounds whereby the sores and corruption of our souls and bodies are cleansed.

In trying to form the *habit* of associating your interesting work with its counterpart in the Spiritual Sphere, you will find it to have a softening and hallowing effect upon you—and you will be perpetually hearing God's wonderful sermons.

And now, with kind regards and prayers that God's blessing may rest upon you and your work,

Believe me,
Yours most sincerely in our Blessed Lord,
John B. Dykes

Desire for the Religious Life

St. Oswald's, Durham
Nov. 8, 1870

My Dear____,

Notwithstanding what you say in your note, I still think you are doing rightly in reverently cherishing (though in perfect subordination to the Will of God) the idea of entering the "Religious Life." Do not long for it, or be in a hurry for it, lest you should out-run the slow, gentle march of God's Will. But the wish may at least prove a stimulus to you, and furnish you with a fresh and definite object for subduing in yourself any habits or tendencies which you feel to be inconsistent with a life of that character.

Thank God for clearly showing you the existence in you of those latent failures to which you allude, which recent circumstances have had the effect of bringing to light.

It is a great mercy to be able to see a failing sharply and definitely.

The next thing is to take all pains slowly, patiently, prayerfully, determinedly, to overcome it.

Try to picture to yourself our Lord in your position. How would He take the little slights? (if they *are* slights) which I have no doubt they are *not*.

Try to forget *self*: it will make you so much more happy and peaceful and useful. The Cathedral clock warns me that I must go. I shall be very thankful to have a line from you after the Retreat.

May God ever bless and keep you,
Yours most sincerely in Christ,
John B. Dykes

We are all out of the Vicarage now, and are in lodgings, while the house is purified, papers, etc.

On Frequent Confession

St. Oswald's Vic., Durham
Jan. 9, 1871

My Dear____,

...

I do think, however, that in your case too frequent Confession is not desirable.

If there is no honest striving to overcome sin, to act out our Confession, and show God by our *deeds* that our acknowledgments of guilt and unfaithfulness were genuine, frequent Sacramental Absolution may become simply injurious to the soul.

Mr. Carter says that Confession "may be an occasion of scrupulosity of self-consciousness, or perplexity, and is a hindrance to Grace. It may be used merely for temporary relief, without any purpose or endeavour after a higher life, and so become even an encouragement to sin, or at least an alleviation of the sense of fear and self reproach attending it, and thus a means of self-deception."[1]

Far better have the soul braced up to carefulness and watchfulness, by a sense of fear and uneasiness, than lulled into a false and nerveless security.

A mere feeling of disquiet, then, is not by any means a proof that God means you to try and remove it by resorting at once to Confession, but that He is looking for some practical results in you, some faithful exercise of the powers of self-mastery which you possess; some honest conscious response to the expressed Will; some co-operation with the Grace, which, as yet, He sees not, and the absence of which is preventing the influx of His Love, and Peace.

Of course, for instance, if you are cherishing any feelings of bitterness or want of Charity against ___, God's Love in you will be chilled. Except we Love, we cannot experience His Love.

At these times, of course, careful introspection is quite necessary. Also, you should daily go through an act of honest self-examination. But, apart from this necessary devotional self-scrutiny, the less you think about yourself the better. Do not dwell on fancies or feelings,—they vary infinitely with every change of bodily health, or sometimes even of weather.

I advise you therefore to think and speak and write about yourself as little as possible (except when really necessary) and to give your thoughts and your energies to your work. Keep yourself well employed, with a certain amount of healthful light reading and society, and never mope and brood. Have your time so well filled up that you have no leisure to think much about yourself. Now pray forgive what you will think an unsympathetic

---

1. So that if Confession is used in any way as a substitute for stern self-discipline, and is not accompanied with a strict and persevering endeavour to master the faults which are known and acknowledged and for which God's forgiveness is sought, it may prove most dangerous to the soul.

letter, and with all good wishes for the new year, believe me ever, my dear friend, yours most sincerely in our Blessed Lord,

John B. Dykes

Interruptions in Work

St. Oswald's Vic., Durham
Jan. 23, 1871

My Dear____,

. . . Your greater longing for Confession is, I trust, a mark of God's Grace working in you. Only take care that it is accompanied with honest and sustained endeavour on your part to free yourself from the love and dominion of those sins, from which you seek Absolution. The caution I gave you last time I wrote is needful to be borne in mind, that we must not rush to Confession simply to free ourselves from a feeling of restlessness.

As the Sacred Leaven works, it will cause inward disturbance.

You speak of the constant interruptions of your life. Well, Who sends these interruptions? It surely can be none other than He, without Whom not a sparrow falls to the ground, and Who, by the secret ordering of His Providence, permits you to be so tried. You *must*, my dear sister, try to forget the creature, and to see the Wise, All-Loving Creator, acting through the creature.

There is a secret meaning in every interruption you have, and although your day may appear broken and disjointed and objectless, yet if you have simply tried to go through each passing phase of it, serenely, and dutifully, as in the presence of God, it will leave its own abiding Blessing behind.

About your Confraternity petition—I am not quite sure. Might it not assume this form—"A Child—Grace to know and accept her Lord's Will"?

When God sees it good for you to embrace a Sister's life, He will make your way plain. It is He perhaps Who is secretly moving your Mother to withhold her consent. Balaam only sees the creature stopping his way. It is not until his eyes are opened, that he sees the mysterious Form in the background, influencing the creature. I am rejoiced to hear your work grows so steadily.

Ever yours sincerely in our Blessed Lord,
John B. Dykes

On Shrinking from the Religious Life

St. Oswald's, Durham
Palm Sunday, 1871

My Dear____,

I am very sorry to have been quite unable to answer your letter hitherto. I have been so busy with necessary Parochial duties (partly arising out of our large Confirmation) that I am ashamed to think how many letters are still remaining unanswered.

I cannot quite understand your now seeming to draw back, when God seems so unexpectedly to have placed the object of your long wishes, within your reach.

Is there not something of waywardness about this, longing anxiously after something, so long as you think you cannot obtain it—and then as soon as you find you can, feeling doubtful whether or not to reject it?

Still at the same time, I do not altogether wonder at your hesitation. It *is* a very important step—and you do well to balance all considerations for, and against; but I candidly tell you that, under the circumstances, it appears to me that you should *close in with* the mother's offer, and at least enter the sisterhood as a *Probationer*.

Of course, you cannot become a confirmed sister for a considerable time—you will then have had opportunities for testing your powers; and also seeing what course circumstances which might affect you, are taking.

I shall hope to see you (please God) on Wednesday week; but my feeling is, that you should not relinquish your long cherished wish for the Religious life, and that "having put your hand to the plough, you should not look back." Of course there will be difficulties, but earnest Faith "removes mountains." Go forth in the strength of the Cross, and the strength of the Crucified shall be *yours*. In haste,

Yours ever sincerely in our dear Lord,
John B. Dykes

On Cherishing Times of Brightness

St. Oswald's Vic., Durham
Sep. 1, 1871

My Dear___,

I return your Retreat Resolutions. May God help you so to keep them as best to further your growth in holiness. The plan of going through portions of your Retreat meditations on the two days which are left free in your Resolutions would I should think be a good one. Take care and devoutly cherish the remembrance of the Meditation on the "Prodigal Son"—in which God vouchsafed you a special realization of His Love in Redemption. These bright moments—these sensible Inspirations or Revelations, do not come frequently—God gives them at times, and the recollection of them should be reverently cherished, to cheer us in seasons of dryness and deadness, or temptation.

The three on the Mount of Transfiguration did not know the special and immediate purpose (in reference to themselves)—*why* the wondrous Vision was granted. The dread time for which it was meant to prepare them—the time of our Lord's Agony—came on, and they missed and forgot the lessons which "the Holy Mount" had been mercifully designed to teach them.

Seasons of illumination often precede seasons of gloom. There is an alternation of moods and feelings in the Spiritual Life (and this quite consistent with general *progress*), not wholly unlike the alternations of times and seasons—darkness and light, evening and morning, winter and summer—in the natural world.

Neither in Nature or in Grace are we to expect that the sun is always sensibly to shine.

I did not forget you on your birthday. To-day is the "Birthday into Eternity" of my darling little child "Mabel Hey," who fell asleep in Jesus this day last year. May we all meet her ere long in that Home of Rest and Peace to which I am sure she has gone.

Believe me
Ever yours most truly in our Blessed Lord,
John B. Dykes

Self-Imposed Penances

St. Oswald's, Durham
Jan. 12, 1872

...

I think little acts of self-imposed penance—discreetly chosen—may often be very useful. They should generally be of the same *kind* as the sin they are meant to correct.

You speak of your temper "often showing itself in saying little *hard* things—often, in an offended *cold* manner; and with a want of brightness." Well now, for the "little *hard* things" say something *soft* and tender; for the "offended *cold* manner," force yourself to show a kind, *warm* manner; for "the want of brightness" exhibit a little extra brightness, so as to make what reparation you can, in kind, for the special fault. And never be above asking pardon for any hard, or sharp saying.

I envy you having time to read aloud quietly *The Life of St. Francis*. It will be a mutual benefit to yourself and your sister.

May God bless and guide you.
Yours affectionately in Our Blessed Lord,
John B. Dykes

Reserve in Teaching

St. Oswald's, Durham
May 11, 1872

My Dear____,

Your last letter found me at Weybridge. I had to go up to London every day and was very busy.

I am glad you have not given up your class. It is a mistake to suppose we must always teach *all* we know, or else are unfaithful. Our Blessed Lord never did so. He always "spake the Word, as they were able to hear it." He always spake the Truth, but not the whole Truth. All religious teachers must exercise reserve in the communication of Truth. "*Pearls*" are not to be cast before "*swine*." High Sacramental Mysteries must not be thrust upon those who barely know the rudiments of the Faith. Moreover, we are told to be "wise as serpents" and "harmless as doves." We must let our teaching be modified by the circumstances under which we teach . . . We must not exaggerate our differences with other good Christians, or get into the habit of fancying ourselves more "Catholic" than all the Churchmen and Churchwomen around us. Probably many of them are in God's sight a thousand-fold better "Catholics" than ourselves. Your little rules are very simple and nice. God bless and prosper you in your work.

Believe me,
Yours ever sincerely in our Blessed Lord,
John B. Dykes

Love in Trials

St. Oswald's, Durham
Jan. 15, 1873

Just a line to say that I have sent off your intercession and to express my sorrow at the last trouble that has befallen you.

It is in mercy that God has allowed this last trial to come upon you while you are away from the ordinary distractions of life, and able to give more time to meditation and prayer.

How did Hezekiah meet his sorrow? He took the letter containing the fatal intelligence, and spread it out before the Lord. And God gave him a happy issue out of all his troubles.

But he was humble and submissive before God—not "rebellious." Do not give way to any rebellious or desponding feelings; you have something else to do. You are called upon to the practical exercise of Faith, Hope, and Love. *Faith* in God's infinite Mercy and Power. *Hope*, that He not only can, but *will* bring good out of this seeming evil; and *Love* towards Him, and the offender—a Love which shall practically exert itself in earnest, persevering, hopeful prayers.

By "Prayer and supplications, with thanksgiving, let your requests be made known unto God," if you wish to recover, or retain His "Peace."

On the Use of Discipline

St. Oswald's Vicarage, Durham
Feb. 28, 1873

My Dear Sister,

. . .

In reference to the subject of your letter, I think I must adhere to what I have already said on the subject of the discipline. I cannot feel justified, at all events, at present, in sanctioning your regular use of it. As an occasional penance, in certain particular cases, I could not object to recommend it—but *not* as a regular and self-chosen exercise, as suggested in your letter.

You say that you long for some form of bodily suffering. Our Blessed Lord does not sanction such longing. *Suffering*, we know, is an occasion of temptation, and He teaches us to pray not to be led into temptation. Unsanctified pain is most dangerous to the soul, and self-chosen pain has not the promise of His Benediction.

A restless longing for pain, as for something food in itself, seems rather like charging the Great Refiner with not looking after, and neglecting to try you in His purifying fires.

Probably the particular kind of pain He sees you need, is not mere outward physical pain, but more keen and searching, which *He* and He alone can administer. You may endure agonies of physical pain, yea, "you may give your body to be burned," and if you are wanting in charity, may not be one whit better for it.

No: offer yourself unreservedly to Him, to do, or to suffer, just what *He* calls upon you to do, or to suffer. Do not seek to rectify His mistakes. Depend upon it, He will look after you.

Perhaps you may find the practice of *Love* in all its phases,— towards your Mother, sister, brother, and others, as wholesome discipline, and a much harder discipline too, than the occasional castigation of your body.

Perhaps you might find it useful during Lent, if you awake during the night to get up *once* and say *one* of the Penitential Psalms—with your hands stretched out in the form of the Cross. May He Who died for you, accept and direct your yearnings after greater conformity to Himself in His Passion. Believe me

Yours affectionately in Him,
John B. Dykes

On the Active and Contemplative Life

St. Oswald's, Durham
May 6, 1874

My Dear Sister,

I am sorry to have been unable to answer your letter before.

In reference to the question you have asked me, concerning your choice of an active or contemplative life, I feel that, so far as I can see at present, I *dare* not take upon me the responsibility to advise your seeking the latter.

You speak of the contemplative life being the highest. I am not sure that we are warranted in saying this. Was our dear Lord's a contemplative life only? "My Father worketh hitherto, and I work." His was a busy, active life—full of distractions, full of work, and yet full of rest, for He rested in the Will of His Father. His Rest, His Peace, His Joy, was *doing* what the Father had given Him to do, and "Finishing His Work."

Which, too, of the Apostles and New Testament Saints or worthies lived a mere contemplative life? They all *worked* and worked hard. No doubt the active life is full of danger. The work itself may very easily distract us, and make us forget Whose work it is. But I should conceive the danger of the contemplative life to be much more subtle and real. Contemplation may so easily degenerate into dreamy, morbid, self-introspection.

The *tendency* of the mere life of contemplation must be to make one rather self-centred—at least to make one forget all but God and oneself.

The active life rather takes one *out of self* and so helps one to overcome this deadly enemy of the Soul. "It is more blessed to *give* than to *receive*." It is better and higher to be a source, than a mere recipient of Blessing.

It appears to me that, so long as God gives you health and strength, and voice, and power of work, you are bound to use these faculties for the good of others, and not to bury your talent in a napkin. God shuts out many from the possibility of active work. These He calls to work of another kind, to pray and meditate and suffer and intercede. God may call *you* to this some day, but you must not anticipate this call, you must "work while it is day." When you speak of work being a *hindrance* to the spiritual life, I think that is hardly a right way of putting it. If the work is work to which we are called by God—it must be no hindrance, but the very greatest help to the spiritual life.

Everything, of course, in itself may become a hindrance to our spiritual life. You say that you find the very "offices" of Devotion in themselves a distraction. All things which God designs to be most for "our health," may become to us occasions of falling.

When, therefore, you say that the various failings, distractions, etc., of which you are conscious are *caused* by your work, you do not seem to me to go deep enough for the real cause.

If you allow the devil to make your *work* for God a source of temptation, and instead of mastering him, merely seek to relieve yourself of your labours, depend upon it he will make your *want* of *work* a more serious and dangerous source of temptation.

No, my dear child, like thousands of others, you are sighing for *rest*. But you must *"labour* if you would enter into rest." With such sin and misery and ignorance all around, God cannot spare any of His fellow-*workers*. He always keeps a staff of contemplatives. But *He* places them in that order. They do not place themselves there.

Think then less of self, and try what you can do for JESUS. You will find Him sick: visit Him—you will find Him ignorant; teach Him—you will find Him needing your aid at every turn. You must not think only of your own soul, you must not hide your light, but let it *shine out*, to the Glory of your Father in Heaven. May God teach you to know His Will, and help you resolutely to choose it!

Affectionately yours in our Blessed Lord,
John B. Dykes

Low Church Missions

Langham Hotel, London
Oct. 29, 1874

My Dear Sister,

Your note has just reached me here, whither I have been summoned to attend a meeting of the *Hymns A. and M.* Musical Committee.

I am grieved, but not surprised, at what you state about the Mission preaching. I have heard something of the kind before. But do not be too critical. Try to throw yourself into the spirit of the Mission. The special Mission teaching is not for you, but for others to whom teaching which might be appropriate for you, would be altogether hurtful.

Trust in the Love of the Holy Ghost to correct any erroneous teaching on the part of His Missioners, and to bless the Word spoken to the conversion of souls.

He speaks in "divers manners," and He speaks the Truth to us "as we are able to hear it," and He makes use of defective teaching, no less than the most orthodox teaching. Therefore I would rather urge you to suspend criticism, than prayer and sympathy. During the progress of the work, give it all the help you can, with your prayers.

Yours ever affectionately in our Blessed Lord,
John B. Dykes

On the Sacraments

S. Oswald's Vicarage, Durham
Sep. 8, 1873

I presume you have seen a notice of my present controversy with my Bishop. I send you a copy of the correspondence. It is very sad, but I cannot help it. I can only trust that God will bring good out of it. I have just received Counsel's opinion from the Attorney General, Dr. Stephens and Mr. Bowen, as to the Bishop's right to exact these pledges. They give it as their opinion that he has "no such right," and advise me to apply to the Court of Queen's Bench for a mandamus, compelling the Bishop to grant the licence. I have sent the "Opinion" to his Lordship, but he has not vouchsafed any reply.

I was much grieved to hear of poor Uncle Fred's blindness: one can only hope and pray that, as his eyes are closed to the natural light, the Celestial Light may flow inwards more abundantly; and that his last days, while his darkest, may be his brightest.

And now, my dear ___, just one word about a sentence in your letter, in which you say—"How infinitely small all our squabbles and disputes about *Sacraments* and *vestments* and *sundry other matters* appear, when any great personal trouble faces us," etc.

Now had you left out the word "Sacraments" here, I should fully have endorsed your remark. But, in the first place, is it quite reverent thus to mix up the Divine and the human—"*Sacraments*," and vestments and divers *other* matters?

And, secondly, when we consider that the Sacraments of the Church were ordained directly and expressly by our Lord Jesus Christ Himself—that they are the "Golden Pipes," the Divine Channels, whereby the streams of Life from the fountain of life flow into the Church; that the "Water and the Blood" are the great Mysteries in the Church, in which and through which the Holy Ghost testifies of Jesus, and brings and maintains us in vital Communion with Him, surely we cannot regard them as "matters of mere secondary moment."

God's Watchmen, the Ministers and Stewards of His mysteries, must be ready *earnestly* to *contend* for and jealously to guard these great Mysteries.

The whole history of the Church teaches this: that low views on the Sacraments are only one stage removed from low views of Christ Himself.

Socinus always follows in the train of Calvin. Let the whole state of Protestant Germany—let the state of Geneva—Calvin's own city—testify.

To shield the Citadel, we must defend its outworks. There is a deeper meaning (as many of us know) even in what seem our most trivial "squabbles,"—*e.g.* the present one, as to the position of the Priest at the "Holy Table"—than the world thinks of. Be thankful . . . that you are not *called upon* to fight, and pray for those who *are* called upon, that they may seek nothing but only the glory of God, and may be guided by His Holy Spirit into all Truth.

To His Sister Lucy, on the Death of Her Husband, the Rev. John Cheape

Durham
June 23, 1857

I can well imagine that you will not be much disposed for reading letters; still I cannot refrain from writing to tell you how deeply we all sympathize with your in your sad bereavement.

How little I thought, when I left Ilkley so lately, and bade your husband goodbye, that I should see him no more in this world.

God's ways are indeed mysterious, and past finding out: we can but bow our heads, lay our hands upon our mouth, and say "Father, Thy Will be done," confiding in His unerring Wisdom and unfathomable Love—*fully* persuaded that all *He* does is best, and that had it been otherwise it would not have been so well.

That you will find it hard actively to realize this at first, I can well conceive, but yet you will not the less, in your innermost soul, acknowledge it.

You will feel *sure* that he has been taken away, in Love, that it is better, (oh! how far better!)—for *him* to have been removed; that it is better even for you, better for all:—else he would have been still preserved to us.

Nay, you know that if the choice were now offered you, you would not call him back again from the Presence of his Saviour, merely to drag out for a longer term of years a weary existence in this body of frail, weak mortality. He is not lost to you, only removed, for a little time; taken before to that Everlasting Home, where you shall ere long follow him, to part no more, but to enjoy with him the Presence of your common Redeemer for ever.

Try then, amid your sorrow, to thank God for His Fatherly Goodness, and you shall find the very stroke "joyous," rather than grievous; and discover that the Angel of Death who has visited your dwelling and snatched away from you your dearest earthly friend, has been but a Messenger of Mercy, sent to sever you from a terrestrial love, that your soul might be wholly possessed with a Divine Love and that you might be folded in the Everlasting Embrace of Incarnate Love.

May the unutterable consolations of Him Whose name is the Comforter, which are mostly realized in seasons of earthly affliction, be yours, dear L., in your present bereavement: and may you have cause to thank God through Eternity, for this sharp stroke, which, loosening the cords which bind you to earth—has strengthened the ties which unite you to Heaven. God bless you!

To His Sister Lucy, on the Death of Her Little Child, Born Five Months after His Father's Death

Durham
Nov. 23, 1859

I need not tell you how surprised and shocked we were at hearing last night from F., of the death of your little boy.

Poor dear little Johnnie; with those funny twinkling eyes of his—I can hardly imagine that they are closed for ever in this world. It must indeed have been a sad blow to you; and I can assure you, you have our warmest and most affectionate sympathy, in your bereavement. It seems cold work, perhaps, offering consolation when the grief is fresh. But I am sure that you will see that there are real solid grounds for comfort. In the first place you are sure, quite sure—that the stroke has been sent in Love, and that the little fellow would not have been taken Home, had it not been for *his* good, and for *your* good, and for the good of all.

You know and feel in your inmost soul that it is *really* for the best, otherwise it would not have happened. And you feel that you have an opportunity offered you of receiving rich Grace and Blessing from God, by the thankful and entire surrender of your will to that of God—assured that He can and will, (if you only throw yourself trustfully upon His mercy) far more than compensate for the loss you have sustained.

It is a hallowing and refreshing thought that, though another tie is sundered that bound you to Earth, there is a new and powerful link uniting you to Heaven! and it cannot but be a source of *sweet*, tho' sad comfort, to reflect, as the little family group is thinned in this world—"How grows in Paradise your store."

It is impossible to help picturing to oneself the meeting in that Peaceful Shadowy Land, between the father and his little boy—who never knew each other in this world, and who will never look on each other with bodily eyes, till they see one another in the Beauty and Glory of their Resurrection Bodies. One cannot help thinking of that Mysterious Communion which their disenthralled Spirits are now enjoying, and of the earnest interest and affection with which they will be contemplating and aiding (so far as is permitted them) the two so closely connected with them—still left behind.

I am sure, dear L., you would not have either of them back, if you might—back from their Redeemer's Presence—to the miseries and temptations of this sinful world—back to the tremendous possibility of falling away and being lost for ever.

Oh, no, they are both safe now, at Rest in the Arms of Christ, where neither men nor devils, nor sins, can touch or harm them for all Eternity. No! In God's good time you shall go to them; not they come back to you.

Kiss my little brotherless Goddaughter for me. Tell her I hope and pray to God to make her a good girl, that she may go and live with little Johnnie in Heaven.

On the Death of His Father

St. Oswald's Vicarage
Jan. 11, 1864

My Very Dear Mother,

Though partially prepared for the sad intelligence contained in L.'s letter this morning, yet I confess it was a heavy shock to hear that he was *no more*, and already gone to his rest. Everlasting Peace be with him!

I need not say how deeply I sympathise with you in this irreparable loss, which God has willed that you should sustain; and yet I feel sure that you have been already too well and gently schooled by Him, not to see *Love*, and Love only, even in this His heaviest stroke. Had it pleased God to take him away in his prime, in the midst of his vigour of mind and body—one can hardly realise the terrible blow it would have been to yourself and to us all. But, little by little, and as you have been able to bear it, God has prepared you for this last issue.

He has been gently and gradually worn out . . . And now at last, when his work is done—and the evening come when he could no longer work—His Heavenly Father has tenderly taken him to his Rest. And I feel sure that you would be the very last to wish him back again to battle with all his pains and weaknesses in the weary world.

It is sweet to feel *sure* that he is safe, for ever safe; that he has entered upon an Eternity of Rest and Peace and Joy.

Nor is he lost to you, even now, he is probably far nearer to you *now*, than even when on Earth—though your eyes are holden that you cannot see him. And but a little time and you shall be re-united to part no more for ever. I hope, please God, to be with you on Wednesday. I may either walk from Arthington or come by the evening coach. If you are full at Moor Lodge, I will go to the little Inn. I presume the funeral will not take place before Thursday.

Praying that God's richest blessing may rest upon you, and the special comforts He has promised to those that mourn, be abundantly realized by you,

Believe me ever
Your most affectionate son,
John

To His Brother Arthur, Laid up at Eastbourne

St. Oswald's Vicarage, Durham
Feb 29, 1864

It seems a long time since you and I wrote to each other, but you are not the less often in my thoughts: the letters which have lately come from Eastbourne have been sent to me—and I have been much concerned to hear how ill you have been latterly. But I am sure you will feel that "all is well" with you, and that your chastisement is all sent in tender Love.

From the accounts I hear of your present bodily state, I cannot but think that your sojourn on this Earth cannot now be long; and that you should be preparing (it may be) for a very sudden summons.

Well, dear Arthur, you are sure the summons will not come before its time. He who has ordered, and is gently and wisely ordering, every minute circumstance and accident of your trial—will not fail you at the last. His Presence will be with you, His Everlasting Arms will support you. Do not allow yourself for one moment to lose confidence in Him.

Satan will try to fill you with distressing doubts and anxieties. Steadily resist him. Keep your eyes fixed upon Jesus. He has passed through pain and weakness, and weariness and desolation of Spirit. Through temptations and Agony and Death. He knows what it all means. He feels and sympathizes with you. He has pledged Himself to send you no more than He will enable you to bear and to proportion His grace to your needs. The Father "perfected" His beloved Son through suffering.

Try more and more to see in *your* Sonship, that *you* are one of God's beloved ones—that He is dealing with you as with His Own Child. Try to repose in the sweet consciousness of His Love. Seek to have no wish, no desire, save only that His Blessed Will may be wrought out in you and that you may be perfectly conformed to His Image and Likeness, Who "went not up to joy, but first He suffered pain, Who entered not into Glory before He was Crucified."

So long as God spares your life, you *must* remember that He has *work* for you. You have something either to *do*, or to *suffer*. Pray to Him to show you what that work is; and to enable you faithfully and thankfully to perform it. Never mind if it is *hard* work. Toil and work and pain will be all soon over, and *then* Everlasting rest! Try to keep as much in prayer as you can; it will be a protection against Satan and all his host, who will be hovering near to assail you. Prayer, again and again for pardon, for all the sins of omissions, and commission, in thought, word, or deed, known or unknown, in your past life—"Wash me thoroughly from my wickedness and cleanse me from my sin." And pray for larger outpourings of the Holy Ghost the Comforter.

This is the Great Gift of God which He has so specially encouraged us to seek: without Whom we can do nothing—with Whom we can do all things.

And continue interceding for others. You may not live to see the answer to those prayers; but they *shall* be heard and answered—and the answer to them shall form one element in your Cup of Joy, in the world to come.

And now, dear Arthur—God only knows whether we shall ever meet again in *this* world. May He grant that we meet Hereafter.

May the Blessing of the Everlasting Trinity rest upon you in Life in Death and for Evermore. Assuring you of my prayers,

Believe me,
Ever your loving brother
John

To this his brother Arthur was too ill to reply; but the following answer was sent at his request:

Arthur thanks you much for your very kind letter to him; he says he should much like to have written to you himself, but he is too weak. He wishes you to be told how much he feels indebted to you for all you have done for him; and says he feels he owes more to you, than almost to any one else—for the way you have watched over him in Durham; and all the interest you have taken in him since, also the kind advice and help you have given him. We have thought him decidedly weaker the last two days, and his face looks so deathlike, I cannot think he will last long now. Poor dear Arthur, I fear he suffers very much, though he will not allow it himself. He says he cannot call *that* suffering which is bringing him nearer to God. His body is so fearfully swollen, and as he can only lie on one side, the water seems to collect there.

He is so thankful to have us here, and has no wish to see any one else now, as he says the pain of parting would be too great. He has done with *that* now; and like only to think of the Glorious Meeting, when we are all together again.

He says he feels like a child going home for his holidays, and shall be so glad when the time comes, though he is willing to wait, and suffer whatever God thinks best to lay upon him.

He has often regretted that he could not talk more; but it was not in him to do so—He *felt* too deeply to talk. He would like to write to all his friends, and thank them for all they have done for him.

C.D. has been over, and seems so anxious we should all feel at home. They are most kind in wishing us to stay as long as Arthur lives; she keeps him constantly supplied with beautiful flowers and all the delicacies she can think of.

To His Cousin, Mrs. E. Wawn, on the Death of Her Husband, the Rev. E. B. Wawn

S. Oswald's Vicarage, Durham
Oct. 4, 1866

I cannot send my letter off without enclosing a line to yourself to assure you of my prayers and heartfelt sympathy in the heavy bereavement with which is has pleased God to try you. Although God has dealt very tenderly and mercifully with you, in gently preparing you, little by little, for dear Edward's removal, yet I can well imagine how keen your sorrow when called upon actually to resign him, and lay him in his grassy bed, asleep in Jesus, till the glorious morning.

Still, how full of rich comfort the thought that your seeming separation is but for a very short time.

He has only gone Home a little before you. The time of blissful everlasting reunion will soon come. And even now, the separation *is* only seeming, not *real*. Dear Edward is probably nearer to you now, than he was while on earth, even although invisible. Although his *body* lies mouldering till Jesus calls it into new Life, his spirit is already instinct with new energy and new power. He has not forgotten those he loved on earth. His Love has only become purer and deeper, and more efficacious. He prayed for you while on earth. His prayers cannot have ceased. They have only become more acceptable and availing. In the mystical Communion of the Body of Christ, the members in Paradise do not forget, or lose their interest in, their poor struggling fellow members on earth, but yearn after them and aid them, and doubtless are permitted by the Divine Head and Lord, to exercise ministries of mercy towards them. In Christ you and Edward can yet hold sweet and holy Communion. May He, the Father of the fatherless, and the Husband of the widow, have you and your little ones in His holy keeping, and fill you with His Heavenly Comfort.

To a Friend, on the Loss of Her Little Children

Durham
Oct. 24, 1870

My Dear Mrs.____,

You will not, I am sure, think it an intrusion if I write a line to tell you how deeply Mrs. Dykes and myself sympathise with you and Mr.____ in your present sad trial. We have lately ourselves been called upon to part with one of our darlings, and another one, poor Gertie, was for a long time hovering between life and death: and even now, is only very slowly regaining her strength, and still causes us anxiety. So that, having had some recent experience in what you are yourself undergoing, we are better able to enter into your sorrow. To lose two dear little treasures almost at a blow, is, I deeply feel, a loss and trial of no ordinary kind. And yet, my dear friend, I am sure you will soon begin to realise that the picture has its bright, as well as its dark side.

Would you have your little darlings back even if you might? No! I am sure you would not. You would never wish to bring them out of Paradise, from the companionship of Holy Angels, of the spirits of the Blessed, and from the Bosom of Jesus—to this weary world, to be exposed again to pain and weakness, and sickness, and most of all, to *sin*.

Oh, no, they are far, far better looked after now, than they could be under your tenderest care.

Moreover, you have them safe for ever. Had they lived, they *might* have fallen: they might have finally forfeited their Heavenly Inheritance. You might have had the bitter pang of parting from one, or both, for ever. But this *cannot* be now, as far as they are concerned. They are everlastingly secure.

The great Physician Himself has undertaken their case. He has not only healed them of their weakness and sickness, but has placed them beyond the reach of ever being sick or in pain again. They have gone home to wait for you; it may be to repay already your motherly care and pain for them, by ministries of mercy towards you. They will be not less near to you—perhaps much nearer—now, than they were before.

I am sure you will find the truth of our Lord's Words realised; and having some more of your earthly "treasure" removed from hence to the dear Home in Paradise, you will find your *heart* more readily settling there, and thus gently lifted up from this world and its fleeting interests. In this, and other secret ways, perhaps known only to yourself and God, you will find this heavy trial instinct with blessing, and have cause to thank God for His tender Love, in sending it to you.

Tomorrow, at about three o'clock in the afternoon, your little ones (at least, all that is mortal of them) are to be laid in their last earthly resting place, to sleep safe and sound till Jesus comes to wake them in the Morning. Oh, what a blessed awakening!

And now, I have only to assure you that you and your husband have not been, and shall not be, forgotten in my poor prayers; and with kindest regards to you both, and sincerest sympathy from my wife and myself, to beg you to believe me,

Ever yours most truly,
John B. Dykes

**REQUIEM AETERNAM DONA EIS DOMINE
ET LUX PERPETUA LUCEAT EIS.**

Appendix 1

The Bishop of Durham and the Vicar of S. Oswald's

Durham County Advertiser
Friday, July 25, 1873

Sir,

May I ask you to do me the favour to publish the following correspondence. It must tell its own tale. It is not without intense repugnance that I place it before the public. But it seems due to myself, due to my friends and parishioners, and due also to the diocese that I should do so. On the one hand, I cannot bear the thought of seeming to oppose my Bishop without openly stating the grounds on which I have acted; and, on the other, as regards the diocese, I cannot but think that it has become necessary that some voice, however feeble, should be raised against a one-sided system of administration which, if not kept in check, bids fair to produce much unhappiness and mischief.

In explanation of the first letter I have only to add that, after a long and most anxious search for a fellow worker in the place of my old friend Mr. Wray, who is on the point of leaving the curacy for the Vicarage of Ovingham, I succeeded in securing the services of a clergyman, most highly recommended, now working in the diocese, the Rev. G. E. F. Peake, and wrote to the Bishop, asking him to be so good as to grant him the usual licence.

Faithfully yours,
John B. Dykes

Appendix 1

I

Auckland Castle
July 4, 1873

My Dear Sir,

I have received your letter with reference to Mr. Peake. The extent to which some of the clergy of the present day, in their public ministrations, disregard the law which they have pledged themselves to obey, has become very serious. Grievous offence is thus given to many right-minded churchmen of the laity; whilst this open defiance of lawfully constituted authority, by the ministers of the Church, greatly strengthens the efforts of those who are striving to effect the disestablishment of the Church of England.

I have, therefore, after much serious consideration, come to the conclusion that the time has arrived when it has become my duty to do what I can to protect curates from the unlawful requirements of some incumbents, and to protect parishioners from the follies and lawlessness of some curates.

To accomplish this I must require of an incumbent, on his nomination of a curate, that he give me his written pledge that he will not require of such curate—

1. That he wear coloured stoles.
2. That he take part in, or be present at, the burning of incense.
3. That he turn his back upon the congregation during the celebration of the Holy Communion, except when "ordering the bread."

I must also require of a curate a written promise that he will offend in none of these things. I know not what has been your practice in these matters, but on receiving the documents I have mentioned, I shall be prepared to accept your nomination of Mr. Peake.

Yours truly,
C. Dunelm

II

S. Oswald's Vicarage
July 5, 1873

My Dear Lord Bishop,

In reply to your Lordship's letter, received this morning, to the effect that you refuse to license Mr. Peake or any other curate to this parish without a written pledge from myself, and also from him, that he will not do certain things named in your Lordship's letter, I have no alternative but to decline most respectfully, but firmly, to sign, or require a curate to sign, any such document whatever. The request is one which your Lordship has no right to make, and I have no right to grant.

A curate is needed for the wants of this parish. A clergyman of irreproachable character and orthodoxy has offered himself. I am ready to fulfil all the antecedent conditions which the law requires, in the shape of declaration, nomination, etc. But I can consent to nothing further. The law does not require, and never has required, the supplementary document which your Lordship wishes to demand; and I must be pardoned if I decline to take any step which may tend to the imposition of this new yoke about the necks of the incumbents and curates of the diocese.

The points referred to in the proposed paper, I observe, are (1) stole, (2) incense, (3) the position of Celebrant.

1. With regard to *stoles*, your Lordship must be fully aware that coloured stoles are every whit as legal, or illegal, as black stoles or scarfs. The surplice and hood are the only permissible ordinary vestments: black gowns, black stoles or scarfs, are all equally unauthorised. Therefore, if the law is enforced, it should be enforced all round; and the Archdeacons' scarfs, and the clergy's stoles and black gowns must all go; and (forgive me for adding) we must see your Lordship celebrating in your Cope.

2. As regards incense, your Lordship, I think, must know that it is not used in any church in the diocese—at least *I* have never seen it used (if I am in error on this point I will gladly apologise). This insertion, therefore, seems made apparently for no other purpose than to give *point* to the declaration, as it cannot have been rendered necessary by the prevalence of the practice of censing in the diocese.

3. As to the eastward position of the Celebrant, your Lordship must be aware that the recent judgment of the Judicial Committee which ruled that point, having been pronounced in an *undefended* case, did not finally settle the law for the whole Church. It affected one individual, and one individual only. The judgment itself has been torn to shreds again and again as worthless in point of law. The Bishops, as a body, have refused to act upon it. Why, then, is it to be the law in this diocese, and nowhere else?

But it is not on the ground of the *details* of the proposed paper or declaration that I object to it. I object to the *principle* of the paper, as an endeavour to thrust the High Church clergy of the diocese into a corner, and subject them to an utterly unfair pressure.

Suppose another Bishop were to refuse to license any curate where the incumbent did not pledge himself to have *daily service* and *weekly Communion*. These certainly are infinitely more the "Law of the Church" than a private decision of a lay court which nobody respects. Does your Lordship think that clergymen, of Mr. F___'s stamp for instance, would quietly acquiesce? Would your Lordship have acquiesced when you were an incumbent?

I can see nothing in your Lordship's unhappy proposition in store for the diocese but confusion, rebellion, and heartburning, and grievous hindrance to the work of the Church in this teeming population.

Your Lordship may think it wise and right—instead of adopting a liberal policy of acknowledging the fact that there *are*, and always have been, and always *will* be, more than one narrow school of thought in the Church, and allowing to all parties who are striving to work for Christ according to their several lights, generous recognition and scope within certain fair limits—to adopt the exterminating policy, which your Archdeacon thought it becoming to thank God at a public meeting you *were* adopting, viz., of "using every opportunity to *stamp out* Ritualism" (the cant expression of the day for distinctive Church teaching and practice) in your diocese. But depend upon it, my Lord, you will not succeed.

Your Lordship, I observe, charges first one of the High Church clergy, then another, with being dishonest, with being Jesuits, and the like. You will, I trust, however, find them honest enough to stand up for their principles, even although your Lordship should cruelly endeavour to "stamp them out" one by one by refusing them curates. For this is what your Lordship's proposition comes to. Where are the High Church clergy of the diocese to find curates? Certainly not amongst men who would consent to make such preliminary pledges as your Lordship wishes to exact of them. How could I ask Mr. Peake, or any good Churchman, to sign this document? He would simply refuse, and say, "Thank you, I prefer to go to some other diocese." And he would be quite right. Already the High Church clergy have the greatest difficulty in obtaining curates. The diocese has got the reputation of being administered simply in the interests of one narrow party.

If the new programme is carried out, we may as well give up the attempt as hopeless.

I could say much more, but for the present I refrain. I have simply to renew my request that your Lordship will be so good as to license Mr. Peake to this curacy, after I have sent in all the necessary papers.

The only alternative will be (provided there is no appeal to the Archbishop) to endeavour to do the best I can, until my health again breaks down, without a curate, and to leave the colliery district, with its rapidly increasing population, for which the Commissioners have made a grant for a second curate, to take care of itself.

I beg to remain,
Your Lordship's faithful servant in Christ,
John B. Dykes

III

Auckland Castle
July 7, 1873

My Dear Sir,

I will make no remarks on the tone of your letter just received. I can make allowance for a person writing under feelings of irritation and annoyance.

With regard to your statements respecting myself, or the law, I have simply to say that they are altogether incorrect, and are not justified by the facts of the case.

Yours truly,
C. Dunelm

IV

S. Oswald's Vicarage, Durham
July 16, 1873

My Dear Lord Bishop,

Yesterday afternoon I received the accompanying papers from Mr. Peake. I venture to forward them to your Lordship, and once more, after earnest thought and prayer, to renew my request that you would be so good as to license him to this curacy—the Licence to take effect on the avoidance of the Curacy by Mr. Wray.

The Law requires certain papers, and certain papers only. These I have sent; and thereupon respectfully claim my rights.

Your Lordship, on your own showing, has no fault to find with me. You state that you do not even know what my practice is in reference to the matters noticed in your first letter; therefore you can have had no formal complaint against me. Nor does your Lordship know anything against Mr. Peake. Hence there can be no valid reason why your Lordship should hesitate or refuse to grant the Licence for which I ask.

I have told your Lordship I cannot sign the supplementary paper you have sent. The Law knows nothing of it. It has never been required of me before. It is not required in any other diocese. I should consider myself acting unfairly to my brethren were I quietly to acquiesce in its introduction here. Is each diocese to have its own arbitrary and conflicting set of rules for the discomfiture of curates?

If your Lordship refuses, I shall be driven to appeal to the Archbishop's Court, or else to apply for a Mandamus to compel your Lordship to put your office in force. For I shall have a legitimate ground of complaint. Your Lordship's refusal will injure myself and my parish to the amount of £240 a year, the two grants of £120 from the Commissioners depending on your Lordship's Licence. It will involve also a slur on the character of Mr. Peake and myself, to say nothing of the grievous spiritual injury done to the souls of my people.

I need not assure you, my Lord, that it will be only with the *extremist* reluctance that I shall be compelled to adopt such a hateful course, and have the matter made public. The Church cannot bear these unseemly quarrels. I shrink from such a line of action for my own soul's sake, for my people's sake, yes, and for your Lordship's sake; for I feel sure that in your declining years it can be no pleasure to have to waste time and energy in fruitless contention. But I see no other course open to me. It is not for me to set my hand to a document the object of which is, to injure that great party in the Church to which it is my happiness to belong; to cause distress and annoyance to many of my dear brethren in the Ministry; to abridge the liberties of the clergy; to foster disorder and profanity in God's house, by introducing two sets of Ritual; to recognise invidious distinctions between Incumbents and Curates; and thus to bring elements of confusion and discord into many parishes now at peace.

If your Lordship, then, is determined to press this point, I can see no other course but to leave the results in God's hands, and reluctantly but firmly resist it.

I solemnly affirm, my Lord, it is from no feeling of insubordination, or desire to withstand lawful authority that I so act. It is thoroughly contrary to my nature and to all my deepest instincts so to do. It is simply burdensome and odious to me. But it is plain that resistance to authority may become a duty. Where would the Reformation, or the present Old Catholic movement have been, had there been no resistance of authority? Where would our present wonderful Church Revival—our open Churches, daily offices, restored surplices, choral services, hymns, multiplied early Eucharists; nay—to turn to an earlier time—where would the great Evangelical Movement have been, if the clergy had simply determined to do no more, and to do no less, than their Bishops sanctioned or approved of?

But it may be said that the points insisted on in your Lordship's Paper are really so trivial, that this is not a case in which resistance is justifiable.

My Lord, I must again suppose a parallel case. A very short time ago it seemed almost certain that not only the Eastward position of the Celebrant, but also the Eucharistic Vestments were legal. There seems a strong probability that both questions will speedily have to be tried again; and your Lordship, no doubt, is aware that it is the opinion of lawyers of the greatest eminence that the Purchas Judgment would be reversed.

I will not ask the question whether your Lordship would at once feel bound to *reverse the terms of your Paper*, and visit the Low Church clergy as you now wish to visit the High Church. But I will suppose that in some neighbouring Diocese the Bishop *were* to make such a rule—refusing to license any curates who would not sign a written pledge (the incumbents signing the same) that they would never stand at the north end of the Altar, but only at the centre (or at the "North-side" of the centre, facing east), and that they would never celebrate but in the legal vestments. How, I ask, would my brethren of the Low Church School relish such a document? Would they think it only a *trivial* matter, and one in which they were *bound* simply to obey their Bishop? I think we may gather something as to their then attitude from the recent fanatical speech of Lord Shaftesbury, which was so enthusiastically applauded by the party:—"If the rubrics allow it; well then, away with the rubrics." "If the Church of England sanction it; let the Church of England go, and the Bishops with her!" It is very easy, my Lord, for either party to uphold episcopal authority when they have the Bishops with them; not quite so easy, when the Bishops are in opposition.

But in view of this by no means improbable reversal of the Purchas Judgment, what would be the result? Why, I presume, there would be a strong Memorial sent to the Bishops, as in the case of the former Judgment, requesting them not to enforce it. And no doubt they would *not*; unless, indeed any unfair pressure of the former judgment had rendered a Nemesis unfortunately inevitable.

Your Lordship speaks of "disestablishment." I will tell you, my Lord, what will soon precipitate disestablishment. If that outrageous "Minute" just sent by the "Church Association" to the Archbishops and Bishops in answer "to the Archbishop's" letter—a document which for cool impertinence and malignant intolerance I have rarely seen equalled—if this "Minute" were to be acted on, the Establishment would go in a year. If the Evangelicals (so-called) think to "stamp out" or persecute the Church party, or the Church party the Evangelicals, the days of the Establishment are numbered. The only *possible* chance for the safety of the Church is to allow *both* the great parties—who are each doing real work for God, but not in exactly the same way; who are each zealous for God's Truth, but have affinities with different sides of Truth—fair play and scope within reasonable bounds.

In our towns, where there are several Churches, this is pre-eminently needful; for here there *can* be no grievance. In Durham, for instance, many of S. Nicholas' people come to S. Oswald's, and many of S. Oswald's go to S. Nicholas', many to the Cathedral, etc., etc. And so it should be. There is no practical grievance. There will, of course, be extreme cases of excess or defect in the way of Ritual and order which must be dealt with singly. But each party must be fairly left to take its own general line. God knows there is abundant room for both. There *can* be no Procrustean uniformity of Ritual. It would be a most disastrous thing for the Church. The Church of a great and intelligent and free people must provide for considerable divergence in the outward expression of her teaching and allow for minds and tempers of very different kinds.

But you may say, my Lord, "All this is true to a certain extent. So long as Ritual is a question of mere taste and aestheticism I do not much mind it. But when it is used as a cover for inculcating false doctrine, here is a matter of life and death. It must be put down."

Now, my Lord, I well know this feeling lies at the bottom of your present action. And, believe me, I deeply respect you for being jealous for God's truth. A Bishop is worth nothing who is *not*. And God forbid that this should for one moment be a ground of complaint on my part against your Lordship.

But I must tell you honestly—and I would tell you with all the reverence due from a son to a Father in God—that it does *not* seem to me to be simply God's Truth that your Lordship seeks so energetically to defend, but a perversion of that Truth. Your Lordship's teaching on the subject of the Holy Eucharist appears to myself irreconcilably at variance with the teaching of Holy Scripture, of the Church of England, and of the Primitive Church. It presents itself to my mind as simply the teaching of Zuinglius, and not as that of the Catholic Church. Your Lordship has employed some strong writing and words in your last Charge, and your oral addresses from time to time, in condemning teaching which is *not* that of the High Church Party, which would be rejected by them quite as earnestly as it is by your Lordship. *e.g.* Such teaching as that there is in the Eucharist a "*material*" Presence of Christ, a "*carnal*" Presence (*Charge*, pp. 31, 41, 36); the doctrine that the sinner is "as much a partaker of Christ" as the saint (p. 33); that the elements "change their Nature" [*i.e.*, I suppose, that they *cease* to be, after the order of nature, "verily and indeed," bread and wine after Consecration] pp. 41, 43; that the Eucharist is the "one exclusive channel by which Christ's Death is imparted to the believer" (p. 35); that "the elements are to be worshipped " (p. 23), etc., etc.

But when I look for your Lordship's own teaching, which is to supplant that of the Church, and which we, the clergy of this Diocese, are expected, out of deference to our Bishop, to teach our people, I am startled by reading that the elements are not "*in* ANY *sense, or manner*, converted into the Body and Blood of Christ" (p. 37); that they are "BUT *symbols*" (p. 43); that the mere object of the Institution is "to cherish in the mind of the recipient a grateful sense of the love of Christ" (p. 39); that the elements "remain" after Consecration "IN EVERY RESPECT *the same* as they were before" (pp. 49, 50) ; that the communicant is fed "*not* by the hand of the Priest administering the bread and wine, but by faith laying hold of the promises of the Gospel" (p. 44); although the Article distinctly speaks of the Body of CHRIST being "*given*" as well as "*taken* and *eaten*"—*given* by the Priest, taken and eaten by the people; and the administering Priest is ordered, as he gives it, to say "the Body of our Lord JESUS CHRIST, which was given for thee, *preserve thy body and soul to everlasting Life*: take eat," etc.

My Lord, it is a matter of the profoundest astonishment to me that those who can so treat the plain statements of Holy Scripture and the Church, as your Lordship seems to me to treat them, should be ever charging their brethren with dishonesty.

If the most solemn and emphatic words of Him who is *the* Truth, who cannot speak more and cannot speak less than the Truth—if His explicit words "This *is* My Body, this *is* My Blood" are to be glossed away into meaning "This is *not* My Body, This is *not* My Blood:"—If the words of the HOLY GHOST explaining to us that—just as, under the Old Covenant, the *death* of the victim was not enough, but there must be a sacrificial *eating of* and communion with the victim, as well as a memorialising of its blood or death before GOD, both inside and outside the Holiest—so, under the New Covenant, the *Death* of the great Sacrifice on Calvary was not enough, but there must be a sacramental *feeding on* and communion with the Sacrifice, as well as a Memorialising of it in Heaven and on earth; and that the Holy Eucharist is the divinely ordained means wherein that sacrificed Flesh and Blood are communicated to us (I Cor. x. 16), and also wherein we Memorialise and "show forth" before GOD and man "the Lord's Death, till He come" (I Cor. xi. 24–26):—If, I say, these words of the HOLY GHOST and other like words which speak of "the Lord's Body" (I Cor. xi. 29), and "the Blood of the Covenant" (Exod. xxiv. 8; S. Matt. xxvi. 28; Heb. x. 29, xii. 24; I S. John v. 8) as awful realities mysteriously existing in the Church, capable of being impiously "profaned," or devoutly "discerned" and used—if they are to be treated as unmeaning figures of speech, evacuated of all their profound and tender mystery, insomuch that it shall be an adequate explanation of the words "This is My Body"—"this is a *symbol* of My Body, or a '*photograph*' or likeness of My Body"![1] then, farewell to faith, farewell to all reverence for Holy Scripture! My Lord, I cannot

---

1. The allusion is to an illustration often made use of by the Bishop in Confirmation Charges.

thus play fast and loose with the words of Inspiration. I must either believe all, or disbelieve all. I have been taught from my earliest childhood to revere this Blessed Book. I love and reverence it with all my heart's best love and reverence. And I do from my soul protest against any attempt, from whatever quarter, to improve upon it, to explain it away, and "make it of none effect" by human "traditions," be they Roman or be they Protestant. I have no wish to teach *more* than Holy Scripture teaches on the Mystery of the Eucharist; but *I will not teach less*. I have for several years made it my daily prayer—under the deep sense of my ignorance and liability to get wrong on a subject of so much controversy, and an earnest wish not to be led astray myself or lead my people astray—that "God would by His HOLY SPIRIT "help me ever to *speak* and *write*, ever to *act* and *think* and *feel*, on this Holy Mystery as shall be best pleasing to Himself, and for the benefit of my own soul and the souls of my people; and would preserve me from holding or teaching *anything* thereon, but what is fully in accordance with His Revealed Truth." What I hold, then, I do not hold lightly or thoughtlessly. I am bound to add that I have hardly ever heard your Lordship speak on this sacred subject without feeling pained and shocked. You have almost always seemed to adopt the reasoning of the Jews of old, "How shall this Man give us His flesh to eat?" (S. John vi. 52), appealing to carnal reason and "common sense," and not to the assured Word of Him who "speaks, and it is done"; forgetting the grave caution of Jeremy Taylor that "If it is *hard* to do so much violence to our *sense* as not to think it *bread*; it is more *unsafe* to do so much violence to our *faith* as not to believe it to be CHRIST'S Body." Your Lordship tells us that our Blessed Lord's Body CANNOT be present at the Christian Altars; that such Presence is inconsistent with any "*rational* idea of a body" (p. 39). Has your Lordship ever thought that it was inconsistent with the "rational idea" of two little fishes to be capable of indefinite extension so as to feed just as many thousands or millions as CHRIST *willed* them to feed? And are the properties and powers of that Body which is taken into Hypostatic union with Godhead—that "Spiritual" and glorious Body—to be judged by the standard of human reason?

In expressing, then, my earnest dissent from your teaching, I will not return upon your Lordship and those who think with you the words in which you deem it right to speak of your High Church brethren;[2] and which you have in substance too often

---

2. "It is one of the most painful features of the School, that its members, in their

repeated. But I will merely say, that if I were to bring myself to adopt your Lordship's mode of interpreting Holy Scripture on this great subject (to say nothing of the same mode as applied to the Church's formularies), I must give up the doctrines of the Incarnation and Atonement as well; in fact, I must drift into infidelity.

Moreover, if I held your Lordship's view, I could never argue against a Roman Catholic. He would have me down in a moment. Holding what I do, and what I am humbly convinced is the teaching of the HOLY GHOST and the Catholic Church, I feel I am impregnable against him.

But I will not proceed. I have not written all this for the sake of mere theological disputation; but simply for the purpose of showing (for I wish to keep nothing back) that independently of the strong sense I have of the injustice of your Lordship's present demand, I have grounds also for a deeper underlying feeling against it, a feeling which seems to divest it of any moral claim on my obedience *in foro conscientiae* which it might otherwise possess.

I cannot help interpreting it by the light of your Lordship's expressed utterances on the subject of the Holy Eucharist, and regarding it, in some sort, as associated with, and an outward sign of, a wish on your Lordship's part to disparage and degrade that sacred Mystery in the Diocese. People who have been accustomed for years to see the Holy Sacrament celebrated in one way—the Priest maintaining his true and proper position at the Altar—are suddenly to find the Ritual arrangements of the Church interfered with by a new curate. He and the Rector are to be exhibited in antagonism; one standing "before the Holy Table," the other going round the corner to the north end—a position unknown throughout Christendom, never adopted by any branch of the Church of God since the Church has existed, and never *contemplated* by the framers of our own Ritual. A slur is thus cast on the Incumbent. The Holy Sacrament of Love is made an occasion for the display of disunion and disagreement. The minds of ministers and people are kept in a perpetual fret.

---

constant efforts to excuse to themselves their gradual departure from the teaching of the Prayer-book, have as gradually *destroyed their moral power of discerning in these matters between truth and falsehood, between honesty and Jesuitry*, and are ready to adopt the most unnatural meaning of plain words, or to hazard the most unscrupulous assertions, if by such means they may palliate their advocacy of doctrines which *they know in their inmost heart to be directly and essentially* at variance with the formularies of our Church."—*Charge*, pp. 47, 48.

The parish is condemned to a state of *chronic* change. The sore is to be re-opened every week.

I repeat, my Lord, that I must respectfully decline to take any part in the introduction of this state of things into our parishes. I must decline to co-operate in what would be equivalent to throwing a stone at, inflicting a wound upon, interfering with the work of, branding with a mark of unfaithfulness, just those clergy in the diocese whom I most love, and whom I believe to be most faithfully, most loyally, most successfully working for CHRIST. One of them has for (I believe) fifty years maintained without change the ancient position of the Celebrant "before the Holy Table." He will probably be soon wanting a curate. Am I not to think of him, and other of my dear brethren, as well as of myself?

If your Lordship thinks it wise to break in upon the peace of the diocese with a measure which *can never do any good*, which can only breed discontent and bitterness, you must take the consequences, and accept the sad responsibility. The diocese is at peace now. In Durham we are in perfect harmony: we have fallen each into our own groove, and with mutual respect and forbearance are endeavouring to do our work to the best of our power, and fairly to meet the wants of different classes of Church people.

But alas! alas! If here, and throughout the diocese we are to be at war again! Your Lordship, I know, will meet with the loud approbation of that Persecuting Association which takes to itself the name of "Church." But will that be any compensation for the thought that many of your clergy are left without curates; that thousands of the people are deprived of the spiritual supervision of the Church, and are left to the tender mercies of Dissenters and Roman Catholics; that discord and rebellion are doing their bitter work in the Diocese? My Lord, I implore you in God's Name not to force this upon us.

I have only most humbly to crave indulgence for the length and tone of this letter, written amid incessant interruptions—written not under feelings of "annoyance and irritation" as your Lordship says of my former letter, but in all seriousness, and not without earnest prayer. I cannot face the responsibility of seeming to defy my Bishop without fully and unreservedly stating the convictions under which I act.

I am, my Lord,
Your Lordship's faithful and obedient son and servant in CHRIST,
John B. Dykes
To the Right Rev. the Lord Bishop of Durham

V

Auckland Castle
July 19, 1873

Dear Sir,

I regret that I must decline to license the Rev. G. E. F. Peake to the Curacy of St. Oswald's, Durham.

Yours faithfully,
C. Dunelm
To the Rev. Dr. Dykes

Appendix 2

Dr. Dykes' Published Hymn-Tunes

HYMNS ANCIENT AND MODERN

(W. Clowes and Son)

"O Strength and Stay"	Strength and Stay
"Sun of my Soul"	Keble: No. 2
"Sweet Saviour, bless us ere we go"	In tenebris lumen: No. 3
"Saviour, again to Thy dear Name we raise"	Pax Dei
"Sweet flow'rets of the martyr band"	Salvete Flores
"Christian, dost thou see them?"	St. Andrew of Crete
"O come and mourn with me awhile"	St. Cross
"At the Cross her station keeping"	Stabat Mater: No. 2
"And now, belovèd Lord, Thy Soul resigning"	Commendatio
"Light's glitt'ring morn bedecks the sky"	Easter chant: No. 2
"Joy, because the circling year"	Glebe Field

Appendix 2

"Come, Holy Ghost, our souls inspire"	Veni Creator: No. 2
"Holy, Holy, Holy, Lord God Almighty"	Nicaea
"Praise to the Holiest in the height"	Gerontius
"Jesu, Lover of my soul"	Hollingside
"The King of Love my Shepherd is"	Dominus regit me
"O quickly come, Great Judge of all"	Veni Cito
"Our blest Redeemer, ere He breathed"	St. Cuthbert
"Ten thousand times ten thousand"	Alford
"Hark, hark, my soul"	Vox Angelica: No. 1
"O Paradise! O Paradise!"	Paradise: No. 2
"Art thou weary, art thou languid?"	Christus Consolator: No. 1
"Come unto me, ye weary"	Come unto Me
"I heard the voice of Jesus say"	Vox Dilecti
"Nearer, my God, to Thee"	Horbury
"Lo! The Angels' Food is given"	Ecce Panis
"Draw nigh and take the Body of the Lord"	Sancti venite: No. 3
"O Food that weary pilgrims love"	Esca viatorum
"Hosanna we sing like the children dear"	Hosanna we sing
"Thou, whose Almighty Word"	Fiat Lux: No. 1
"Lord of glory, Who hast bought us"	Charitas
"Eternal Father, strong to save"	Melita

"God, the Father, Whose Creation"	First Fruits: No. 2
"Day of wrath! O day of mourning"	Dies Irae
"Now the labourer's task is o'er"	Requiescat
"Forsaken once, and thrice deceived"	Derry
"How bright those glorious spirits shine"	Beatitudo
"Litany of the Incarnate Word": No. 1	
"Litany for Children": No. 1	

The above list comprises the tines that were especially written for *Hymns Ancient and Modern,* or that had been composed before, and given by Dr. Dykes to the Committee; but the following sixteen were obtained from other sources, and make the number of his tunes in all fifty-five in this Hymnal.

"Behold the Lamb of God"	Ecce Agnus: No. 2
"Days and moments quickly flying"	St. Sylvester
"Father of heaven, Whose love profound"	Rivaulx
"Fierce raged the tempest"	St. Aëlred
"Hark, my soul! It is the Lord"	St. Bees
"Hark! the sound of holy voices"	Sanctuary: No. 3
"Jesus, the very thought of Thee"	St. Agnus: No. 1
"Shall we not love thee, Mother dear?"	St. Agnes
"Jesus lives! no longer now"	Lindisfarne: No. 2
"Lead, kindly Light"	Lux Benigna
"O Lord of heaven, and earth, and sea"	Almsgiving

"Ride on, ride on, in majesty"	St. Drostane: No. 1
"God the Father, God the Son"	Litany of the Passion
"The day is past and over"	St. Anatolius: No. 1
"Thou art gone up on high"	Olivet: No. 1
"Through the night of doubt and sorrow"	St. Oswald
"We pray Thee, Heavenly Father"	Dies Dominica

In the remaining lists, only the numbers composed for each Hymnal are given.

THE CONGREGATIONAL HYMN—AND TUNE—BOOK

Compiled by the Rev. R. R. Chope
(Simpkin and Marshall)

Lo! He comes with clouds descending"	St. Andrew
"Jesu! Redeemer of the world"	Finchale
"Days and moments quickly flying"	St. Sylvester
"All hail the power of Jesu's name"	Laud
"From Heaven to earth glad tidings I unfold"	St. Joseph
"Lord, we raise our cry to Thee"	Milman
"Lord of the worlds above"	St. Godric
"Lord, have mercy and remove us"	Arundel
"When our heads are bowed with woe"	Butterby
"In the hour of trial"	Magdalene

"Ride on! Ride on in majesty"	St. Drostane
"O'erwhelmed in depths of woe"	Waterbrook
"Creator! Spirit, Lord of Grace"	St. Barnabas
"O God of life, Whose power benign"	Cilicia
"Jerusalem the golden"	Jerusalem
Rock of Ages, cleft for me"	Gethsemane
"Hosanna to the living Lord"	St. Constantine
"The strain upraise of joy and praise"	Dykes
"Jesus! Name of wondrous love"	St. Bees
"Jerusalem, my happy home"	St. Oswin
"Fierce raged the tempest o'er the deep"	St. Aëlred
"The day is past and over"	St. Anatolius
"O Jesu! God and man"	St. Helen
"Lord, shall Thy children come to Thee"	St. Werburg
"Spirit of Wisdom! guide Thine own"	Elvet
"When on Creation's morn"	Croxdale
"Where Angelic Hosts adore Thee"	Pittington
"O, who are they so pure and bright?"	St. Oswald

Appendix 2

HYMNAL

Compiled by the Hon. and Rev. John Grey, of Houghton-le-Spring (Mozley)

"The Lord will come: the earth shall quake"	Tenebrae
"Brightest and best of the sons of the morning"	St. Ninian
"It is the holy fast"	St. Oswald
"O Maker of the world, give ear"	Magdalene
"Father of all, Whose wondrous grace"	Rivaulx
"Sing, O my tongue, devoutly sing"	St. Christopher
"The judgment o'er, see now," etc.	St. Lawrence
"Come Holy Ghost, our souls inspire"	Veni, Creator
"Christ! Of the Holy Angels' light and gladness"	St. Winifred
"Spouse of Christ, for Him contending"	All-Hallows
"Lo! Christ stands at His martyr's side"	St. Chrysostom
"Our Lord the path of suff'ring trod"	Saxham
"O God Most High! Creator! King!"	Anningsley
"Day of wrath! O day of mourning"	Dies Irae
"All is o'er, the pain, the sorrow" "Who are these like stars appearing"	St. Chad
"Jesus lives! no longer now"	Lindisfarne
"Saviour, when in dust to Thee"	St. Edmund
"Praise the Lord! ye heavens adore Him"	St. Ambrose

"Jesu! the very thought of Thee"	St. Agnes
"For thee, O dear, dear country"	Morlaix
"Hail the day that sees him rises"	Ascension

THE SONG OF PRAISE

Compiled by Lady Victoria Evans-Freke
(G. Routledge and Sons.)

"The radiant morn hath passed away"	Crespusculum
"Holy Father, cheer our way"	Vesperi lux
"Now God be with us," etc.	Deus noster refugium
"Low at Thy feet I lie"	Salvum me fac
"Oh! dark and dreary day"	Dies tenebrosa: No. 2
"Welcome, happy morning!" etc.	Pascha
"O Holy Jesu, Prince of Peace"	Eucharistica
"On the Resurrection morning"	Resurrectio
"Rest of the weary, joy of the sad"	Salvetor et Amicus
"O Jesus, I have promised"	Jesu, Magister bone
"Thy life was given for me"	Quid retribuam

THE HYMNAL COMPANION

Compiled by Dr. Bickersteth, Lord Bishop of Exeter
(Sampson and Low)

"Thou art gone up on high"	Olivet
"Lord, when before Thy Throne we meet"	Eucharist
"Rest in the Lord!—from harps above"	Irene
"For ever,'—beatific word"	Semper cum Domino
"Lord, I hear of showers of blessing"	Etiam et Mihi
"We would see Jesus," etc.	Visio Domini

THE HOLY YEAR

Compiled by Dr. Christopher Wordsworth, Lord Bishop of Lincoln
(Longmans)

"Father of all, in Whom we live"	Confirmation: Part 1
"O God, in Whose all-searching Eye"	Confirmation: Part 2
"Awake! awake! the Apostle cries"	Illumination
"Holy of Holies, awful Name"	Mercy-seat
"The wounds which Jesus once endured"	Resurrection
"O Lord of heaven, and earth, and sea"	Almsgiving

HYMNS FOR INFANT CHILDREN

(J. Masters and Co.)

"Oh! What a blessed child am I"	
"Jesus, Holy, Undefiled"	Ferrier
"How bright the sun shines overhead"	
"I have a Christian name"	
"How many things I read and hear"	
"Where is the Holy Jesus?"	
"One day dear children, you must die"	
"How glorious is our God Most High"	
"O come, dear child, along with me"	
"At God's right hand, in Heav'n above"	
"I have seen the setting sun"	
"Baby brother, baby brother"	
"Heavenly Father, from Thy Throne"	Deliverance

Appendix 2

THE CHILD'S BOOK OF PRAISE

(Novello and Co.)

"Holy Jesus! We adore Thee"
"Now to Bethlehem haste we"
"Alleluia! Now all the bells are ringing"
"Reverently we worship Thee"
"The Holy Angels sing"

THE ANGLICAN HYMN-BOOK

(Novello and Co.)

"Angels, roll the rock away!"	Resurrection
"Jesu, to Thy Table led"	Panis Vivus
"Jesu, my Lord, my God, my all"	Amplius
"Awake! awake! put on Thy strength"	Exsurge

THE PEOPLE'S HYMNAL

(Metzler and Co.)

The Reproaches (prose version)
"Now my soul, thy voice upraising"
"Onward in God's name we wend"
"Holy Ghost, come down upon Thy children"

A BOOK OF LITANIES, PROSE AND METRICAL

(Longmans)

"Litany for Advent"

"Litany of Penitence": No. 1

"Litany of the Blessed Sacrament"

"Litany in any calamity": No. 1

THE PARISH CHURCH HYMNAL

Edited by R. Minton Taylor, Esq.
(Novello and Co.)

"Dayspring of Eternity!" etc.	Oriens exalto
"Lord dismiss us with Thy Blessing"	Dimissal
"Father, Thy way, not mine"	Domine, dirige me
O Brightness of the Immortal Father's Face"	Lux vera

THE SARUM HYMNAL

(Brown, Salisbury)

"Hark! The voice of Love and Mercy"

"Lord of Life, prophetic Spirit," etc.

"Every morning the red sun"

Appendix 2

A SUPPLEMENT TO THE COLLECTION OF PSALMS AND HYMNS USED AT READING

Compiled by the Rev. S. M. Barkworth, D.D.
(W. H. Strickland, Reading)

"Christ is gone up with a joyful sound"	Jesus Victor
"Lord of my life, Whose tender care"	Malton
"May days are gliding swiftly by"	Tenbury

CHURCH HYMNS

(S. P. C. K.)

"My sins have taken such a hold on me"	Credo, Domine
"God the Father, from Thy Throne"	Litany Irregular

HYMNS FOR THE CHURCH OF ENGLAND

Compiled by the Rev. Thomas Darling
(Longmans)

"Hosanna to the living Lord"	Hosanna
"Behold the Lamb of God!"	Ecce Agnus

A SUPPLEMENTAL HYMN—AND TUNE—BOOK

Compiled by the Rev. Brown-Borthwick
(Novello and Co.)

"Hark! the herald angels sing"	Bethlehem: New
"Father, I know that all my life"	Slingsby

THE CHORALE-BOOK

Edited by H. H. Bemrose
(Bemrose and Co.)

"When gathering clouds around I view"	Durham
"O let him whose sorrow"	St. Barnabas

THE BRISTOL TUNE-BOOK (FIRST SERIES)

(Novello and Co.)

"Rise, my soul, and stretch thy wings"	St. Hilary

THE NEW MITRE HYMNAL

Compiled by the Rev. W. J. Hall
(Longmans)

"Hail to the Lord's anointed"	Eleutheria

Appendix 2

PROCESSIONAL HYMNS WITH TUNES

Edited by J. Biden, Esq.
(J. Biden, Northampton)

"Children of the Heavenly King"	

HYMNS FOR ADVENT AND LENT

Compiled by the Rev. R. Tomlins
(Jackson, Manchester)

"And is it Thy voice, patient Saviour, yet calling?"	St. Leonard

POPULAR CONGREGATIONAL MUSIC

Edited by W. H. Jude, of Liverpool

"Hark! the herald angels sing"	

THE CHURCH OF ENGLAND HYMNOLOGY

Compiled by G. P. Joyce, Esq., Newport, Isle of Wight

"O Lord Jesus, at Thy coming"	Parate Viam

THE ST. ASAPH TUNE-BOOK

Edited by W. J. Hughes
(J. Morris, Rhyl)

"Bosnia." Set to Welsh words.	

CONGREGATIONAL CHURCH MUSIC

Edited by Dr. W. M. Cook
(Hodder and Stoughton)

"Lord of mercy and of might"	Hodnet
"Lowly and solemn be"	Southfleet
"Gird on Thy conquering sword"	Trent
"My God, my Father, while I stray"	Shoreham
"Thou art the everlasting Word"	Catford
"Lord, in this Thy mercy's day"	Rutland
"We sing His love, Who once was slain"	Eastgate

CHURCH PRAISE

(J. Nisbet and Co.)

"O for a heart to praise my God"	Burton Agnes
"When gathering clouds around I view"	Barrington
"The Lord Himself, the mighty Lord"	Faith
"Hail, Thou once despisèd Jesus"	Bamborough
"There is a land of pure delight"	Canaan
"Go to dark Gethsemane"	Glastonbury

THE CONGREGATIONAL PSALMIST

Compiled by Dr. Henry Allon
(Hodder and Stoughton)

"Come, let us anew our journey pursue"	Mizpah
"The way is long and dreary"	Via Crucis

THE WESLEYAN TUNE-BOOK

Edited by Dr. Hiles
(Novello and Co.)

"None is like Jeshurun's God"	Beatus Israel

REID'S PRAISE-BOOK

(J. Nisbet and Co.)

"Lord we are Thine; in Thee we live"	Consecration

HYMNAL WITH TUNES NEW AND OLD

Edited by the Rev. J. Ireland Tucker, D.D., of Troy, New York.
(Huntington and Co.)

"I would not live always"	Bethany
"Inspirer and Hearer of prayer"	St. Editha
"Rock of Ages, cleft for me"	Faith

THE CHILDREN'S HYMNAL

Edited by the Rev. J. Ireland Tucker, D.D., of Troy, New York (Huntington and Co.)

"There's a friend for little children"	
"It came upon the midnight clear"	

STRAY TUNES WHICH HAVE BEEN FOUND IN PRINT

"Faithful in Thy love." (F Pitman.) "As the seasons move"	
"O day of rest and gladness"	Dies Dominica
"The Lord of Harvest let us sing"	Thanksgiving
"God the Father, God the Song"	Litany of the Passion
"God that madest earth and heaven"	Vespers
"Jerusalem, thou city blest"	St. Cecilia
"Day draws to evening," etc.	Hora Novissima
"Great and Glorious Father," etc.	Oswestry
"The tide of time is rolling on"	Dunholme
"Of the Father's love begotten"	Corde natus
"O Thou Who sitt'st enthroned above," etc.	Church Consecration
"Beneath the Church's hallow'd shade" "We consecrate, O Lord, to Thee"	Churchyard Consecration
"O sing to the Lord with a psalm of thanksgiving"	Synods and Conferences with Choral Festivals

Appendix 2

"God the Father, God the Son, Holy Spirit Three in One"	Dismissal
"Holy is the seed time"	
"Come, our Father's voice is calling"	Our Father's Voice
"We lift our hearts to Thee, our Head"	
"Sun of my soul"	Ilkley
"My God, I am Thine"	Jesmond
"The night is gone" (Church Music Press)	
"The Voice that breathed o'er Eden"	Blairgowrie
"Gladsome year of Jubilee"	Missionary Hymn
"Holy, Holy, Holy Lord"	Trisagion
"Sing to the Lord a joyful song"	Cantate Domino

The following tunes are in MS., besides many others:

"Bread of Heaven, on Thee we feed"	
"And now, O Father, mindful of the love"	
"Tender Shepherd" (Two Settings)	
"For all the saints" (Two Settings)	
"The Son of God goes forth to war"	
"Of the Glorious Body broken"	Coena Domini
"Bound upon the accursèd tree"	
"There is a blessèd home"	
"The strife o'er, the battle done"	

"Day of wrath": No. 3	
"The Heavenly Word"	O Salutaris Hostia
"The roseate hues of early dawn"	
"Alleluia! sing to Jesus"	
"Forward! be our watchword"	
"At Thy feet, O Christ, we lay"	
"O Jesu, Thou art standing"	
"To Thee our God we fly"	
"Just as I am"	
"O Paradise" (in F)	
"Hail, Gladdening Light"	

In addition to about three hundred Hymn-tunes Dr. Dykes wrote five Carols, in Canon Bramley's and Sir John Stainer's collection of *Christmas Carols New and Old* (Novello and Co.).

"From far away we come to you"	
"Infant of days, yet Lord of Life"	In terra pax
"Once again, O blessed time"	Christmas Song
"On the Birthday of the Lord"	
"Sleep, Holy Babe"	

He also wrote several Anthems and Introits, the two most important being—

"These are they which came out of great tribulation"
"The Lord is my Shepherd"

Others remain in the Durham Cathedral Choir-books, and are unpublished.

Dr. Dykes also composed a *Burial Service, Services* for Morning and Evening Prayer, and Holy Communion, besides songs and part songs, sacred and secular.

Index

The format of the original 1897 index has been retained in this edition. It is notable that there are so many references to Dykes' travels and equally the particular styling of personal titles. Fowler's edition consistently followed his own transcription of Dykes' references. Inconsistencies and omissions in the original publication have been amended in this edition where possible.

Active and contemplative life, Letter on the, 198
"Adoro te devote," 132
"Agnus Dei," 111, 112, 125, 126
Aira Force, 101
Airey, Rev. J. A. L., 27, 30, 34
Albert, Prince, 22
    His visit to Cambridge, 12–14
Alder, Rev., 46
Alderson, Sir James, 7
Alderson, Mrs., 6
    Her hymns, 6
    Letter from her brother Arthur, 60
    Her Almsgiving Hymn, 109
    Letter from Dr. Dykes, 110
    Her Christmas Carol, 93
    Words for part of a song, 137
    Passion Hymn, 138
    Suggested alterations, 139
Alexander, Mrs., 49, 139
Allon, Dr., 111, 146
    His *Congregational Psalmist*, 152, 240
    On Dr. Dyke's hymn-music, 155
Amplius, 98, 234
"Angels, roll the rock away," 98, 234
Anglican Hymn-Book, 234
Annotated Prayer Book, 68

Anthems composed by Dr. Dykes, 41, 49, 51, 54, 110–15, 124, 243
Archibald, Judge, 127
Arthington, 57
"Asaph Tune Book, St." 329
Ashwell, Canon, 82
    His account of Dr. Dyke's funeral, 150
    On the obituary notice, 44, 152
"At the Cross her station keeping," 49, 112, 225
"Awake! awake! put on Thy strength," 98, 234

Baker, Sir Henry, 48, 76, 78–81, 99–101, 118, 119, 127, 129, 132–34, 138, 146
    Letters from Dr. Dykes on receipt of cheque, 129
    On Dr. Wordsworth's Almsgiving Hymn, 102
    Letter to Dr. Dykes, 100
    His objection to Mrs. Alderson's Passion hymn, 139, 140, 142
    On the death of Dr. Dykes, 158
Bangor, 19
Baring, Bishop, 117

Index

Barnard Castle, 111
Barnby, Joseph, 81
Barnsley, 45
Barrow House, 20
Beachy Head, 63
Belmont, 115
Bemrose, H. H.: *The Chorale-Book*, 237
Ben Rhydding, 150
Ben-y-Vracky, Ascent of, 124
"Benedictus," 111, 125, 126
Benson, Father, 70, 73
Beresford-Hope, Mr., 119, 121, 136
Bernard, Mount St., 26
Bickersteth, Rev. E. H., 101
    The Hymnal Companion, 86
    His poem, 87
    His marriage hymn, 87
    Requests Dr. Dykes for a hymn-tune, 108–9
Biden, J., *Processional Hymns with Tunes*, 238
Birmingham Festival, 75
Birnam, 124
Bishopthorpe Parish Church, 29
Blackburn, Judge, 127
Bland, Archdeacon, 38
Blow, 14–16, 19
Blunt, Professor, 11, 68
Blunt, Rev. J. H., on the death of Dr. Dykes, 160
Bodley Family, 4, 13, 45
Bombay, 125
Bournemouth, 37, 62, 115
Bowen, Mr. C., 121, 124
Boy's enthusiasm as a worker for Christ, Letter on a, 167–68
Braan, Falls of the, 124
Brechin, Bishop of, 126
Bright, Dr., 95, 97, 140
Brighton, 64
Bristol Tune-Book, 237
Browdie, John, 30
Bullock, Mr., 147
Burial Service, music for the, 82, 244
Burn, Jane, 32
Buttermere, 137

Cadge, Mr., 70
Camberwell, 20
Cambridge, Duke and Duchess of, 22
Cambridge, 9, 11
    Fire at, 23–24
Cambridge University Musical Society, 15
    First concert, 15
    Its early history, 15
    Jubilee Commemoration, 15
Camidge, Charles, 66
Camidge, Dr., 98
Capes, Bessy, 4
Carlisle, Earl of, 32
Carols composed by Dr. Dykes, 93, 97, 243
Carruthers, Mr. David, 8
Carter, Rev. William, 26, 28, 83, 140
Carus, Mr., 11, 14
Castle Hill, 136
Castle Howard, 97
Cat bells, 101, 137
Catherine's Hall, Cambridge, St., 11
Cattley, Canon, 83, 111
Chamberlain, Rev. Thomas, 37
Character, Letter on, 173
Charitas, 109, 226
Charity, Letter on, 172
Chaytor, Mary, 56
Cheape, Rev. John, 39
Cheape, Mrs., 15, 63, 149
    Letters from Dr. Dykes on the death of her husband, 202
    On the death of her little boy, 203
Cheape, Miss, 74, 149
Cheltenham College, 72
Cherishing Times of Brightness, Letter on, 195
Chevalier, 82
Children's Hymnal, 241
Children's Hymns, 80, 233
Child's Book of Praise, 234
Cholera, Epidemic of, 38
Chope, Mr.: his *Congregational Hymn- and Tune-Book*, 54, 228
Choral Festival, Birmingham, 75
    Doncaster, 114
    Durham Cathedral, 55–56
    Worcester, 83, 111

Index

Chorale-Book, 237
"Christian, dost thou see them?" 85, 225
Church Congress, Manchester, 56
    Norwich, 69, 70
    Nottingham, 101
Church Hymns, 237
Church music, Lectures on, 79, 84–85
    Paper on, 101
Church of England Hymnology, 238
Church Praise, 239
Church Psalter and Hymnal, 115
Clare Hall, Cambridge 9
Clayton, Hannah, 79
Clouds in the Spiritual Life, Letter on, 173
Coatham, 138
Coffin: his Transfiguration hymn, 136
Coleridge, John Duke, 124
Colwith Force, 111
Communion fasting, Letters on, 164–65, 184–86
    Preparation for, 168
    Spiritual and sacramental, 186
Confession, Letters on, 165–66
    Frequent, 191–93
Congregational Church Music, 86, 239
Congregational Hymn-and Tune-Book, 54, 228
Congregational Psalmist, 240
Cooke, Dr. W. M., 87, 121
    Editor of *Congregational Church Music*, 86, 239
Cowley, Retreat at, 83
"Creed in G," 36
Cromer Terrace, 147
Cross, St., 49, 225
Crossgate Moor, 117
Croxdale, 148
Cuthbert, St., 49, 226

"Dark shades of night," 43
Darling, Rev. Thomas: *Hymns for the Church of England*, 236
Darlington, 26, 136
Datchet, 43
Davidson, John, 69
Davies, Rev. C. G.: Incumbent of Holy Trinity Church, 9

    Vicar of Tewkesbury Abbey, 26
"Day of wrath, O day of mourning," 49, 227, 230
Denison, Archdeacon, 119, 138
    His letters to Dr. Dykes, 120
Dictionary of Music and Musicians, quotation from, 15
Dies Dominica, 98, 228
Dies Irae, 48, 49, 73, 227, 230
"Dikes Scholarship," 11
Discipline, Letter on the use of, 197
Dissenters, Letter on dealing with, 190
Dockwray, 101
Dodsworth, Mr., 9
Doncaster Choral Festival, 114
Dowson, Mr. Joseph, 62
Dresden, 147
Druid's Circle, 138
Dulwich Hill House, 20
Dunkeld, 124
Dunn, Sarah, 74
Durham, 27, 30, 111, 132, 138
Durham, Bishop of, 129
    On Dr. Dykes' pamphlet, 133
    His letters to Dr. Dykes on licensing a Curate, 75, 116, 117, 211, 215, 223
Durham Cathedral, 29, 30
    First Choral Festival in, 55
Durham, Cordelia, 50
Durham, Lady, 98
Dykes, Arthur, 43, 57, 80
    His letters on the death of his brother Charles, 58–62
    Failing health, 62
    Death, 63
    Simple faith, 63
    Letter from Dr. Dykes on his illness, 205–6
    His answer, 206–7
Dykes, Caroline, her death, 7
Dykes, Caroline Sybil, 70, 86, 91, 147
Dykes, Charles Edward, 8
    Death, 45
    Funeral, 46
    Character, 46, 47
Dykes, E. O., 90 *note*, 99
Dykes, Edward, 57, 63, 74, 112

Index

Dykes, Eliza, 29, 57, 74
Dykes, Ernest Huntington, 36, 74, 82, 91, 92, 101, 110, 111, 115, 127, 129, 132, 136
Dykes, Ethel, 70, 91
Dykes, Fanny, 12, 20, 50, 57, 74, 90
Dykes, Frances, 20
Dykes, Frederic, 10, 56, 57, 63, 74, 105, 114, 119, 121, 124, 126
Dykes, George: his illness, 42
    Death, 43
Dykes, George Lionel Andrew: birth and death, 43
Dykes, Gertrude, 70, 81
    Her illness, 90, 91, 92, 95, 96, 97
Dykes, Jack, 90, 92, 115, 126
Dykes, John Arthur St. Oswald, 56
Dykes, John Bacchus, 1
    Birth, 1
    Grandfather, 1, 2
    Parents, 2
    Education, 2, 8
    Talent for music, 3, 5
    Organ-playing, 3, 6
    Daily life, 3
    His voice, 5
    Juvenile hymns, 6
    Serious illness, 6
    His letter to Samuel Knight, 7
    Death of his sister Caroline, 7
    Testimonial on leaving Hull, 8
    Death of his brother Philip, 8
    In Plymouth, 9
    His first musical composition, 10
    At Cambridge, 11
    The Dykes Scholarship, 11
    Account of the visit of the Queen and Prince Albert, 12–13
    The University Musical Society, 13
    Evening party at Trinity Lodge, 16–19
    At Bangor, 19
    Keswick, 19
    His impressions of Jenny Lind, 20–22
    The "silver spoon," 22
    The Yorkshire Fellowship, 22–23
    Fire at Cambridge, 23–24
    Delight at hearing *Elijah*, 25
    Death of his grandfather, 25
    Curacy at Malton, 26, 28
    His gift for acting, 27
    Ordination, 28
    Parochial work, 28, 54, 85, 160
    His lecture on "Sound," 29
    Ordained Priest, 29
    Minor Canon of Durham, 29
    His duties, 30, 32, 37
    Appointed Precentor, 31, 32
    Daily life at Durham, 33
    Plays the organ, 34
    On his fault of procrastination, 35
    His new home, Hollingside Cottage, 35
    Marriage, 36
    Birth of his eldest son, 36
    His "Creed," 36
    Distress at his brother's secession, 36
    Literary work, 37, 39, 68
    List of his articles, 37 *note*
    Sermon on Ash Wednesday, 37
    On the sanitary condition of Durham, 38
    His review of Rowland Williams' "Rational Godliness," 39
    Sympathetic character of his musical compositions, 41
    His hymn-tunes, 41, 43, 49, 54, 68, 69, 74, 78, 86, 87, 88, 91, 92, 98, 104, 108, 109, 112, 113, 114, 115, 122, 126, 130, 132, 133
    Anthems, 41, 49, 51, 54, 55, 110, 111, 112, 114, 115, 124, 243, 244
    Visit to the Farne Islands, 42
    Death of his brother George, 43
    Birth and death of his boy, 43
    Sermon on "Natural and Supernatural life," 44
    Death of his brother William, 45
    Charles, 45
    His contributions to *Hymns Ancient and Modern*, 47
    Number of tunes published, 48
    Honorary degree of Mus. Doc. conferred, 49

Index 249

On the death of Cordelia Durham, 50
Presented to the living of St. Oswald's, 53
Resigns the Precentorship, 54
Choral Festival in Durham Cathedral, 55
At the Manchester Church Congress, 56
Birth of his son, John Arthur St. Oswald, 56
Death of his father, 57
Of his brother Arthur, 58, 63
On the services at Brighton, 64, 65
On the anniversary of his wedding day, 66
His article on "The Manner of Performing Divine Service," 68
On the tune of "Lead, kindly Light," 69
Retreat at Horbury, 70
Nis paper at the Norwich Church Congress, 70
On the resignation of the Rev. E. B. Wawn, 72
His *Te Deum*, 73, 84
Dies Irae, 73
Retreat at Wykeham, 73
Illness and death of his mother, 74
At the Birmingham Festival, 75
St. Michael's Festival,
Appendix to *Hymns Ancient and Modern*, meetings in connection with, 78, 79, 80, 99
New edition, 133, 136
Value of his assistance, 80, 109
Lecture on Church Music, 79, 84
Hymns for Infant Children, 80
On the proposed *Hymnary*, 81
At the Worcester Musical Festival, 83, 111
Retreat at Cowley, 83
Number of applications for hymn-tunes, 86, 87, 107, 109, 113, 115
His tunes for *The Hymnal Companion*, 87–90
Illness of his children, 90
Death of his daughter Mabel, 91
Her funeral, 91, 92
On Mrs. Alderson's Christmas Carol, 93–96
On her Almsgiving Hymn, 109, 110
Tunes for other carols, 97, 243
Amount and variety of his musical work, 98, 110–12, 113
At Monklands, 99
Patterdale, 101
Nottingham Church Congress, 101
Paper on Church Music, 101
On Dr. Wordsworth's Almsgiving Hymn, 101–4
On an anonymous hymn, 105–7
Doncaster Festival, 114
Correspondence on the Bishop of Durham's refusal to license a Curate, 116, 211–24
"Defence Fund," 121
Proposal for establishing a Sisterhood, 122
Counsel's Opinion, 122, 123
At Birnam, 124
Revision of his Anthem, 124
Sacred compositions, 126, 132
Letter to his son on the collapse of his case, 127–28
Letters to Sir H. Baker, 129–30, 140–41
His pamphlet, "Eucharistic Truth and Ritual," 131
Letters to Mr. Monk on hymn-tunes, 133–36
At the Lakes, 136
On Mrs. Alderson's Passion Hymn, 138
Suggested alterations, 138–40, 142
Death of his uncle, 142
Failing health, 144, 146, 148
His Offertory paper, 144–46
At Leeds, 147
Last Sunday at St. Oswald's, 148
In Switzerland, 149
Return to England, 150
His death, 150
Funeral, 150, 151
Reason of the success of his tunes, 151

Dykes, John Bacchus (*cont.*)
    His last hymn-tune, *Via Crucis*, 153–54
    Keen insight into human nature, 162
    His Spiritual Letters, 164
    To an invalid on fasting communion, 164–65
    On confession, 165–66
    On a boy's enthusiasm as a worker for Christ, 167–68
    On preparation for Communion, 168–69
    On Retreats, etc., 169–70
    On humility, 170–71
    On a rule of fasting and abstinence, 171–72
    On charity, 172–73
    On character, 173
    On clouds in the spiritual life, 173
    On the wedding of a sister, 174
    To an invalid on keeping Lent, 175–77
    On temper, 177–78
    On carelessness in prayer, 178
    On a rule of life, 179–80
    On temptation, 180–81
    On the value of obedience in the spiritual life, 181–83
    On keeping Lent, 183
    Submission to God's will, 183–84
    On fasting Communion, 184–86
    Spiritual and sacramental Communion, 186–87
    The Fruits of the Spirit, 187–89
    On nursing and on dealing with dissenters, 189–90
    Desire for the religious life, 191
    On frequent confession, 191–93
    Interruptions in work, 193
    On shrinking from the religious life, 194
    On cherishing times of brightness, 195
    Self-imposed penances, 196
    Reserve in teaching, 196–97
    Love in trials, 197
    On the use of discipline, 197–98
    On the active and contemplative life, 198–200
    Low Church Missions, 200
    On the Sacraments, 201–2
    To his sister Lucy, on the death of her husband, 202–3
    On the death of her little boy, 203–4
    On the death of his father, 204–5
    To his brother Arthur, 205–6
    To Mrs. E. Wawn on the death of her husband, 207
    To a friend, on the loss of her little children, 208–9
Dykes, Lucy, 14, 20, 49, 74
Dykes, Mabel, 70
    Her illness, 90
    Death, 91, 101
    Funeral, 91
Dykes, Mary, 2, 74
Dykes, Mrs., 38, 90, 97, 132, 142, 149, 150, 152
    Letters of sympathy on her husband's death, 158–59
Dykes, Philip, 8
    His death, 8
Dykes, Rose, 1
Dykes, Rev. Thomas, 1, 78 *note*
    Incumbent of St. John's Church, 2
    Master of the Charter House, Hull, 3
    Death, 25
Dykes, Thomas, 2
Dykes, Rev. Thomas, 8, 12, 57, 74
    Ordination, 8
    Received into the Romish Church, 36
    Death at Bournemouth, 37
Dykes, William Hey, 2
    Manager of the Yorkshire District Bank, 2
    Superintendent of Christ Church Schools, 6
    Manager of the "Wakefield and Barnsley Union Bank," 7
    Presentations, 8
    Resigns the Bank, 56
    His death, 57
    Funeral, 57

Dykes, William Hey, 9
  Illness and death, 45
Dykes, Mrs. William Hey, 2
  Illness, 74
  Death, 74
  Letter from Dr. Dykes on the death of his father, 204–5
"Dykes Defence Fund," 121

Eastbourne, 62, 63
Ecce Panis, 80, 226
Edwards, Professor, 51
Elliot, Mr. 55, 56
Elvey, Sir George, 125
"Eternal Father, strong to save," 49, 226
Eucharist, 89, 231
"Eucharistic Truth and Ritual," Pamphlet on, 131
Excelsior, 51, 86
Exsurge, 98, 234

Faraday, Professor, 21
Farne Islands, 62
Fasting and abstinence, Letter on a rule of, 171
"Father, I know that all my life," 74, 237
Fennell, Dr. and Mrs., 8, 10
Few and Co., Messrs., 121, 122, 125
Filey, 43
Flamborough, 49
Flowers, Dr. G. F., 80
Folkestone, 149
"For ever' beatific word," 114, 232
Forbes, Professor, 37 *note*
Fowler, C. Hodgson, 122, 126, 150, 161
  Letter from Dr. Staunton on the death of Dr. Dykes, 160
Fowler, J. T., 148
Francis, Mr. Henry Ralph, 2, 3
Francis, Sir Philip, 2
Freke, Lady Victoria Evans, 146
  Her *The Song of Praise*, 115, 231
Friar's Crag, 101
Friend, Letter from Dr. Dykes to a, On the loss of her children, 208
Frost, Mr. Percival, 19, 20
Fruits of the Spirit, Letter on the, 187–89
Funchal, 58

Garvey, Mr., 8
Gauntlett, Dr., 49, 101
"Gentle Shepherd," 91, 92 *note*, 242
Gilly, Dr., 31, 34, 51
Gladstone, Mr., 136
Gleadless, 9
Glebefield, 78
Glencoin, 101
Gobarrow Park, 101
God's will, Letter on submission to, 183–84
Goldsmith, Oliver, 29
Goodwin, Dr. Harvey, 11
Grange, 101, 136
Grasmere, 111
"Great and glorious Father," 87, 125 *note*, 241
Great Gable, 137
Greatorex, Rev. Edward, 29, 31, 42, 80
  His recollections of Dr. Dykes, 50–52
  Precentor of Durham Cathedral, 54
Greenwell, Alan, 55
Grey, Earl, 32
Grey, Lady Elizabeth, 32
Grey, Lady Georgiana, 69
Grey, Rev. and Hon. Francis, 32, 116, 117, 118
  Letter to Dr. Dykes on the death of his daughter, 97
Grey, Hon. and Rev. John, 69 *note*
  His *Hymnal*, 44, 230
Grey, Mr., 70
"Groves, The," 1

"Hail, Gladdening Light!" 122, 127, 130, 243
Hall, Rev. W. J., *New Mitre Hymnal*, 237
"Hark! the herald angels sing," 112, 237, 238
"Hark! the sound of holy voices," 98, 227
Harland, Rev. Edward, his *Church Psalter and Hymnal*, 115
Hatfield Hall, 16 *note*
Henley, 115
Henshaw, Dr., 34, 35
Hereford, 84, 85
Hermitage Bridge, 124

Hexham, Epidemic of cholera at, 38
Hey, Mr. William, 2
Hiles, Dr.: *Wesleyan Tune Book*, 240
Holden, Dr., 56
Hollingside, 36, 49, 226
Hollingside Cottage, 32 note, 35, 38
"Holy, Holy, Holy, Lord God Almighty," 49, 226
Holy Trinity Church, Hull, 5
    Musical festival, 8
    Wakefield, 9
Holy Year, The, 68, 232
Holywell Lodge, 62, 64
Honister Pass, 136
Horbury, 43, 49, 226
Horbury, 43, 147
    Retreat at, 70
Houghton-le-Spring, 44 note, 75, 122
"How bright those glorious spirits shine," 41, 227
How, Dr. Walshain, 87, 125
Hughes, W. J., *The St. Asaph Tune-Book*, 238
Hull, 2, 8, 25, 143
    River, 1
Hullah, (John?), 83
Humility, Letter on, 170–71
Hungerford, 78
Huntingford, Mr., 99
Huntington, Bacchus, 2
Huntington, Elizabeth, 2
Huntington, Mr. Frederic, 6, 7, 143
    His death, 143
Huntington, Rev. George, Rector of Tenby, 69
    "Random Recollections," 69 note
Huntington, Rev. William, Vicar of Kirkella, 2
Huntington, William, 57, 75
Huntington, 14
Hymnal, 230
Hymnal Companion, The, 86, 87, 90, 232
Hymnal with Tunes, New and Old, 240
Hymnary, The, 81, 82
Hymns composed by Dr. Dykes, 41, 43, 49, 54, 66, 68, 69, 74, 80, 84, 85, 87, 88, 92, 93, 98, 99, 104, 108, 109, 112, 113, 114, 122, 125, 127, 130, 132, 133, 134, 153–54, 225–44
Hymns Ancient and Modern, 47, 48, 78, 80, 99, 104, 109, 118, 225
    Appendix, 78, 80
    New edition, 133, 136
Hymns for Advent and Lent, 238
Hymns for the Church of England, 236
Hymns for Infant Children, 49, 80, 233

"I am the Way," 111
Ilkley, 56, 57, 67, 75, 149
Ingelow, Jean: her poems, 57
"Inspiration stone," 138
Invalid, Letter to an, on fasting Communion, 164–65
    On keeping Lent, 175–77
"Invitation to Rest: 'Come unto Me,'" 113
Irene, 87, 133, 232
Islington, 78

Jarratt, John, 143
Jebb, Dr., 77, 99
Jenkyns, Professor, 51
"Jerusalem the golden," 54, 229
"Jesu, lover of my soul," 36, 226
"Jesu, my Lord, my God, my All," 98, 234
"Jesu, to Thy table led," 98, 234
John's Church, St., 2, 4
    Services, 4
    Missionary Society meetings, 4
    Sunday-school anniversary, 6
Joyce, G. P.: Church of England Hymnology, 238
Jude, W. H.: Popular Congregational Music, 238
"Just as I am," 132, 243

Keary, Rev. W., 4
Keble, Rev. J., 156
Keighley, 56, 67
Kelvin, Lord, 14 note
    His account of the Cambridge University Musical Society, 15
Kempe, Rev. J. W., 68, 71, 85, 97, 100
Keswick, 20, 101, 136, 138

Kingsley, Charles, 37 *note*
Kingston College, 2
Kingston, George, 28
Kingston, Mrs., 56
Kingston, Miss Susan, 28
    Her marriage, 35
Kingston-upon-Hull, 1
Knight, Mr., Vicar of St. James's Church, 6, 8
Knight, Samuel, 7

Ladislaus, Johannes, 93
Lake, Dr., 82
    His sermon on Dr. Dykes, 157
Latin Cross, 56, 57
Latrobe, Mr., 14
"Lead, kindly Light," 41, 69, 227
    Origin of the words, 69
    Of the tune, 69
Leeds, 69, 74, 79, 90, 99, 132, 147
Lent, Letters on keeping, 175–77, 183
Leominster, 81, 99
Leonard's, St., 150
Leonard's, St., 113, 238
Levett, Mr. N. D., 114
Lewes, 63, 64
Lichfield Cathedral, 114
Liddon, Canon, 75, 127
Lincoln, Bishop of: his complaints against the compilers of *Hymns Ancient and Modern*, 102
Lind, Jenny, 20, 22
Lindpainter, 32
Litanies, Prose and Metrical, A Book of, 235
Literary Churchman, Obituary notice in the, 44
Little Hereford, 77
Littledale, Dr., 86
Lodore, 101, 136
London, 25, 69, 80, 125, 127
Londonderry, Marquis of, 34
Longley, Bishop, 43
"Lord, I hear of showers of blessing," 114, 232
"Lord, when before Thy Throne we meet," 88, 232
Louis Napoleon, Prince, 22

Love in trials, Letter on, 197
Lowe; Rev. Julius C., 148
Lucerne, Lake of, 150
Ludlow, 76
Lunatic Asylum, West Riding, 43
Lux Benigna, 69, 227
Lyte, Henry 156

Mackonochie, Alexander, 80
Maltby, Bishop, 34, 38
Malton, 26, 28, 29, 39
Malvern Hills, 119
Manchester Church Congress, 56
"Manner of Performing Divine Service," Article on, 68
Manning, Dr., 68
Markham, Archbishop, 2
Marriott, Mr. Charles, 9
Martineau, Rev. James, 143
Mary's Church, St., Lowgate, 2
Masters, Mr., 49, 80, 143
Maturin, Father, 99
Maturin, Miss, 99
Maude, Mr., 42
McDonald, Lady, 31
Meads, 62, 64
Mediterranean Sea, 70
Melita, 49, 226
Mendelssohn, death of, 26
Merbecke: his "*Credo*," 78
Mercer's Hymns, 58
Michael's Church, St., Malton, 36
    Tenbury, 76
Milner, Joseph, 25
Missionary Society meetings, 4
Missions, Low Church, Letter on, 200
Mitchell, D. B.: his death, 25, 126
Mitchell, Mrs., 125–26
Mitchinson, Bishop of Barbadoes, 75, 118
Money, Miss, 74
Monk, Mr., 47, 68, 79–80, 87, 98–99, 119, 132–33
    Letters from Dr. Dykes on hymn-tunes, 133–36
Monkland, 81, 118–19, 132–33
Monsell, Mr., 156
Morris, Professor, 95, 97

Index

Moultrie, Gerard, 156
Musgrave, Dr., Archbishop of York, 28–29

"Natural and Supernatural Life," Sermon on, 44
"Nearer, my God, to Thee," 43, 49, 226
Nelson, Lord, 101
Nessfield, 68
New Mitre Hymnal, 237
New York, Bishop of, 160
Newcastle, 149
    Epidemic of cholera, 38
Newlands, Vale of, 137
Newman, Cardinal, 136
    His hymn, "Lead, kindly Light," 69
Nicaea, 49, 226
Nisbet, 74
Normanton, 8, 84
North Cave, 143
North Cliff, 111
Norwich Church Congress, 69
Nottingham Church Congress, 101
Novello, 70, 73–74, 78, 81, 122, 125
Novello, Clara, 5
    Her first appearance, 5
"Now the labourer's task is o'er," 41, 227
Nursing, Letter on, 189

"O come and mourn with me awhile," 49, 225
"O day of rest and gladness," 98–99, 241
"O God, forasmuch," 51, 54
"O Lord, to Whom the spirits live," 92–93
"O Paradise," 80, 141, 225, 243
"O Trinity, most blessed Light," 129
Oakeley, Herbert S., 64, 70
Oakeley, Mr., 70, 83
Oakeley, Mrs., 70
Obedience in the spiritual life, Letter on the value of, 181–83
Offertory Paper, 144–46
Ogle, Dr., 31, 51
"O God, most High, Creator King, 69, 230
"Old Elvet," Durham, 38
"Old Ivy House," 1

Olivet, 89, 228, 232
Orton, Arthur, 128
St. Oswald's Church, 35–36, 53
    Changes in the ritual, 71, 85
    Population, 115
Oswestry, 125, 241
"Our Blest Redeemer," 49, 225
Ouse, 45
Ouseley, Sir Frederic, 42, 49, 51, 53, 76, 77, 80, 146
Ovingham, 115, 149
Oxford, 83
Oxford, Bishop of, 77–78

Page, Father, 125
Pan-Anglican Synod, 77
Panis Vivus, 98, 234
Paris, 149
Parish Church Hymnal, 98, 235
Parry, John, 24
Parry, Dr., Bishop of Barbados, 67
Patey, Madame, 83
Patterdale, 101
Paul's Church, St., Brighton, 65
Peake, Rev. G. E. F., 116, 118, 123–24
Penances, Letter on self-imposed, 196
Penrith, 138
People's Hymnal, The, 86, 234
Peterborough, Bishop of, 146
"Peterhouse Musical Society," 13–15
Philpotts, Bishop, 51
"Pilgrims, The" 155
Pisheck, Herr, 21
Pitlochrie, 124
Pitman, Rev. Thomas, 63–64
    On Arthur Dykes, 63
Platt, Father, 68
Plymouth, 9
Popular Congregational Music, 238
Portinscale, 101
Powell, Canon, 85
Prayer, Letter on carelessness in, 178
Processional Hymns with Tunes, 238
Proctor, Miss Adelaide: "The Pilgrims," 152
Pusey, Dr., 9, 78

Quain, Dr., 66, 78–79

Index

Quain, Judge, 127

Raine, Mr., 34
Randall, Archdeacon, 77
Randegger, 83
Raymond, Archdeacon, 30, 51
Razor Edge, 20
Redcar, 26, 47
Reid's Praise Book, 240
Religious life, Letter on the desire for the, 191
    On shrinking from the, 194
Resurrection, 98, 234
Retreats, etc., Letter on, 169
Ritual Commission, 77
River Wear, 53
Rivington's, 68
Robson, Mrs., 91–92
"Rock of Ages, cleft for me," 54, 229
Rogers, Dr., 114
Rosendale, Lord, 32
Rule of life, Letter on a, 179
Rumbling Bridge, 124
Russia, Grand-Duke Constantine of, 22

Sacraments, Letter on the, 201–2
Saddleback, Ascent of, 20
St. Asaph Tune-Book, 238
Sanctuary, 98, 227
Sandal Castle Hill, 8
Sarum Hymnal, 235
Scarf Gap, 137
Scawfell, 19
Scholfield, Professor, 11
Scott, Archdeacon, 30
Seatoller, 36
Sharp, Rev. John, 43
Shaw-Stewart, Mr., 121
Sheffield, 9
Sherrington, Madame, 83
Sibthorpe, Richard Waldo, 25
Silcoates fields, 8
Simeon, Charles, 25
Sion College, 127
Sister, Letter on the wedding of a, 174
Skeffington, 114
Skiddaw, 20, 138
Sloman, Dr., 111

Smart, Sir Henry, 5
Smith, G. E., first President of the Peterhouse Musical Society, 15
Snowdon, 19
Snowdon, Mr., 56, 58, 75
"Son of God goes forth to war, The," 133–34, 242
"Song of Praise," 115, 231
"Sound," Lecture on, 29
Southgate, 67
Spence, Miss Harriet, 10
Spiritual Letters from Dr. Dykes, 162–209
Stainer, Dr., 97, 99, 104, 110, 127, 135
Stanton, Father, 79
Staunton, Rev. Dr., on the death of Dr. Dykes, 159
Stephens, Dr. A. J., 121–24, 127–28
Stewart, Professor, 122
Stockton, 34
Stoke Newington, 78, 132
Stoker, Mr., 38, 91
Sullivan, Arthur, 83
"Sun of my soul," 66, 127, 225, 242
Sunday School Anniversary, 6
Sutton Church, 1
"Sweet Saviour," 114, 225
Switzerland, 149

Taylor, Mr. Minton: his *Parish Church Hymnal*, 98, 235
Te Deum, 73, 84, 111–13
Teaching, Letter on reserve in, 197
Tebay, 111
Tell's Platte, 149
Temper, Letter on, 177–78
Temptation, Letter on, 180
"Ten thousand times ten thousand," 41
Tenbury, 50, 76
Tewkesbury Abbey, 26
"The Lord is my Shepherd," 110, 115, 244
    Revision of, 124
"The night is gone," 114, 242
"The roseate hues," 114, 243
"The voice that breathed o'er Eden," 105, 242
"The way is long and dreary," 155, 240

"These are they which came out of great tribulation," 41, 49, 51, 55, 125, 244
Thirsk, 57
Thompson, Rev. Canon, Vicar of Datchet, 43
Thomson, Sir William, 14, 16, 20–21, 26
Thornes churchyard, 45
Thorp, Archdeacon, 51
Thorpe, 34
"Thou art gone up on high," 88, 228, 232
"Thou art the Christ, the Son of God," 105–6
Thun, 150
"Thy way, not mine, O Lord," 122
Tichborne case, 128
Tomlins, Rev. R., Chaplain of the Manchester Jail, 113
Hymns for Advent and Lent, 238
"Too late," 112
Townsend, Dr., 30, 37–38, 51
Townsend, Mrs., 30
Tozer, Bishop, 104
Trinity Lodge, Evening party at, 16–17
Trueman, 13
Tucker, Rev. J. Ireland: *Hymnal with Tunes New and Old*, 240
The Children's Hymnal, 241

Ullswater, Lake of, 101
"Unto Him that loved us," 112

Via Crucis, 153, 240
Victoria, Queen, 22
    Her visit to Cambridge, 12–13
The Village Organist, 86

Waddington, Dean, 51
    His death, 82
Wakefield, 8, 29, 43, 84
"Wakefield and Barnsley Union Bank," 7
Walla Crag, 138
Walmisley, Professor, 13–14, 19

Wawn, Rev. E. B., Theological Master in Cheltenham College, Resignation, 72
Wawn, Rev. John Dale, 2
Wawn, Mrs. E.: letter from Dr. Dykes on the death of her husband, 207–8
"We would see Jesus," 108, 232
Welling, Mr., 76
Wellington, Duke of, 22
Wesleyan Tune-Book, 240
Wharfe, Valley of the, 56
Wharfedale, 150
"When I had wandered from His fold," 156
Whewell, Dr. and Mrs., 16
Whinfield, E. W., 16, 112
Whittington Rectory, 125
Wilberforce, Archdeacon: his secession, 36
Wilberforce, William, 2, 25, 78
Wilkinson, Anthony, 38
Wilkinson, Rev. Dr., 147
Wilkinson, G., 73
Wilkinson, Major, 122
Wilkinson, Percy, 148
Williams, Isaac, 37
Williams, Rowland, 37
    His "Rational Godliness," 39
Wilson, Mrs., 136
Winchester, Bishop of: his death, 118
Windermere, 111
Winkworth, Miss, 92
Wood, Mr. 42
Worcester, 76
    Musical Festival, 83, 111
Wordsworth, Dr., 11
    The Holy Year, 68, 232
Work, Letter on interruptions in, 194
Wray, Rev. W. M., 14, 19–21, 26, 100, 115, 121, 149
Wykeham, Retreat at, 73

York, 9
York, Archbishop of, 23, 29, 118–19, 136
"Yorkshire Banking Company," 2

www.ingramcontent.com/pod-product-compliance
Lightning Source LLC
Chambersburg PA
CBHW050344230426
43663CB00010B/1988